A
Celebration
of
American
Family
Folklore

Tales and Traditions from the Smithsonian Collection

Steven J. Zeitlin
Amy J. Kotkin
Holly Cutting Baker

○ YELLOW MOON PRESS ○

A
Celebration
of
American
Family
Folklore

Some of the stories and photographs in this book were previously
published in booklet form by the Smithsonian Institution.

Grateful acknowledgment is made to the following for permission to
reprint previously published material:
MARYLAND ARTS COUNCIL FOLKLIFE PROGRAM: Excerpt from "Family
Folklore: A Model Course Outline." Copyright © 1977 by Amy. J.
Kotkin, Holly Cutting Baker, and the Maryland Arts Council Folklife
Program. Reprinted by permission of the Maryland Arts Council Folklife
Program, Baltimore, Md.
SANGA MUSIC INC.: Excerpt from "The Ranger's Command" by Woody
Guthrie. Copyright © 1960 by Sanga Music Inc. All rights reserved.
Used by permission.
SATURDAY REVIEW: Ballad by Frank Warner, quoted in "Growing Up in
Greenwich Village." Copyright 1943 by *Saturday Review*. All rights
reserved. Reprinted by permission.
TEMPLE UNIVERSITY PRESS: For permission to adapt material that appeared
originally in *Children of Strangers: The Stories of a Black Family* by
Kathryn L. Morgan. Copyright © 1980 by Temple University.
THE WASHINGTON POST: Excerpt from "Interview with Maria Katzenbach"
by Kevin Scott, *Book World*, January 15, 1978. Copyright © 1978 by The
Washington Post. Also for excerpt from "Fifty Ways to Meet Your Lover"
by Michael Kernan, *Washington Post*, December 29, 1976, p. B-3.
Copyright © 1976 by The Washington Post. Reprinted by permission of
The Washington Post.

○ Yellow Moon Press ○
P. O. Box 1316 Cambridge, MA 02238
(617) 776 - 2230
Fax: (617) 776 - 8246

ISBN: 0-938756-36-2

BOOK DESIGN: ELISSA ICHIYASU
Manufactured in the United States of America

For our parents:

Irving Zeitlin
Shirley Stein Zeitlin

David Kotkin
Eve Goldfeld Kotkin

Dick Cutting
Ruth Murray Cutting

*My grandfather mentioned that
his ancestors had been, perhaps, for the
most part honest — traveling peddlers
and merchants — but perhaps with a
little bit of piracy. They were in Latvia
and Lithuania on the Baltic Sea.
I'd like to think they were pirates, but
when I think about it seriously, they were
probably all hard-working people,
to be perfectly honest.*

JOHN BISHOP

❧

*The history of my family is like the
history of the country: good people, and
bad people, and famous people, and
people nobody ever heard of.*

SUSAN BERRYMAN BOBROW

❧

*I remember my relatives talking and
talking and talking, and yet as a kid,
I didn't listen. I'd love to go back
now and listen.*

WAYNE DIONNE

CONTENTS

ACKNOWLEDG-MENTS

Since the first family folklore tent was erected at the Festival of American Folklife on the National Mall in 1974, we have been the grateful recipients of scholarly guidance, encouragement, and sound advice from many distinguished folklorists, colleagues, and friends. That the tent appeared at all is a tribute to Dr. Robert Byington, former deputy director of the Smithsonian's Office of Folklife Programs. His acceptance of the idea and support for our collecting and early publications has enabled us to gather a rich corpus of folklore and to begin to interpret its meaning. We are deeply grateful to him.

A special thanks is also owed to Sandra Gross. As a founding member of the Family Folklore Program, her perspectives on the material and her creativity enabled us to communicate our findings to the public through exhibitions and publications. She helped to edit our earlier publications, and, in that way, helped to shape this one. We value her insights; they are very much a part of this book.

We would also like to thank the Office of Folklife Programs, Smithsonian Institution which sponsored this project, and its director, Ralph Rinzler, for his encouragement throughout the years and his advice on our exhibitions and presentation techniques. We would also like to thank Barbara Strickland who cheerfully responded to thousands of inquiries for our earlier pamphlets and Richard Derbyshire for organizing the collection of photographs. The Smithsonian's Office of Fellowships and Grants also deserves thanks for Steven Zeitlin's predoctoral fellowship during which portions of this book were written. Our sincere appreciation also goes to the National Institute on Aging for its support of our continuing research on the folklore of older Americans.

Dr. Kenneth Goldstein, Department of Folklore and Folklife at the University of Pennsylvania, has also been a longtime supporter of the program and an invaluable resource for fieldwork methodology. We are likewise indebted to Bess Lomax Hawes, director of the Folk Arts program at the National Endowment for the Arts for her enthusiasm and advice on the program through its many incarnations.

Folklorists Margaret Yocom, Karen Baldwin, and Kathryn Morgan were pioneers in the field of family folklore. Their thought-provoking and detailed research on their own families provided us with new methods of inquiry and, most importantly, an understanding of the ways in which folklore evolves and functions in family life.

A number of other people have been generous with their support and encouragement at crucial times over the past seven years. Wilton Dillon and Charlene James of the Smithsonian Institution gave us opportunities to test our ideas in workshops across the country and at related programs in Washington; Suzanne Roschwalb helped us to collect the photos from local residents which were used in our exhibits and this book; Ethel Mohamed showed us how family memories could be beautifully embroidered on cloth, and graciously allowed us to use her works in our exhibitions and our publications; John Baker and Dan Berger were very supportive during the endless days of preparation for the festivals; Jeff Warner endured constant revisions of the manuscript, and lent his advice on each successive draft.

We would also like to acknowledge our gratitude to Wendy Wolf, our editor at Pantheon, for seeing the potential in this collection and encouraging us to undertake this project. Her enthusiasm and ability to give new expression to our familiar thoughts is much appreciated. We would like to thank Nan Graham at Pantheon for taking over the book when Wendy departed on her trip around the world. Thanks also to Milly Daniel for copyediting the book and Elissa Ichiyasu for designing it.

Finally, our deepest thanks goes to the many hundreds of families who interrupted their summer holiday to share their stories and traditions with us. This book is a tribute to their heritage.

Family folklore collectors: Deborah Autorino, Holly Cutting Baker, Linda Burack, Robert Clayton, Susan Davis, Lorrie Gross, Sandra Gross, Amy Kotkin, Carolyn Mitchell, Jack Santino, Rosemary Scanlon, Amy Schuman, Andrea Shelton, Paul Wagner, Linda Watson, Mark Workman, Steven Zeitlin.

Assistant editor: Amanda Dargan.

Over three summers leading up to and including the Bicentennial in 1976, Amy Kotkin, Holly Cutting Baker, Sandy Gross and I, along with a team of fellow folklorists, recorded thousands of family stories and traditions at the Festival of American Folklife in Washington, D.C.. While the rest of the Festival featured fiddlers, blues musicians and craftspeople from around the country, the Family Folklore tent consisted of a few card tables with a cassette recorder on each. Anyone who came into the tent was invited to record their family stories.

Among those who wandered in was anthropologist Margaret Mead—she didn't exactly wander in, but approached on a golf cart filled with Smithsonian dignitaries. Awed in the presence of one of my true heroines, I gave an earnest speech about what we were trying to accomplish. When I finished, she stood up, brandished her legendary cane and launched into a tirade—did I think I had invented families? Invented oral history! She had been doing it for 50 years!

Margaret Mead's cane notwithstanding, much was accomplished in the years leading up to the Bicentennial, whose importance is now apparent in retrospect. Not just in that tent, but in many parts of the country, Americans were recognizing the importance of stories and storytelling, and in a larger sense, of folk culture—it remains one of the lasting legacies of the 1960s and '70s.

Two decades earlier, in the 1950s, Allan Nevins at Columbia University argued that modern communications, particularly the telephone, were eliminating one of the great repositories of the American past, the letter and diary. Technology, he suggested, could help to fill the gap in historical evidence by using the tape recorder to create "an oral document." Oral history caught the popular imagination with Studs Terkel's *Division Street: America* (1966) and *Hard Times* (1970). One of the early influential works to use oral history was *The Saga of Coe Ridge: A Study of Oral History*, written by folklorist Lynwood Montell in 1970. In 1974, Theodore Rosengarten published *All God's Dangers: The Life of Nate Shaw*, based on interviews with a black sharecropper. During the same period as we were collecting stories, Alex Haley, intrigued by some African words passed down in his family, researched his family's history back to Africa. Both the book and television mini-series, *Roots*, inspired thousands to explore their genealogies and family histories.

In l966, while teaching ninth and tenth grade English in a 250 pupil high school in Rabun Gap, Georgia, Eliot Wiggington helped his students start a quarterly magazine, "Foxfire". In 1972, articles from the magazine were published in book form by Doubleday and, along with its successors, sold more than six million copies. In the first book, Wiggington writes:

Daily our grandfathers are moving out of our lives.... When they're gone...the eloquent and haunting stories of suffering and sharing and building and healing and planting and harvesting—all these go with them, and what a loss. If this information is to be saved at all, for whatever reason, it must be saved now; and the logical researchers are the grandchildren.

His students became folklore collectors and oral historians, collecting narrative accounts of mountain culture from neighbors and relatives. Today, more than 200 Foxfire-like magazines exist across the country, in inner cities ("Cityscape"), small towns ("Bittersweet", "Loblolly") and suburbs (from "Snake Hill" to "Spring Bank"). There are Eskimo, Navaho, Mexican-American, Choctaw and Cajun Foxfire-based magazine projects.

The Foxfire project, along with books such as this one, began to give teachers the tools that enabled them to use the background of their students as a resource in teaching. Many teachers who came into contact with these projects began asking their students to collect stories, in some cases to transcribe and then develop them into more polished tales and essays. Some teachers have used these stories as touchstones, asking their students to write about how their own lives may differ from those of their grandparents, or working with students to create personalized books that combine family stories and photographs. Many teachers began bringing parents and grandparents into the classroom to tell stories. Family folklore is also a valuable resource for the new Whole Language approach to education, which emphasizes the importance of drawing on the students' own experiences to teach reading and writing skills.

This resurgence of interest in folk culture received new impetus in 1967, when Ralph Rinzler, who performed with the Greenbriar Boys during the folksong revival in the early 1960s, established the Festival of American Folklife at the Smithsonian, which later sponsored the Family Folklore Project. The Folklife Festival presents personal experience stories in "narrative sessions" held alongside the Festival's multicultural presentations of music, dance and crafts. The Festival emphasizes the context for performance traditions, and encourages performers to talk as well as play, placing their music and art within the framework of their lives through stories. The Smithsonian's Festival, and the folklorists who worked for it, helped provide the impetus for the National Endowment for the Arts' funding program in Folk Arts which, in turn, spread this same sensibility to state and local programs across the country.

Then in 1973, others began to create venues for sharing folklore and stories when Jimmy Neil Smith, a high school journalism teacher founded the National Storytelling Festival in Jonesborough, Tennessee. The traditional coon hunting stories of Jerry Clower were the initial inspiration, and traditional Jack tale teller Ray Hicks participated in the first Storytelling Festival. However Smith realized that the future of his program was not in this country's handful of traditional folktale raconteurs, but in the new generation of revivalist storytellers who cropped up as a by-product of the sixties.

Traditional cultures also benefitted from the revival. In 1976, Congress authorized the creation of the American Folklife Center at the Library of Congress, which holds many of the invaluable recordings of American folk culture, among them Francis Denzmor's early cylinder recordings of Native American chants and songs recorded at the turn of the century. One of the American Folklife Center's first initiatives was to duplicate those cylinders and turn them back to the tribes from which they were originally collected—the Seminole, Omaha, Pawnee, Iroquois, Teton-Sioux, Ojibwa, Chippewa, Cheyenne, Cherokee, and Eskimo, among others. Today young tribal singers flock to the Center to recapture the endangered music of their forefathers. Folklorists at the Library recall the jubilant face of one Native American on discovering that the singer he was listening to was his great grandfather.

In 1979, Barbara Myerhoff published *Number Our Days*, a compelling, beautifully written study of a senior center in Venice, California. Inspired by the work of psychiatrist Robert Butler on the "life review process," which emphasized the positive role of reminiscence in the aging process, Myerhoff's book became a classic not only among anthropologists but also social workers; and Myerhoff's students and colleagues developed social programs that drew on her ideas. For instance, Susan Perlstein founded Elders Share the Arts to develop living history storytelling plays for and by older adults. Marc Kaminsky and Arthur Strimling evolved storytelling programs for the Brookdale Center on Aging in New York City. "What makes the recent reevaluation of reminiscence so culturally significant," writes Marc Kaminsky, "is that nothing less than our attitude towards old people is at stake." Storytelling became a tool for social workers and therapists who, in turn, became witnesses for the life stories of the elderly.

Often these programs include an intergenerational component where students and seniors exchange stories. As 80 year old Moishe Sacks said, "it's an osmotic process, the young get a little bit of wisdom, a little bit of knowledge from the old, and the old get a bit of vigor, a little youthfulness from the young."

As the Family Folklore Project was nearing completion, I began a program to document the stories of America's elderly. Along with Marjorie Hunt and Mary Hufford, I worked on a book and documentary film called *The Grand Generation*. We began to observe that many family traditions are tied into patterns of aging and the life cycle. For example, Alan Jabbour described for us the pattern in the lives of traditional fiddlers. Frequently the instrument was learned from parents or grandparents in childhood, played as a young man, then put away for a number of years, to be revived in old age. "I was not simply finding a few [older fiddlers] who still played," he writes. "Rather, I was learning that old age was precisely when one played the fiddle." We heard the same stories from many aging practitioners of family traditions — cloggers, woodcarvers and quilters. All of these arts seemed in danger of dying out, but never did. As one folklorist observed, there at the feet of the older cloggers, small children were dancing, later to revive the tradition at the other end of the life cycle.

As I was working on *The Grand Generation*, I had the opportunity to interview an elderly Hmong immigrant musician for a documentary on older Americans. When he arrived at Washington's National Airport, Mr. Buo Xuo Mua carried with him a queej, the instrument on which he preserves the ancient funeral music of the Hmong people. His grandson was carrying a home video camera with which he would document his grandfather's music. As the grandson put it, "We each have our instruments for preserving the past."

Since the Family Folklore book went to press in 1982, we have seen the proliferation of home video. As a result, more than ever before, ordinary people and communities can readily document important occasions in their own lives and histories. People like the D'Agnese brothers, a tailor and a deli owner from Long Island, become homegrown anthropologists documenting the folk customs of their home town in southern Italy. With the VCR and home video recorder, storytelling has come full circle. It is once again up to us to actively participate in our own myth making.

As we conducted interviews in the Family Folklore tent, another shift was occurring in our culture as a result of the 1965 revisions to the Immigration and Naturalization Act. Today, one in four Americans traces their ancestry to non-European sources, and, in 65 years, it is estimated that the majority of us will trace our descent to Africa, Asia or Latin America. With this influx of people has come an influx of stories that we could not begin to collect for this book. But many are, indeed, new migration stories. A Mexican immigrant mentioned that in the city of Puebla there was so much immigration to the US that a saying grew up in the town, " Last one to leave turn out the light."

In more recent years, escaping over the border from Mexico, fleeing on boats from Haiti or Cuba, or catching the last choppers out of Saigon, a new generation of immigrants has enriched this country with their experiences and stories. A number of Hmong immigrants, refugees from the Vietnam war, began to embroider their migration story in cloth, using needlework to tell the tale of crossing the treacherous Mekong River to safety in Thailand, then traveling to America. In some of the tapestries, the last embroidered image is of the immigrant crying into a tape deck, recording cassettes to send back home.

Since the 1970s, a number of ethnic groups have begun to reclaim their heritage as a birthright. In a "cultural democracy," they argue, each group must have the right as well as the forums in which to tell their own story. Often it is a story of oppression and disenfranchisement. One of the earliest of these efforts was New York's Chinatown History Project started by John Kuo Wei Tchen and Charles Lai in 1977. They sought to reclaim Chinatown's history through an exploration of the Chinese laundry workers, so often neglected in official histories. From an ignored and satirized occupation, they told a story of heroic resistance against discrimination.

In the days before radio and television, storytelling was the major source of family entertainment, and traditional folktales were commonly handed down across the generations. These traditional tales continue to be told in certain parts of this country. But in the twentieth century movies and later television began to tell us stories in powerful visual images. Costing millions to produce, today's films employ an extraordinary technology and draw on the nation's most gifted actors, directors and writers. Next to them, a grandfather telling stories about his childhood hardly seems as amusing.

Replacing one form of entertainment with another is perhaps a change we can live with. But stories are more than entertainment. Their displacement creates a larger gap; for the different forms of storytelling are also, we are discovering, a way of expressing a regional, a family and a personal identity. Stories offer ways of teaching values, developing a shared humor, shaping a collective experience, teaching about the past, or, simply putting children to bed. Since the sixties, teachers, scholars, and parents have reached back into that cultural storehouse to redefine and reinvigorate storytelling, to fill the void that was created when television and movies became our major forms of entertainment.

This movement to reevaluate the role of stories in our

lives is greater than the sum of its parts. In its totality it uses the stories of ordinary Americans as a voice speaking softly— but with a deep clarity and power— into the roar of our commerce driven media. Taken together, these populist initiatives in oral history, folklore, gerontology, anthropology and education have affected hundreds of communities across this country with a similar message validating the culture we live in and our effect on it. They have created a resurgence of storytelling, not only in places such as Rabun Gap, Georgia, Beech Mountain, North Carolina, or the family folklore tent in Washington, D.C., but in local communities across the country. We have recognized that it is possible to recycle, revitalize, and, in some sense, reinvent folk culture for our times. One folklorist interviewing an aging storyteller asked him, "when you're gone, who is going to be left to pass on these stories?" He answered, "well, you're listening to them, aren't you?"

Stories well told bear power, the power to affirm the individual, the particular, what is distinctive to a particular place and time. Ultimately, schools, museums, festivals and libraries are as valid a setting for the transmission of stories as a grandmother's kitchen, the front stoop, or the barber shop. The recounted story—one voice unfolding a narrative in spoken words—offers one of the tools we need to address a central challenge of our time, the creation of a humanistic society in a media age.

As I look back over those three summers between 1974 and 1976, I recognize that they were the beginnings of my lifelong interest in this field of storytelling and folk culture. Through family folklore, I met my wife, Amanda Dargan, who independently was completing a fine master's thesis on her own South Carolina family. She became a collaborator on this book in the late 1970s (her essay appears on p. 222). When I worked on the project, however, I was single, as were most of my colleagues. Now, married to Amanda, with two children, I see that many of the ideas we had about family folklore and the crucial role it plays in family life were true. We find ourselves passing on stories to our children not only about their ancestors, but about our own childhoods (their favorite is about how Amanda put her pet kittens in the refrigerator to cool them off one hot day); and we love to watch our children create their own folklore, much of which revolves around their stuffed toy penguins — Big Sam, Little Sam, Tantrum Louie, and the rest (none of whom can ever grow older than four in Animal Village).

I also realize that the Family Folklore project was one small part of a larger movement: it represented a way of looking at our culture, one that is concerned not only with families — traditional and non-traditional — but also with American culture in the largest sense. Along with a number of other parallel efforts, it envisioned folk culture as a resource for educating young people and restoring in a self conscious way a sense of community in an often rootless society.

With its publication in 1982, the Family Folklore book was frozen in time, and the world changed around it. We would love to have collected and included the stories of the new immigrants, and the many groups from other parts of the country whose experiences are not represented here. Nonetheless, we hope this book as it stands will continue to inspire others to further the work we started, finding new and constantly evolving ways to foster this gentle, humanistic vision of the world.

Anthropologist Barbara Myerhoff, in her essay "Stories as Equipment for Living," tells of a student, a physical education major who received an assignment from her to conduct a life history with a person who was part of his life but to whom he had never paid any mind. He chose a quiet, illiterate woman who was a maid in his family and taped her life story for eighteen hours. She told about how she had been poor, she had never married, she had put a brother through school, she had been a prostitute, she had struggled with hunger. When he finished, he went to her room, and said, "How can I ever thank you for what you've taught me?" And she said, "Oh, you mustn't thank me. You know, ...every night when I go to sleep... I lay here on my narrow cot... and I memorize my life, in case anybody should ever ask."

Steve Zeitlin
City Lore: the New York Center for Urban Folk Culture

A
Celebration
of
American
Family
Folklore

Family Folklore: The Creative Expression of a Common Past

Families travel light. As the greater part of our experience slips beyond our reach, we clasp a mere handful of stories, expressions, photographs, and customs. Our photo albums, attic trunks, even our memories can only hold so much: Aunt Ida's fading wedding photo or a pair of unused tickets for the fateful voyage of the Titanic may be all that remain of whole generations in a family. From countless incidents, families choose a few stories to pass on, the funniest or perhaps the most telling. From all of the garbled baby talk, a single utterance may become a family expression. Yet these time-honored images do more than recall scattered people and events; they come to represent the unremembered past, the sum total of a family's heritage.

Like the folktales collected by the brothers Grimm, or the songs collected by Cecil Sharp in the Appalachian Mountains, family stories, expressions, customs, and photographs are examples of folklore, the informal and expressive traditions of close groups.[1] These traditions spring up whenever Americans gather their kinfolk together to talk, to celebrate, or to play. For every famous literary and photographic work, there are hundreds of thousands of stories and snapshots in which Americans have invested a large portion of their creative genius. Family tradition is one of the great repositories of American culture. It contains clues to our national character and insights into our family structure.

For an individual family, folklore is its creative expression of a common past. As raw experiences are transformed into family stories, expressions, and photos, they are codified in forms which can be easily recalled, retold, and enjoyed. Their drama and beauty are heightened, and the family's past becomes accessible as it is reshaped according to its needs and desires.

A family's folklore differs from its history. Its stories, photographs, and traditions are personalized and often creative distillations of experience, worked and reworked over time. When a family tells of that glorious moment when a relative just missed the sailing of the Titanic, or a great-grandmother held off a band of outlaws, or a grandfather tricked a border guard on his departure from the old country, the lore is precisely that: a glorious moment carefully selected and elaborated through the years, tailored to the demands of the present. Even photographs are not unbiased slices of life.

We look at a picture of a child in the family, and we think, "that is it, this is the way it was," but it is simply the way the world looked for a single moment through a mother's or a father's eye.

This is a book about those stories, expressions, keepsakes, and customs which characterize family life. It is a book about Uncle Velvl, the horse thief, lynched according to one yarn in "Lynchburg," Virginia; about Max Blum, pictured in a photograph as "One Gun Blum the Jewish Cowboy"; about Ethel Mohamed who embroidered her memories of great storms and her peddler husband's pushcart in cloth; about the Janneys who invented their own holiday, "St. Grunes Day."

But it is also a book about some prominent themes in American culture. The interviews we conducted with more than two thousand family members at the Smithsonian's Festival of American Folklife from 1974 to 1977 can help us understand how Americans interpret their history, the subjects they celebrate in their stories, photographs, and customs. General patterns emerge. Americans like to photograph themselves in front of their new cars or in pastoral settings, but rarely in their daily routine. They tell stories about eccentric rather than conventional souls; about up-

HOLLY CUTTING BAKER

MARY GOODWIN

heavals, natural disasters, migrations, supernatural occurrences, not ordinary events. And they are especially fond of tales which tell of how their ancestors lost a great fortune which would otherwise have gone to them.

This is also a book about five particular American families. Following our collection of stories and traditions, folklorists from different backgrounds reminisce and contemplate the lore which shaped their family lives. One talks about the proverbs told to him by his great-grandmother, passed down from slavery times, another tells of a Russian dance still performed at his Jewish family weddings. One focuses on storytelling at Pennsylvania German weddings and funerals. One centers on the expressions of small children growing up in a Greenwich Village family in the forties, while yet another concentrates on the "characters" in a rural South Carolina clan. At the end of the book, a brief interviewing guide and sample questionnaire offer suggestions for starting one's own family folklore project.

The past is a dark screen occasionally lit by vivid images. Families perpetuate only a few of the radiant scenes from their histories—jubilant weddings, hilarious practical jokes, terrifying earthquakes and fires—bright, flashing images indeed. We think the ones we've assembled here come together like the frames of a film which expresses the artistic side of family life, and hope that the reader will be able to watch it like a dazzling and yet familiar home movie, a chronicle of what American families choose to remember and preserve about themselves.

The Forms of Family Lore

Man has been called the time-binding animal. The development of language, the invention of writing, and the advent of photography have each altered man's relationship to his past. Language gave him oral tradition; now he had the ability to tell another person what happened to him in a story or reminiscence. Writing made it possible for him to record his own account of his past; now his experiences could be transmitted across the generations in his own words. Photography and taping made it possible to record the past at the moment of its occurrence, to record the present at the moment of its transformation into the past.

Families make use of all of these. We tell stories, write letters and memoirs, take pictures to document our shared experience and later to relive it. In the same way that we take a different kind of vehicle — automobile, luxury liner, jumbo jet — depending on that portion of the globe to which we wish to travel, so the varied forms transport us to different segments of our past, for different purposes.

Birthdays, for instance, are a common scene preserved in American family pictures. A collection of these images can be a fascinating record of a person's growth. A story about those experiences, however, might fall below the threshold of interest: "first they brought out the cake, then they blew out the candles. . . ."

Oftentimes, a photograph just can't convey what a story can. The birthday party with its sweetness and its fragile hold on time makes a good subject for a picture. Yet one woman remembers and tells a story about only one birthday, an embarrassing party where her family ran out of spaghetti. Appropriately, that is the birthday at which no photos were taken. Stories are most often told about out-of-the-ordinary events, those which harbor some excitement and conflict. Photos are more idealized, and would not have served to preserve this incident in her past. How does one communicate running out of spaghetti in a snapshot?

Each form of family lore can convey only one portion of the family's past. It skews reality in a particular way. For instance, on looking through the Williamson family photographs, we might figure that they lived in a snowy northern climate. The truth is that all of the family's pictures were taken on those rare occasions when it snowed on their tobacco farm in sunny South Carolina. That is when they were inspired to take out their camera.

We have met a number of women who, like Ethel Mohamed of Belzoni, Mississippi, have begun to stitch their family history into cloth. They discover that their thread moving through cloth cannot convey scenes with the detail of a photograph or the movement of a family story. Their work becomes symbolic: family background is symbolized by a coat of arms, occupations by a shovel or a pushcart. In Mrs. Mohamed's work, the symbolism becomes quite elaborate, with the happiness she found in family life represented by her children pouring out of a treasure chest. Stitched into cloth, a family's past seems far more impressionistic and dreamlike than in their photographs and stories.

Events like the Civil War live on outside the history books in the traditions and remembrances of countless individual families. Yet each form of folklore conveys a different perspective. In one southern family, for instance, the photographs of grey-clad soldiers serve to unravel mysteries of family resemblance, while a single surviving story focuses not on a soldier but on an ironic incident that befell a well-intentioned great-aunt. Apparently, this ancestor felt sympathetic towards the Union soldiers starving in a nearby prison camp. She brought them greens and a dish called clabber, a kind of sour milk. Soon afterwards the soldiers began to die in great numbers. Some claimed they starved to death, but in the family the legend persists that their great-aunt's clabber

JOAN BERNICK

killed them, and that, inadvertently, she killed more Union soldiers than her husband and the rest of the family together.

Diaries and letters from the Civil War often record the everyday, discuss such issues as the quality of the army's food, the weather, an amusing incident; the tales in oral tradition pay little attention to dates, places, or ordinary events and center on character, particularly on heroes and cowards; a family's memorabilia, swords, uniforms, and medals suggest only the heroics; an ancestor who was court-martialed may be a fine subject for a family story, but his dishonorable discharge papers are unlikely to be hung on the wall.

Folklore represents one of the important ways we give life meaning beyond the immediate present. If we were simply to list all the events of a person's life in chronological order, it would look as much like a shopping list as a lifetime. Using the forms of folklore, we order our lives into eras, and organize and dramatize incidents within them. We become able to both understand and communicate our experiences through our photo albums, our stories and celebrations, the objects we have collected.

One of the most telling uses of the past came in a set of stories made up by a father for his young son. Each night before going to bed, Saul wanted to hear a story. After trying a number of formulas, the father discovered that his son's greatest preference was for a recounting of his own day. So the father began each evening: "Once there was a little boy named Saul, and he woke up in the morning and had a bowl of Cheerios. . . ." Then he told of this young child's activities throughout the day.[2]

For this boy, the goings-on of his last twelve hours became wonderfully pleasing when recast in story form. Certainly the events were not the source of the appeal; the magic was in the telling, in the transformation of a daily history into story, of life into art.

Many of the episodes in a family's past are exciting and memorable; still, much of their magic derives from the forms in which the past is expressed—stories, photographs, celebrations. They hold secrets—about the past, of course, but also about the way we choose to think of ourselves, about the dreams we project backwards on our ancestors concerning what we would like them to have been, and what we need from them now.

1903.

JOAN BERNICK

Family Stories

A man is like a phonograph with half a dozen records," George Bernard Shaw once said, "You soon get tired of them all; yet you have to sit at a table while he reels them off to every new visitor." We like to think of family tales as those narratives which we don't mind hearing over and over again. For this book, however, we have considered a family story any incident retold by one family member about another over a period of years.[1]

A family generally believes its stories to be true, at least in part, for they are a rendering of history in which it has a definite stake. One person suggested that as we grow older our yarns are more likely to be accepted as fact:

That's one of the privileges of age. You get that old and you get to have all your stories be true. You could have been a liar all your life, but when you get old enough, all your stories become true. My grandfather lived by that privilege as he got older.[2]

Family stories are usually based on real incidents which become embellished over the years. They are relevant to American history not only because they convey some factual information, but because they often capture the ethos of an era.[3] A family story may epitomize a certain time period even if the details are false. They also tell us much about the storytellers and how certain episodes in our national history bear upon their lives today.

By combining fact and fiction expressively a family can shape its own history. Consider these contrasting anecdotes about the Civil War:

I have a great-great-grandfather who did not fight in the Civil War. He lived in Boston, and he looked just the way someone who fought in the Civil War would have looked, but his mother had bought him out. For three hundred dollars she got somebody to take his place. My mother used to tell me that when she was a little girl and they had the Memorial Day parade, in Boston, when all the old veterans who were alive were honored, my great-great-grandfather who had a little goatee and who looked like Colonel Sanders, but skinnier, used to have to hide in the house. And they would close the shutters and lock the door to hide their shame because he had not fought in the Civil War.[4]

A gentleman in Portland, Oregon, told quite the opposite story. His great-great-grandfather had not only fought in the Civil War, but had apparently been wounded so that he was remembered as having walked with a limp for most of his adult life. In fact, he started a long tradition of military heroism in the family. His grandson had fought in World War I; his great-grandson, in World War II; and his great-great-grandson, whom we interviewed, in Vietnam. All had been decorated soldiers.

Recently, this young man became inspired to do some research into the history of his family only to discover that his great-great-grandfather had been bought out by his mother for three hundred dollars—just like the great-great-grandfather in the earlier tale! Rather than face closing the shutters on Memorial Day, he simply relocated out west, walked with a limp, and passed down heroic stories.

The first story contains useful information for historians about the process of buying exemptions for military service, and the pressures on those who had done this once the war was over. The second, though patently false, is historically important because of the way it shaped subsequent events; the military history of the family is incomprehensible without knowledge of this story—regardless of its inaccuracy!

ANN HAWKINS

Until recently, folklore collectors were interested more in traditional folktales than in family stories. They gathered the legends and jokes which appeared in only slightly altered forms in many different locales, and were not grounded in the actual experiences of the tellers and their families. They set down the classic American tall tales about the giant killer mosquitoes of Texas, for instance, and the legends about our heroes such as Jesse James and Davy Crockett. These were often told in families, but did not concern the family's past.

Occasionally, traditional tales of the sort gathered by these well-known American collectors such as Vance Randolph and Frank C. Brown are told about members of one's own family. Jokes, floating legends, and traditional folktales sometimes appear as family stories. A grandfather, for instance, may tell a joke about a numbskull; when his grandchildren retell it, he may well become the numbskull. A traditional joke is thus transformed into a family story.

When we first collected this next story we thought it had no currency outside of one particular family:

My great-grandfather lived in Scotland, and he had a habit of going into a little pub or tavern in the evening and getting a little messed up and then he'd come home. One night he got to talking to this barmaid and she went with him over to the field and they had a little sport and then he passed out. She wanted to tell him how much she had enjoyed it and she couldn't talk to him so she took a blue ribbon from around her hair and tied it on his tool and left his kilt rolled up. My great-grandmother waited for several hours and he didn't come home. So she started toward the tavern in town and found him lying on the hillside with his kilt rolled up and the blue ribbon on his tool. And she said, "I'll not be knowing where you've been or what you've been doing, but I'm proud to see that you won the first prize."[5]

The folklorist who transcribed this tape for us was a young lady unfamiliar with the risqué meaning of "tool", and she transcribed it as "toe". Even with this alteration, she felt the story was funny. Sometime later she retold it at a dinner party at her parents' home in a different part of the country where an elegantly dressed woman told her, "Oh, you don't have to say the word 'toe.' We all know what you mean. We've heard that story before." This was an education for our interviewer, but reminded us, too, that traditional folktales can be told as family stories.

Despite such exceptions, family stories are usually particular to individual families. Hearing many different narratives about courtships or great fortunes lost in the family, members may mold their stories and memories to fit a traditional pattern. But for the most part tales are created anew in every family, and only occasionally travel between them.

America's diversity shapes its folklore: stories told in New England have their own distinct style and subject matter, as do the tales of Texans or Jewish-Americans. Whereas third-generation Americans often tell of perilous escapes from the old country, westerners recall their ancestors' journeys across the Oregon trail. Appalachian families often tell stories of long-standing feuds, black Americans of heroic action taken against oppression, and urban dwellers of poverty-

stricken lives in ghettoes and tenements. There may be individual topics which recur in particular ethnic groups and
regions; yet the general patterns and themes — around which
we've organized our stories here — are national. As citizens
of this country we share many similar experiences — immigration, the Great Depression, Vietnam. We
also share a common language, and, along with it, similar
ways of telling a story, certain ideas about what sorts of episodes are humorous or dramatic.

Grace McDonald lost her memory like a person losing
a set of keys. She was an old lady, a grandmother, and after
one of her bouts with sickness, she couldn't recognize her
children or remember the narrative flow of her past. Through
all her trials, however, she remembered one incident, one
that seems distinctly forgettable. Twenty years before she
had given her grandson some cookies. He didn't want to eat
them at the time, so he hid them in the attic. Several days
later she discovered his stash and chided him. When she took
sick and her memory faded, that incident, that family story
was the part of the past she held on to. Using such stories as

SOPHIE PARKMAN

clues to help her identify each of her children and grandchildren, her memory slowly returned.

Now she remembers each of them with a single story. Neal
is the one who would not pull the weeds when she asked him
to. Jay left the cookies in the attic. "Every time she sees me
she'll say that," Jay said. "You can tell all she has to do is
remember one thing like that and then she gets a whole flood
of things. But you know that's how she remembers you. . . .
It's easier to remember if she has these things as keys.

"She used to remember everything about you," he went
on. "She used to be real sharp, and she used to really take
care of us and she used to be a fantastic cook and a fantastic
baker, bringing up a family of seven people. Now it's almost
like she only has room in her head for one thing."[6]

If an aging woman only has room in her head for one
thing, why would it be a family story? Grace McDonald's
thought process, even in old age, delineates our own. Family
stories are part of the way we remember. They enable us to
simplify the complexities of a family member's personality
into an easily remembered, easily communicated narrative.

Incidents which describe a character, which pinpoint personality are remembered in family tradition; we call this the
character principle in American family stories. One man told

SUSANNE BENDA

us that his grandfather once asked his dad to help out a man whose horse was having trouble pulling a cart up a hill. His dad helped the man, and then lived by the principle of helping others. For the grandson the incident is "the sum total of things, it shows the kind of life he tried to perpetuate through me and my brother. . . . This is just one story," he told us, "it's just one incident, it's the sum total of things."[7]

Occasionally, family stories can pinpoint the subtleties of a personality with astonishing accuracy. We asked Grace McDonald's grandson and his wife if they thought her incidents or "keys" were well chosen.

"Neal is not lazy," Jay's wife said, referring to the story in which Neal put off pulling the garden weeds. Then she thought about it for a moment: "but he is sometimes."

And Jay agreed: "He is, Neal's extremely lazy. I'm sort of sneaky," he added, suggesting that the incident about hiding the cookies harbored a certain truth.

As we read these family stories and contemplate our own, we become aware of a certain irony. If the stories seem to pinpoint character, they simultaneously stereotype it.[8] Simplifying a personality into a single incident automatically reduces it to a character type as well; we must beware of what is lost as well as captured in these incidents. For example, in our collection of stories about memorable relatives, the most common protagonists are mischief makers, heroes, villains, and innocents. All of these celebrated family members must have been complex individuals in their own right. Their lives were probably filled with mundane events and contradictory acts; our innocents may even have been vicious on occasion. But their personalities linger in our memories and family stories in a simplified though satisfying way.

Along with characters, families hold on to episodes which mark the upheavals and sharp changes in their history. Families, like individuals, have a life cycle marked by stages of transition which are often celebrated in story. These include courtships, great fortunes lost in the family, migrations, catastrophes like fires and earthquakes, and family feuds. We call the tendency to retain incidents surrounding radical changes in our history the *transition principle* in family stories.

Sometimes, significant turning points are subtle and hardly seem dramatic at the time. One folklore student, for instance, related a tale about her ancestor Elizabeth and a confrontation she had with her Grandmother Astel on their farm in Wisconsin:

Grandma Astel lived with the family and ruled it with an iron will and a north country accent. Lizzie was something of a tomboy and her grandmother didn't approve of this. As one of her chores, Lizzie was supposed to collect the hens' eggs every morning. One day her grandmother came around to the henhouse and realized that the eggs hadn't been collected. She went looking for Lizzie and found her up in a tree. Grandma Astel extended her arm to the sky and then pointed to Elizabeth and said, "May ye never have a hen!"[9]

Surely this story seems far too insignificant to be passed down across three generations, yet it persisted. As the student explained, the incident marked a turning point in her family's history. Elizabeth left farming and lived in cities all her life; she never did have a hen. "The fact that she left farming was . . . important, because if one were to trace my family back through my matrilineal descent line, Lizzie was probably the first woman to leave farming in perhaps a thousand years." Thus, even this simple exchange between a grandmother and a granddaughter about the morning chores becomes a resonant tale in the context of a family's evolution.

Families, then, are selfish in what they choose to remember and pass on. They are willing to remember incidents which come to epitomize the character of a particular family member; and they are willing to remember an occurrence which marks a turning point in their own life or their family history. In this way, each narrative becomes not a rehash of an event, but a distillation of experience. A single episode comes to represent the entirety of a relative's personality; a whole family history is symbolized by a few dramatic turning points. The stories stand for much larger quantities of experience, and families have at their disposal a heightened form of communication which holds the family together and acts, in one person's words, "as a kind of glue."[10]

In talking about his own family, Donald Collins touches on an important aspect of storytelling—the setting.

JOAN BERNICK

Usually we all get together on Thanksgiving and Christmas. Relatives come in from Chicago, Florida—we've got some that come in from New Mexico. And you should see that house on the holidays. We'll have forty or fifty people come in there. All the women cook and all the men sit out on the porch and booze, you know. And that's when you really hear the stories. When you get them all together like that, you sit back and you hear them. Some of them I've heard so many times, it's just as if I was there.[11]

Meals are common settings for storytelling. They seem to be the time when family members are most at home with each other both physically and psychologically; perhaps it is not a coincidence that we satisfy our emotions along with our appetites. A quintessential family ritual, dinner involves the "ceremonial use of leisure,"[12] often with a ceremony of carving a main course, tossing the salad, and serving. It is often set apart from other meals by the use of more formal silverware and dishes, and often by prayer. As this example suggests, storytelling at the table is often, like the rest of the eating ritual, quite patterned and ceremonial:

My family is Sicilian and we also have a tradition of sitting around a table telling stories. But you can't tell stories except at certain parts of the meal. . . . We have a saying, "when you eat you don't talk." And any of us who talked during the first or second course of the meal were always chastised by grandma and grandpa. . . . After those courses were over, things came out like the artichoke which was not considered a course exactly, but it was kind of something that followed the real meal. Or the chestnuts, or what in Italian families we call the "frutte, dolce, caffè" — the fruit, the sweets, and coffee.

And that part of the dinner would begin with my grandfather eating a chestnut or eating an artichoke, and all of a sudden he would begin to laugh to himself. And inevitably, somebody would say, "Grandpa, why are you laughing?"

And that would begin the storytelling time. And he said, "I'm just remembering the time when. . . ." And that's how one began to tell stories at dinner time. And it happened in the same way almost every night.[13]

Storytelling in American families takes place at family reunions, at holidays, across the table at the evening meal. The very predictability of these occasions helps render them relaxing and enjoyable. Yet the subjects for stories contrast sharply with these recurring activities. Whereas dinners, reunions, and holiday celebrations tend to be peaceful and pleasurable occasions, stories told at those times are often about the unpredictable. They signal disruption or disaster.

Consider this example. During the Depression a grandmother scraped together a meal which consisted of vegetable soup and a salami. Uncle Bill, then a small boy, was alternately throwing a dirty ball against the wall and tossing it to his dog, King. On a misthrow the ball splashed into the vegetable soup. The grandmother was so enraged that she threw the hunk of salami at the young boy. King, mistaking the salami for the ball, leaped up, caught it in his teeth, and ran outside to savor it. The Depression meal was ruined.[14]

The episode is interesting because it marks such a sharp break in the storytelling routine. Ironically, the tale recounts an incident which may have ended a tale-telling session in the past; if any stories were to be told around the table that night they certainly wouldn't be after the dog ran off with the dinner. It is the same with countless similar tales which refer not to the day-to-day routine but to dramatic occasions which disrupt it — ruined meals, burnt turkeys, not the usual fare.

Transformed into story form, the incident of the dog and the salami was occasionally repeated as part of the evening's activities in the Martin family. It became part of the recurring dinner and after-dinner rituals, part of the very routine it disrupted. Through storytelling, the faux pas, the cooking disasters, the Depression traumas, and all the other misfortunes celebrated in family stories become institutionalized; they become part and parcel of holiday gatherings, of long rides in the car or of the evening meal. In this way family stories serve as a way of making the unexpected, the unforeseen, and the disastrous part of the smooth and routine functioning of the family.

We seem to acknowledge this function of storytelling when, after a harrowing or traumatic experience the remark is heard, "at least it will make a good story," or "we'll look back on this and laugh." Our family stories make it possible to laugh over incidents which were anything but funny at the time, and the laughter signals that the trauma has been incorporated into the daily round of family life. At its worst, a bout with poverty in the Depression, or outlaws in the west, or an earthquake or flood might have torn the family asunder. But transformed into stories these incidents become part of the smooth, day-to-day flow of family activities.

Storytelling is part of a number of family rituals and in many ways partakes of their functions. It stimulates healthy family interaction, it provides a technique for influencing and managing family members, it serves as a "family engineered canal" through which culture flows from one generation to the next.[15] Yet storytelling serves one function apart from other traditions.

In the family, as in every community, members gather on certain occasions to share in their leisure. The emotional investment often transforms these recurring activities into a set of binding traditions. Storytelling is a particularly meaningful part of these because it serves to make the critical, the disturbing, the tragic breaks in the cycle of rituals part of the smooth, ongoing life of the family.

HEROES

Tales of heroic action are plentiful in family stories. Their virtuous protagonists triumph over malicious opponents, with wit and wisdom or a decisive physical stroke. These stories are especially common among minorities such as blacks and Mexican-Americans. Many are also told about women who exhibit great courage defending their families, their plots mirroring the lines from a Woody Guthrie song about a cowgirl in the wild west:

When the rustlers broke on us
In the dead hour of night
She rose from her warm bed
A battle to fight.

She rose from her warm bed
With a gun in each hand
Said come all of you cowboys
And fight for your land.[1]

Katherine Morgan in her essay, "Caddy Buffers: Legends of a Middle Class Black Family in Philadelphia" writes about the stories surrounding her great-grandmother Caddy in slavery and in the years following the Civil War. She suggests that they were a "buffer," an antidote against the oppression of white society. One story tells how Caddy would run away from her masters, then get caught and whipped with a cat-o-nine-tails. "Do you think she would cry?" the story goes. "Not Caddy. It would take more than a cat-o-nine-tails to make Caddy cry."[2]

This next story about Caddy, and the examples from our own collection which follow, suggest our fascination with women and other oppressed groups who will not yield to the pressures and conventions of society:

Caddy got married to a Mr. Gordon. Getting married in those days wasn't like getting married today. Caddy never bothered to go to a preacher or anything. It was enough for two people to want to be married. Anyway, Caddy wanted a last name for her children and Mr. Gordon was willing to give them his. It's important for children to have an honest last name. Now Mr. Gordon was not a very good man, but he did have an honest last name and he let Caddy have it for the children. So Caddy put up with his laziness and didn't say too much. Finally though, he left Caddy and got himself another wife. . . . Caddy worked hard and saved her money. One day she heard that Mr. Gordon had gotten himself in some kind of trouble and was going to be sent to jail. Caddy went to the bank. She marched herself right up to the courthouse, marched right up the middle aisle. Stood before that judge. She reached down under her skirt and put the money on the table. She said, "Judge, I don't want no man with my children's name to go to jail so I'm here to bail him out." Now everybody respected Caddy, even the judge, so he let Mr. Gordon go. Caddy was that kind of a woman. Respectable.[3]

MIDGE HEIMER

: THE PAISLEY SHAWL :

My grandmother had an uncle who was the captain of a schooner out of Norfolk and she would go there to visit him. One time she had been down there for an extended stay and she had cast very envious eyes at a paisley shawl which was in one of the stores in Norfolk. Unfortunately, it was far too expensive for her to buy. So she talked about it and mooned over it and finally, when my uncle took her aboard ship, he said to her, "Sarah, you see that yardarm?" And she said, "Yes, Uncle Joe." "If you climb the main mast and touch the yardarm," he said, "I'll buy you the shawl." He thought for sure that she would never think of doing such a thing. After all, she would have to climb up in her dress which in those days had long trains on them. But she just looped her dress up as best she could, climbed the yardarm, and got her paisley shawl!

GERARD E. SHELTON
Vienna, Virginia

: IF IT WEREN'T FOR THAT DAMN LITTLE GIRL :

My grandmother grew up in Shepherdstown, West Virginia, where she lived with her grandfather. He was the head teller of the bank in Shepherdstown and they lived in a brick house right next to the bank. One night—this was in 1885 probably—she heard a noise and looked out the window. She could see some men trying to break into the bank. She woke up her grandfather—which was a gutsy thing to do, I guess, considering that he was like a bear. He took his horse pistol out of his bedside table, pointed it out the window, and fired at the bandits and they ran away. He didn't hit any of them. The bank, in gratitude, gave my grandmother a Smith and Wesson .32 pearl handled special.

She used to take it out into the country in the fall—this is how she tells it—and she'd stand on a bridge. As the leaves blew off the trees she'd go bang! bang! bang! She claimed to be a good shot.

After she got the gun she was again woken up by a noise in the bank next door. This time she skipped her grandfather, the middleman, and just leaned out the window herself. Like roota-toot-toot! It's the bandits!

This lot, I think, got caught at the ferry trying to cross the Shenandoah River. And according to her story, at the trial— when they were tried and sentenced to twenty-five years in jail or whatever—they said, "If it hadn't been for that damn little girl, we would have gotten away clean."

BENJAMIN THOMAS
Exeter, New Hampshire

RUTH COYNE

: THE TRIALS OF AUNT LUCY :

My grandfather was a lawyer, and all it meant to be a lawyer in those days was to pass a test, not to have an education per se. And so he was teaching both his sons to be lawyers, and my aunt Lucy pestered him to teach her. And he couldn't deny her anything, so he did. And everybody was in an uproar over that.

When a family feud broke out Lucy's mother insisted that she not fight, even though she had logged with the boys, and hunted with the boys, and been treated like a son. She apparently wore overalls long after the time it was cute. And Aunt Lucy stood it until the night that Ballard got shot. When that happened and she saw her mother holding her father and knew her father was badly wounded, she grabbed a gun and ran out in her nightgown into the middle of the front yard and just shot at everything and just cursed and sweared and carried on. And the Bakers stopped shooting for a moment, because they thought this was a good time to make fun of her. And as my aunt Neva says, "They called her everything vile and shameful on the face of this earth." But she still stood there and shot at them and wounded two men. Finally they started firing back, and my uncle Andy got the wherewithall to go out there and drag her back into the house so she could at least shoot from beyond the door. And from that point on she fought with them. She would go out in men's clothing.

When she hit about, I guess, twenty, she wanted to set up a law office, so her father helped her set up a law office, but unfortunately no one would come to a woman lawyer. So her father gave her money to buy a farm in southern Indiana. She wanted to leave the area, because she felt so bitter about all these things. And she left with a woman friend of hers and farmed there the rest of her life until she died chasing a cow around a cow lot. Died of a heart attack.

MARY GOODMAN

BEVERLY LEE HOWARD, AGE 24
Washington, D.C.

: ESCAPE FROM IGNORANCE :

My father, Junius Taylor, born a slave, escaped ignorance. He escaped not by the underground railroad, but by the big house. My paternal grandmother, a maid of the slave mistress, took her infant son Junius to "the big house" each day — the slave-master's home was called "the big house." To secure the baby, grandmother placed the child under the kitchen table and used his long shirttail to tie him to the leg of the table. In that manner, she always knew where he was. So Junius grew up at the big house, playing with the master's boys his age and older. When the tutor came and gave the boys lessons, the boys always taught Junius reading, writing, arithmetic, and everything else they learned. That went on quietly for years.

Then one day, rushing through the house, the slavemaster asked his boys playing on the floor, "What time is it?" His boys ignored the question.

Junius looked up at the clock and answered, "It is 10:30, Sir." Running back into the room, the slavemaster demanded, "Junius, didn't you answer that question?"

"Yes, Sir."

TOM THOMPSON

"If you can tell time, you can read!" Grabbing and opening the Bible, he shoved it into Junius' small hands and shouted, "Read!" His face was blood red.

Junius noted that the Bible was open to John 1:5, so he read, "And the light shineth in darkness, and the darkness comprehended it not."

The slavemaster snatched the Bible, and ran to the door calling his wife, "Vinnie, Vinnie, come quickly—I've got a nigger that can read!"

This violation of the anti-reading law had to remain a deep family secret, but one can no more unteach the ability to read than one can overcome and return yesterday's windstorm.

MANIE T. GEER, AGE 78
Durham, North Carolina

: RISING FROM THE RUBBLE :

Uncle Walter who lived down in Waldorf, Germany, was the descendant of Huguenots that had run away from France during the persecution of the Protestants in the 1600s. During the war he wanted to build himself a house, but all the materials for the house, of course, were defense important. You couldn't build a house for yourself. And to a German middle-class guy your house is the most important thing in the world; building your house and getting in it, getting out of apartments, is the crucial thing. And nothing—the world was turning upside down—nothing would deter him from this. . . .

He built a house and he hid it under a junk pile. He bought a lot, and loaned it out for people to throw junk on it. And then he would go there at night and build, layer by layer of brick, and cover it up with junk. When the end of the war came, there was a big pile of junk, but there was a house practically built. All it needed was a roof. In 1946, when the war was over, he raised the roof like a madman. And he was jubilant. He said, "I beat the Nazis, goddamn it, I beat them. I got my house." But the American army took it from him and quartered officers in it for two years, so it was a little delayed in his occupancy of it.

This story always appealed to me because it's an average person's story of what happened during the war. I like it because it's an example of how indomitable certain kinds of

*selfishnesses are even in the midst of great patriotic struggles.
This guy refused to give up middle-class ideals.*

CARLTON FLETCHER, AGE 26
Washington, D.C.

: BEATING THE WRAP :

*There's another one of these narrow escape stories that my fa-
ther always tells. My sisters and I would always make him tell
these stories, and now that I am an adult I know that it was
painful for him to have to relive this by telling these stories, but
we would insist and insist on his telling us. Here's one. Jews
weren't allowed to carry over a certain amount of cash on the
streets in Prague. This was before the war. And my father was
out on the street one day with what he knew was more than the
amount of cash in his pocket that he was supposed to have. And
he was stopped and picked up. The cops took him into the police
station, and he was supposed to empty out his pockets. So he's
desperate, but he got this brain wave. He took his handkerchief
which he had in his pocket and he wrapped it around the money
and pulled it out and blew his nose, and the money was in the
handkerchief. Then cleared his pockets out, and it was okay.
They didn't look in his hand, but the money was in his handkerchief. He just stuck it back in his pocket and walked out free.
So he was very quick on his feet.*

MARIANNE ROSS, AGE 41
Bethesda, Maryland

: COLD FEET :

*As a child growing up, I didn't know much about my paternal
grandfather. He had died before I was born. The only thing I
knew was that he had been a bartender, which didn't exactly
give me much reason to think very highly of him. But the one
story that was told about him meant more to me than I think
anything else could have. One day he was working at the bar
and a tramp came in without any shoes. My grandfather served
him, and the tramp said he had far to go still, and it was a cold
day. So my grandfather said, "Would you like to have my
shoes?" And the tramp said, "Yes." He took off his shoes, gave*

HOLLY CUTTING BAKER

them to the tramp. And in return the tramp said, "I'll draw
your picture for you." So he did a beautiful charcoal drawing
of my grandfather, nearly life size. We still have it in the
family.

Shortly thereafter my grandfather developed what they then
called consumption, which it is felt was really pneumonia, and
died as a result. I have reason to think that perhaps it was from
giving his shoes away, and tending bar for the rest of the day
and part of the night in his stocking feet. But it really endeared
my grandfather to me because I felt if he was nothing more
than a bartender, at least he was very loving and very kind and
very giving. And that to me is important.

SONDRA GORDON BLAZER, AGE 39
Franklin, Ohio

: JESSE JAMES ROBS A STAGECOACH :

This is a story that my grandmother and my great-aunt Patty
used to tell us about one of our great-great-uncles, Alexander
Gregg. Aunt Patty had this portrait of him dressed in his bish-
op's robes in her dining room. He was the first Episcopal
bishop of Texas, and of course everybody in the family thought
he was just a wonderful man. And they told a story about how,
when he was out in Texas, he was riding in a stagecoach and
the stagecoach was held up by Jesse James and his gang and
they stole Alexander Gregg's gold watch. Later Jesse James
realized who he had stole the watch from, and realized what a
wonderful man Alexander Gregg was. And so he returned the
watch, with apologies.

AMANDA DARGAN, AGE 31
Darlington, South Carolina

: IN THE NICK OF TIME :

I had no father, so my grandfather was like a father figure in
our home. He lived with us from the time I was age ten until he
died when I was not quite twenty-two. His name was Edmund
L. Faringhy, and his grandfather's name was John Forsythe,
and he had fought in the Civil War. John Forsythe was half In-
dian, and because he was half Indian when he got out of the

Civil War he didn't have the rights and privileges that the white man had. The only work that he could get was in a cavalry post. During that time they were fighting the Indians. He was kind of an Indian scout, from what I understand from grandfather.

The Indians had captured their captain. So, he took and put flour sacks on the feet of the horse, and he rode into the Indian encampment just as they were getting ready to kill the captain. They had him tied and were going to burn him at the stake. As my grandfather tells me, he rode in and got him off the stake, and rode out while they were having a war party. For doing that he was given the Congressional Medal of Honor. My grandfather still has the pistol he used.

LOU CAMPBELL
Washington, D.C.

ROGUES

Outlaws and horse thieves shoot their way through countless family stories; Americans like to relate to their grandparents, their great-grandparents, and ancestors as notorious characters. John Bishop got to the heart of the matter when he said:

My grandfather mentioned that his ancestors had been, perhaps for the most part honest—traveling peddlers and merchants, but perhaps with a little bit of piracy—they were in Latvia and Lithuania on the Baltic Sea. I'd like to think they were pirates, but when I think about it seriously, they were probably all hard-working people, to be perfectly honest.[1]

The baddest man we encountered in all of our interviews was an ancestor of a Portland, Oregon, family. This rogue migrated west, blotting out his past so well that the genealogical efforts of his descendants proved fruitless. He made one trip back east, chasing after the wife who abandoned him for his cruelty; he tracked her down and shot her in a cheap hotel. In an effort to put a stop to his wanton violence, or at least to give it some direction, he was made sheriff of a frontier town. The brutality continued, only now on the side of the law. Before he died he had gone mad, and he insisted that the family place his deathbed out in the middle of the town square. Then he demanded that his holster and two pistols be brought to him. Sitting in bed, the dying man began shooting leaves off the big tree that shaded the town square. As each leaf split from the tree he called out the name of a man he had killed.[2] This violent, cruel man is removed from the teller by a number of generations—rarely do we find such non-heroic behavior attributed to close relatives.

The Prohibition laws, however, proved a great boon for family storytellers. In 1933 when the law was repealed families could suddenly glorify the illegal act of bootlegging because the sale and purchase of liquor was now perfectly legal. They now had an ideal "notorious deed" by which to memorialize their fathers or grandfathers. As Prohibition began to seem pointless in hindsight, bootlegging qualified an individual as an outlaw when he had never really done anything wrong.

Women are rarely depicted as true outlaws in family stories, but bootlegging was an activity considered honest enough for them. Vera Pratt, for instance, is remembered in her family for smuggling bottles on the Pullman car from Montreal to New York:

She would line the bottles all up and down her body and the customs officers would come around and ask her if she had anything to declare. Since she'd be in bed, nude, they wouldn't want to check her sheets or anything like that, so she'd say, "of course not," and she'd hand them her passport.[3]

As William Humphreys said in his novel, *The Ordways*, the ancestors of a family go "beyond good and evil."[4] Families have a way of accepting their renegades; the black sheep remain part of the flock. As Susan Bobrow put it, "The history of my family is like the history of the country: good people, and bad people, and famous people, and people nobody ever heard of . . ."[5] We pass no judgment on the rogues who follow, except to note that their shadiness, their cowardice, their drunkenness were sufficient to earn them a place in tradition.

PATRICIA BEACH

: LET ME TELL YOU ABOUT
MY UNCLE VELVL :

My mother is famous in our family—in fact all of her sisters are—for telling bobe-mayse. *A* bobe-mayse *is a Yiddish expression for grandmother's tale, so they're all, you know, a little hairy. My favorite one has always been one about her Uncle Velvl.*

Uncle Velvl was a horse thief. After he came to this country from the old country, which was presumably Russia, he continued to practice his trade down in the hills of Virginia. One day, they caught him at it. And you know what they used to do with horse thieves. So they found a nice tall tree, and they did it to Uncle Velvl.

Some time later, a town grew on this site, and there was a lot of dissension over what they should call it. Then someone remembered that a long time ago a horse thief had been tied to a tree there, and they decided to name the town after the occasion of my uncle's hanging. They named the town Lynchburg, Virginia.

Now it just so happens, apparently, that there really was a great-great-uncle in the old country—who never got to this country—whose name was Velvl and who apparently really was a horse thief. But how this story ever grew up about Lynchburg, I don't know. But the assumption is that Burg, being a Jewish name, would fit the story.

ELINOR ABRAMSON
Washington, D.C.

: IT HAPPENED QUICKLY :

We're related to General Porterfield, who was the first southern general to be court-martialed. He lost a big Civil War battle at the beginning of the war. He had been in some of the battles in Texas, and had gone to the military academy. He was one of the few people with military experience at the beginning of the war, and was quickly made general, and quickly lost a big battle, and was quickly court-martialed.

ANNE SAUNDERS GREENFIELD
Alexandria, Virginia

: ELEVEN TO ONE :

I should probably tell you about my great-great-grandfather being killed by the Indians. There were about eleven Texas Rangers—he was one of the rangers—and one Indian. The Indian got about six or seven of them before they finally got him. So that's one of the not-so-brave things in the family.

: MY NOTORIOUS RELATIVE :

My great-grandfather was Italian. His wife came over here with his daughter and they lived in the United States for awhile and while they were here, he died carousing over in Italy. He died by jumping out of his mistress's balcony window and missing his horse. That was my notorious relative.

CATHY TIEF, AGE 18
Camp LeJeune, North Carolina

*At the request of several contributors, we have reprinted this story and all other unattributed stories anonymously.

: THE RAID :

Grandmother had lotto games. All the old ladies from the neighborhood and the parish had lotto games. They took turns having the games in their houses. For prizes, they'd have hand-tatted pillowcases or handkerchiefs, and their home canning, their jellies and their jams and things. And once in a while, a great prize would be a quilt or a jackpot of twenty-five dollars or something. We kids would be allowed to play a little bit but mostly we went around and collected the pot money.

But in those years, St. Louis cracked down on what they called vice. There was a ban on all kinds of gambling, supposedly including gambling in your own home. The ladies at the lotto club were raided by the police! There wasn't a lady under seventy-five there, but they were all herded into the paddy wagon and down to the police station! That was the talk of the town. They thought it was the greatest fun. Of course, they resumed their games the very next week.

SHARON BABER, AGE 42
Arlington, Virginia

: LET US PRAY :

The church meeting was the only place people had to go, and so that's where your courting and your meeting of all sorts went on. My aunt Neva tells me about walking seven miles to Bernan Springs School and walking seven miles back and then eating supper and walking seven miles to the Bernan Springs Church of God. The whole big gang of them would go, and she said they could care less what was said in church. And [she] said there wasn't really any place else for the drunkards to go either, because that's the only place where they'd have a crowd and any audience for their antics.

One evening this boy, Jake — I think his name was — came in and sat down next to my aunt Neva and aunt Lucy, and he was drunk and carrying on. And they were ashamed, so they told him to go outside. So he up and left. Well, he got into the vestibule of the church, and he ran into Bobby. Bobby was dating Jake's sister, Lena. Jake didn't think that Bobby was worthy of Lena. And pretty soon Jake had a knife in Bobby's stomach. And the next thing you knew there was shooting all in the ves-

MARY GOODWIN

tibule of the church; all these drunks that had been sitting out in front of the church and all these boys started fighting.

So the preacher raised the window in the back of the church, and everybody started crawling out through the back. And they were in a single file, and everybody was pressing, and as Aunt Neva says, "There was more screaming going on than a midwife would hear in a lifetime." And she got up to about where the altar was, and Sister Ann Hall, Sister Ann Hall Jones, that's her name, was on her knees there praying, paying no more mind to anybody coming and going. And she looked up when she saw Neva, and she said, "Neva, why do you worry? We're in the Lord's house. Whatever could happen to us here? Why, you may well know that I for one am not surprised. This is just a sign of things to come. Now get down here on your knees and pray with me for these poor souls that are marked to die." Neva said, "Thank you kindly, Sister Hall. I do believe I'll go along here for the ride." And so they crawled out the window and went to a couple of houses nearby.

Bobby was taken up to the local doctor, named Daddy Doc, who said it was only due to his belt buckle that he was alive. The knife had caught him in the belt buckle. So then they went back home, and the next evening they were all back in church at meeting time. I mean, you just accepted the violence along with everything else.

BEVERLY LEE HOWARD, AGE 24
Washington, D.C.

: We All Know the Truth :

This is something my father told me about once. I can't remember if it's my great-grandfather or great-great-grandfather. He'd been a Civil War veteran and after the war he went back to Massachusetts where he was, I think, a minor official of the town. One day they had a large fire at the town hall and it burned down. In the course of it burning down, my great-great-grandfather apparently rushed back in and came out with several things in a bag. Later on they declared him a hero for running into the burning building and supposedly looking to save somebody or something like that. But the story is passed down in the family that he remembered at the last minute to get a bottle of whiskey in his desk drawer. He ran back in to get it, and he was proclaimed a hero. But we all know the truth.

DENISE COOK, AGE 24
Washington, D.C.

: THE SAGA OF ABRAHAM CLARK :

This is a story that I seem to have gotten from my grandfather, Frank Kapple, before I was six years old, because he died shortly after that. I asked him about my middle name, which is Clark. He told me I was named for Abraham Clark, who was one of the signers of the Declaration of Independence. And then grandfather, without any comment, told me this story.

Each of the thirteen colonies had to have three members there for the Congress to participate in whatever was going on. And the Declaration of Independence was one piece of business that had to have at least three delegates who would be willing to sign it. Well, the story went that when they went around counting heads for the signatures, they were missing one person from New Hampshire. And they were frantic because they had to have every colony represented. So they went out into the street, "Anybody from New Hampshire? Anybody from New Hampshire?" Down the street comes Abraham Clark about three sheets to the wind. And he says, "I'm from New Hampshire." So they grabbed him, pulled him in, gave him a pen, and said, "Sign here." So he signed. And if you look at the signatures, you'll see that his is one of the two or three shakiest signatures on the entire document.

Recently I did some research to find out about the signers of the Declaration of Independence. We couldn't find much in our library, but finally we found out that Abraham Clark was not even from New Hampshire; he was from Elizabethtown, New Jersey. His nickname was "Congress Abraham," because he served several terms.

I've always wondered who the toads were who were so tight that they wouldn't put up any money for Washington's troops at Morristown and at Valley Forge and then back at Morristown. As it turns out, the leader of the tightwads was Abraham Clark. That's true.

DAVE KAPPLE, AGE 41
Littleton, Colorado

MISCHIEF
MAKERS

Each society and each culture," writes psychologist Erik Erikson, "institutionalizes a certain moratorium for the majority of its young people. . . . The moratorium may be a time for horse stealing and vision quests, a time to go out west, or a time for pranks."[1] America is no exception. We expect our young, particularly men, to "raise Cain," to "sow their wild oats." We even institutionalize rambunctious, rowdy behavior in mischief night and fraternity rituals.

Parents love to tell their children about their youthful antics—even while discouraging them from the same behavior. One person, for instance, remembered his father warning him not to play with firecrackers while in the same breath telling about the fun *he* had with firecrackers as a boy. Family storytelling often reinforces the mischief-making traditions of the next generation.

Pranks and practical jokes make especially good family stories and are extremely widespread. After all, the tales in their essence depict characters in conflict, A getting the better of B, B sometimes turning the tables and getting the better of A.[2] All family narratives share in this structure, but none fits as snugly within it as the practical joke.[3] The pranks are usually directed towards figures of authority— parents, teachers, drill sergeants, priests, preachers, rabbis— and have, by their very nature, a build-up, a conflict, and a

EARL HIGGINS

climax which can be transformed into a family story with little effort. Turning over an outhouse, for instance, was not only a tempting practical joke, but made for a good story which is told in numerous American families.

DAN BERGER

: THE OUTHOUSE :

I can't lend any authenticity to this story at all, but it has been told a hundred thousand times in the family. Grandpa Hatch was one of the first attorneys in South Dakota. He went to some kind of Methodist college. People are always talking about how rebellious youth are these days. But apparently, one Halloween they were going around dumping over outhouses and being particularly belligerent, and they dumped over the dean's outhouse. Unfortunately, the dean was sitting in the outhouse at the time. The dean identified them and they were about to be expelled from school and they pleaded and carried on and finally the powers that be decided that if they would buy the dean a new outhouse and put it up and build it with their own hands, then they would be reinstated in school. So they built the outhouse and they decided to have a dedication ceremony on campus. And they made a very large deal out of it and probably half the campus was there. They had a prayer and a little speech and then they decided to sing a hymn. And the hymn that they chose was a good Methodist hymn called "I Need Thee Every Hour" and they were expelled from school!

WILLIAM HATCH
Alexandria, Virginia

: THE BEARD I :

My grandfather and many of his brothers and perhaps some sisters emigrated to this country from the northern part of the Ukraine. When they were going to school in the old country they didn't have public schools. They had religious schools if they had any at all, and they went to a Jewish school somewhere in a town in the northern part of the Ukraine.

This school was run by a rabbi who had a long white beard. This old fellow had gone through many generations of young kids, tutoring them in their studies. So it got to a point where he

PAUL REIMERS

got kind of bored with the stuff. My grandfather, his youngest brother, and several other kids from the village were sitting around a very large, round heavy oaken table studying from their prayer books or doing whatever they were doing. As the kids would drone on with their prayers [the rabbi] had a habit of resting his chin on his doubled-up fists so that the beard sort of fell onto this table. My great-uncle said that one late afternoon when it was quite dark and the room was lit by candlelight, the kids got an idea. While one was droning on with his prayer book, another kid picked up a candle and allowed the molten wax to drip on this old fellow's beard till there was a good solid bond between beard and table. Then at the appointed time they all banged on the table, made a lot of noise, and the old fellow picked his head up but left part of his beard on the table. Every boy in the village got punished that night.

SHELDON LIPSON, AGE 42

: THE BEARD II :

My grandfather was the youngest of the three brothers. They were being taught their lessons by a rabbi with a very long beard. And the three boys were really rambunctious. And one day, the rabbi, while he was on a break or something, fell asleep. His beard touched the table. (It hurts to think about it!) The boys dipped tar, and attached his beard to the table. And then they banged the table, and the rabbi jerked up!

The story has got to be at least fifty, sixty years old.

JEFF FRANKEL, AGE 25
Silver Spring, Maryland

: ANYTHING YOUR HEART DESIRES :

When my father was going to college, it was the middle of the Depression. He was very poor and had to work to put himself through college. One of the jobs he had was at the student union which was run by a little Jewish fellow by the name of Goldheimer. Mr. Goldheimer was about five feet two and his arms were about four feet long. He looked like an ape. He walked sort of bowlegged with his arms swinging to and fro.

At that time the student center had a blue plate special, like a twelve-course dinner for sixty-five cents. The advertisement was "Anything Your Heart Desires." So one of those hot shot college kids came in and he happened to be from Newark. And he ordered the blue plate special. He went through all the courses and came to dessert. And the waiter said, "Now what will you have for dessert?" The guy looked at the menu and said, "Well, it says 'Anything your heart desires' and my heart desires a corned beef sandwich." The waiter was a little taken aback and said, "Well, I don't know if we can serve you that for dessert. After all, you've just had four corned beef sandwiches for dinner. I'll have to check with the boss." So he went to Mr. Goldheimer and said, "This character wants a corned beef sandwich for dessert." Mr. Goldheimer was outraged. He came back to the table and said, "What's this about your wanting a corned beef sandwich for dessert?" And the guy said, "Well, on the menu it says 'Anything your heart desires' and my heart desires a corned beef sandwich." Goldheimer threw up his hands, after he had paddled down the aisle like an ape. "All right, you're going to get the corned beef sandwich. Where are you from, son?" And he said, "Newark." And Goldheimer said, "Well, let me tell you something. You may be a big shot in Newark, but in Philadelphia, you're a big peeg!"

DAN BERGER, AGE 28
Philadelphia, Pennsylvania

TOM THOMPSON

: BUTTER I :

My father loves to eat. He likes good food and good cooking. Of course, during the war, certain foods were in limited supply, particularly on board ship where you could only carry so much; not only that, it was also very expensive. One day my father was eating at officer's mess and he was having a great time. He loved butter, and he was putting butter on everything, and the captain was watching. Finally the captain couldn't stand it, and he stood up and he said, "Cutting, do you know that butter costs two dollars a pound?" And my father reportedly looked at him and said, "Yes sir—and worth every damn cent!"

HEATHER CUTTING RAYL, AGE 24
Fall River, Massachusetts

: BUTTER II :

My grandfather told a joke which was repeated so many times that it got to be a tradition. The joke was that the family was sitting around the dinner table one evening, and an uncle was visiting. The uncle kept taking huge hunks of butter and spreading it on his corn. This was many years ago when it was very expensive. So my grandfather said, as sort of a gentle hint, "Butter is fifty cents a pound." And the uncle reached out and took another huge amount of butter and said, "Well worth it!"

JAN MAILON, AGE 28
Falls Church, Virginia

: HELL'S A POPPING :

The story that my grandchildren like most is the one about church a long time ago. We were Baptists, and they had no activities in church then at all; the children just had to sit and be still. That got very, very tiresome, so the boys would walk out of the church occasionally and try to find something to amuse them. One time they went to the church of the white people. There were great big cracks in the old fashioned church, and one of them noticed that a dog's tail was right by one of the cracks. He took a forked stick and pulled it out. He got a hold of the dog's tail, and he put his foot against the wall of the church, and he hollered, "Mad dog!" as he pulled back on the dog's tail. The dog started howling, and he kept it up and hollered, "Mad dog!" Well, the house just emptied itself.

That was so funny they decided that they just had to have some more fun. The church of the white people was completely empty, so they went down to the colored people's church, and they tried to find some meanness to get into down there. They noticed that every time the pastor'd make a good point, he'd say, "Now if I'm lying to you tonight, I hope I go to hell a-poppin'." And so the next week they went in and made the pulpit into a trap door. The next Sunday night they were ready to have their fun. They were listening to the preacher preach, and he made a real good point, and he said, "Now, if I'm lying to you tonight, I hope I go to hell a-poppin'." And so they jerked the trap door and under the pulpit he went. That was down in Louisiana, and the houses were built up high because of flooding. Under the pulpit he went and people went out of the windows and doors and everything saying, "I knew that preacher was lying, and now He's caught him at it!"

It was a crowd of boys, a lot of them. One of my uncles was in the crowd. They were not going to tell it, but it was so funny they had to tell it. So their fathers were the judges, and their fathers got together and decided these boys had to be punished. So they made the boys pick cotton for thirty-five cents a hundred until they made enough money to repair that pulpit and buy an organ for the black people.

CATHERINE NELSON, AGE 83
Little Rock, Arkansas

STEVEN ZEITLIN

: FIVE CARD DRAW :

My dad was always a nonconformist. He and his brothers worked in the oil fields during the oil boom days. One day my dad got hurt on the job and as a result, he said he couldn't bear to put any weight on his heels. The doctors, however, said it was all in his mind, and they sent him to a psychiatrist. This irked him, so my dad said, "If they want to think I'm crazy, I'll make them think I'm crazy." So he goes to the doctor's office, and the doctor brings out the Rorschach ink-blot tests. The doctor laid these cards down in front of my father, and dad reached over, picked them up, shuffled them and dealt them out for a

DALE BROWN

hand of Five Card Draw and said, "I'll open for a dollar."
This was enough to prompt the psychiatrist to report to the
company lawyers, "He's a good old boy, but he's crazy as hell."

DANIEL W. HUMPHREY, AGE 28

Holdenville, Oklahoma

: SUNDAY SUPPLEMENT :

*When my father was working construction, he became an ama-
teur photographer, and a pretty good one too. They were building something in Providence, Rhode Island, and there was a
news photographer on the scene. They wanted to do a feature
story in the Sunday supplement on this building, and the news
photographer wanted to have an aerial shot, but he was scared
to death of heights. So my father, being my father, said, "Well,
give me the camera, and I'll take the picture for you." "Well,
where are you going to take the picture from? There's no
bridge; there's nothing you can look down from." And my father pointed to this crane which was several hundred feet up in
the air. So my father said, "I'll take it from up there." And the
guy said, "You're crazy!" But my father climbed up to the top
of his crane, not thinking anything of it. And he took a picture
of the site, and in doing so he missed, and he took a picture of
his foot. And so my father's foot made it on the front page of
the Sunday supplement.*

HEATHER CUTTING RAYL, AGE 24

Fall River, Massachusetts

: THE HABERDASHER'S CON :

*My grandfather worked for a haberdasher for awhile when he
came here. He was a good salesman and a good hustler. I don't
know if this joke about haberdashers really happened to him.
He said one day, a woman in her late forties came in and said,
"My husband has just passed away. He needs a suit to go to the
hereafter. He never had a decent suit in his life." Apparently,
according to my father, he sold her a suit with two pairs of
pants.*

MYRON BRETHOLZ, AGE 21

Baltimore, Maryland

: ONE LAST FLING :

I never heard a cross word out of either one of my parents. I've never seen such a couple get along in my life. Dad died just before I was nine years old and prophesied his own death. He prophesied his own death in 1904. He told mother at Christmas—he didn't drink then—he said, "I'm gonna get just full enough to have a little fun." She said, "No, you're not." He said, "Yes, I am. This will be my last Christmas. I'll never live to see another." And he was only a young man, only thirty-six years old, when he died. He said, "I'm gonna die before next Christmas, and I'll never see another, so I'm gonna enjoy life."

Well, he was so serious, that she agreed to go along with it. So the first thing he did—he had a quart of whiskey hidden in the kitchen—he called his next door neighbor and said, "Come on in, let's have a drink." He said "Drink fast now, before the old lady catches us." So old man Jolly, he uncorked the bottle and threw a big drink down, and it came right back. And mother had to mop the kitchen, because she had found the bottle and had exchanged it for a quart of vinegar.

So then dad went downtown, and the first thing he did, he threw a big firecracker under the chief of police, and the chief took after him and right through a store they went. Dad squatted down behind a counter, and the chief ran out the back door when the clerk pointed to it. And when the chief got tired afterwards, he told his deputy, he said, "Don't chase Dick Smith, because that's enough, because he's having fun off of us." Well, that took the fun out of the game.

So dad, he bought about a quart of torpedoes, you know, the kind you throw down, that pop? He bought about a quart of them and he paid nine dollars for nine firecrackers. And in 1904 a dollar firecracker was some firecraker. Dynamite wasn't anything. They didn't have taxis then, so he hired a horse-drawn surrey home. He got home and lit one of those big crackers and threw it on the front porch of the sawmill shanty where we lived; it blew the door open, blew out a window, scared the hackman's horse, and he scattered that hack a mile back to town. Dad was really celebrating. Mother confiscated the crackers and put them away before he blew up the house, but he had that quart of torpedoes. He went up and took a double handful and threw them up on the roof and burned all of us kids until mother put him to bed with a broom handle.

C. O. BURNS

Well, he got up next morning, and he was feeling just as good as ever. A few of the neighbors came over to get a drink off him, and Santa Claus had brought me a little steam engine about that long. Dad was trying to fire that up and get steam to run that. Well everything was going just fine until he spilled alcohol on his hands. It caught them on fire, and he wiped his hands on his Georgia knit socks real good and got his socks on fire, tried to beat the fire out with a broom, and said, "Now get out of here and bring me some water." And, "Go bring me some stove wood." So he ran out and the next thing she knew, he had the stove round full of Roman candles. Well those Roman candles had the fuse first, you know, they shot out of the old wood burning cook stove. We didn't have any screen doors. Some of them went out in the yard and shot the chickens out from under the house, shot the cats from under the beds, through the bedrooms. It was a whoopee time. Mother was fit to be tied by then.

But the next June, his picture came off the wall. No frayed string, no broken wire, or anything, it just fell from above the mantle right on the pine floor, a 16 by 20 picture. It was an enlarged photograph and the old gilt frame must have been as big as this table top. It didn't even scar the frame, didn't break the glass. So dad told mother, "Old lady," he said, "see that. Well that means I'm going before the end of the year." "Oh," she said, "Maybe not." "Yeah," he said, "I am, too," and sure enough, he went on and insured his life. He paid one premium, that was all. He died December the eighth, 1905.

ERNEST A. SMITH, AGE 80
Pine Bloom, Georgia

: VOTING FOR SHERIFF :

Dad dropped off the train in his overalls one day, and he found a voting booth set up on the station platform. Wearing his greasy overalls, he went in and voted for the man of his choice, who was the chief of police running for reelection. Then he took the train out of town, went home, came back down again, and he voted again. He'd cleaned up, and they didn't recognize him. Then he went to the barbershop, had his handlebar mustache shaved off, and bought him an overcoat and a derby hat, and he came back and voted again. That time the sheriff, I mean the police, caught him. He said "Dick, don't you think you've voted enough times?" "Well," he said, "What are you kicking on? I voted for you every time." Well, the chief got reelected all right, and he went on from there to become the high sheriff of the county.

ERNEST A. SMITH, AGE 80
Pine Bloom, Georgia

: Dominoes :

I don't know just how true this is. My father related it one way, my mother contradicted. My great-grandmother was Catholic and the rest of the family was Protestant. My great-grandfather wouldn't let her practice her religion. And on her deathbed she of course begged to see a priest. And he finally said OK, it was all right for her to be buried in a Catholic church.

He had to get loaded to go to the church. And supposedly the priest was up there saying his funeral mass and you know they say "Dominus vobiscum." And he misunderstood, being drunk and in the back of the church. And he goes staggering up the aisle and he says "I'll have a game of dominoes."

Like I said, my father was a notorious exaggerator.

JEAN BOURASSA, AGE 50
Oxon Hill, Maryland

: Checkers :

My dad has a really famous story about the first day the Golden Gate Bridge was open. He was about seventeen years old, and he and a friend thought they would be the first people to cross it, so they went down early in the morning. Well, when they got there, they found out that there were five thousand people there, and some of them were in track suits all ready to cross the bridge. My father and his friend thought, "Ah, we'll never make it." So what they did is they went into town, into San Francisco, and they bought a checkerboard. And they went out to the middle of the bridge and they sat down and they began to play. So now they can say they were the first people to play checkers on the Golden Gate Bridge.

ANN REYNOLDS, AGE 22
McLean, Virginia

: THE PIGS :

My mother's uncle Leo always had to feed the pigs when he was a boy, but he didn't like it. Whenever his dad asked him if he had fed the pigs, he said he did when he really didn't.

One day Leo went outside and noticed that two of the pigs were dead. They died of starvation. Leo ran away and didn't come back till dark. Then he started pretending to feed the pigs. Each day he moved the dead ones into a different position so that when his mom and dad looked out the window they wouldn't get suspicious. Since rigor mortis had set in, the pigs were stiff, and their eyes bulged out. Because of the eyes, Leo had to make the pigs face in the opposite direction.

One day when Leo was sick, his dad went out to feed the pigs for him. . . . He called the pigs and when the two dead ones didn't answer, he went to investigate. He tapped one of them, and it fell over. The same happened to the other. Leo was lucky that he was sick because he couldn't get that much of a beating.

JEFF MAJTYKA, AGE 15
Purcellville, Virginia

SURVIVORS

Family members who triumph over poverty and hardship are often remembered in family traditions. Stories about struggles for food, shelter, or clothing are told in every generation, but become especially common with the Great Depression. For all of their needs, Depression children were not to want for good stories with which to discipline their children. "My father," said Sherry Lynn Cocheres, "has always told us about his youth during the Depression. He always tells about his worn blue pants with the green patch, or was it his green pants with the blue patch?"

More often than not, these stories have women protagonists who hold the family together through desperate times. Some believe that whereas men do well in emergency situations, women are more successful in coping with longterm stress. They are celebrated for this quality in family tales.

One person we interviewed suggested that people like to reminisce about their hard times because it makes them feel as if they have accomplished something with their lives. They made it through. They earned the right to look back with laughter and nostalgia on their trials, and tell good stories from hard times.

: THE SHEEP SHED :

This is about my favorite aunt, Caroline. She's had a hard life over the years. When she had probably given birth to about her sixth child, there was a promise from her husband's side of the family of a section of land that they moved to. With that section of land there were already farm buildings but no house. They arranged for a house to be moved down from a county two counties north of there. Well, this was during the Depression, during the early 1930s, and they were just dirt poor. Of course, Caroline, with these six kids, couldn't go up to look it over, but Ed went up and looked over the house and said it was fine. It had linoleum floors, and it was wallpapered, and it had, I think, three bedrooms and a front porch, which at that time was a fairly good house. It was a house they could live in.

There was another old house at this farm, which had been used as a sheep shed. The movers got confused, and they moved the sheep shed down, drove into the yard with the wrong house, with sheep shit all over it and cobwebs. You can imagine the stench which must have accompanied it. And they simply could

46

not afford to have the right house moved down. It would've been another $250, and they couldn't make the workers undo their mistake.

Caroline and her sister Millie helped clean up the worst. She actually scooped it out. It being a sheep shed of course, there were no closets or anything, so the kids would just have to keep their clothes in boxes under the bed. Eventually Ed got hold of some lumber, and he did build closets and raised the roof, in order for the kids to sleep upstairs. But they lived in that house, in a sheep shed, for twenty years.

LOUISE KROESE, AGE 29
Washington, D.C.

TOM THOMPSON

: FAIRY TALE :

There is sort of . . . it's almost like a fairy tale the way it happened to work out when some relatives came over around 1880. Two families settled next to each other. One was very wealthy and had five handsome sons, and the other had sort of a drunken father that no one would talk about and they had a daughter. This daughter went to clean house, to be the maid for the rich family, and she married one of the boys. And these are my great-grandparents. But it's very interesting because it's sort of like Cinderella and the prince.

My parents are now fairly well off, not really rich or anything, but they own an apartment building. They could afford to have someone come in and do the domestic work, like cleaning the stairways, but to this day my mother insists on doing the scrubwork. And we've talked about how it's perpetuated, this thing that she thinks she's just a scrubwoman even though she really is very comfortably well off.

SUZANNE GIBSON, AGE 30
Alexandria, Virginia

: DOWN IN ALABAMA :

In Alabama—Talladega, Sylacauga, Goodwater—in the late thirties, early forties, people worked very hard. Farming was their way of life. It was difficult because, being black, a lot of them were sharecroppers; my dad was a sharecropper. When I was born, he didn't have the money to pay for the delivery which was thirty dollars, so he gave the doctor a suckling pig and fifteen dollars. Doctors and lawyers were accustomed to taking something in trade in those days.

I was born the year that Joe Louis defeated Max Schmeling; many black parents named their male children "Joe Louis." My father dubbed me Joe Louis Thomas, but the man he sharecropped from, Mr. Fred Burroughs, who ran a jewelry store in town, insisted that I be named after him, so I was named Fred Louis. He didn't have too much of a choice; he didn't want to alienate the man.

I don't know if it was a black-only kind of thing, but I do remember that by the time my grandfather harvested his crop and went in town to sell the cotton and things like that, he ended up owing the man money. And he would have to go into debt to get enough seeds to go start all over again. It was a very traumatic experience to see a man who you consider stalwart stand and cry and have to swallow it.

That's all they did—they worked. They worked and went to church every Sunday. One would carry one's shoes over one's shoulders till you got to the church, because the roads were not covered, so you got a lot of dust. And what you did was use Vaseline to polish your shoes, give 'em a high gloss. Some of the guys would slick their hair down with a pomade, but use soot from the chimney or the stove to make it very black and shiny.

Part of the tradition was to teach us how to survive under white domination. So you were taught little expressions, "If you're white, you're all right/ If you're brown, hang around/ If you're black, stay back." And you begin to accept that as part of your lifestyle. "Don't mix in white folks' business," we were told all the time. "Mind your tongue around white folks." It was almost like an eagle teaching their young ones how to feather their nest, you know.

The fireplace was a gathering place at night. It was the greatest source of light because we only had kerosene lamps. And the older people would sit around and tell stories. They were primarily ghost stories or stories of black people running into trouble with white people—the time they really saw the Ku Klux Klan, how they came and got this or that person. Sometimes there were stories about how the Klan would come in and there would be a standoff.

I remember I lived with an Indian doctor in Talladega—his name was Dr. Peavy—and he ended up getting most of the patients in town who were not able to be helped by trained physicians. He cured a lot of people using roots and herbs. I was one of them, 'cause I had a serious case of athlete's foot when I was a child, and I couldn't walk. The doctor at Talladega College was giving me a treatment, but it wasn't working and the root doctor made a salve out of roots and in three or four days I was back on my feet again.

But one of the stories was that the Klan came after him one time. I don't know for what reason. He was sitting on his porch with a shotgun, knowing that they were coming. They were threatening to kill him, but he didn't back down; he just said that he had a doublebarreled shotgun, and the first one that moved to try to take him—well, he would take a few with him. He was ready to die. And they finally said, "Oh, he's crazy!" and they left him alone.

And that became part of instilling some kind of pride, you know, here was a man who stood them off. But it didn't help you overcome the basic fear. I remember once, after having moved to Brooklyn, New York, going back on a vacation to a place called Tallapoosa, Georgia, which was just across the Alabama line. I had forgotten the racial fears. I was walking down the streets with some former childhood schoolmates, and I bumped into this elderly white man by accident. And he turned and he drew back to hit me (but he didn't)—he just ver-

bally threatened me. And all of a sudden the fears came back. And I said, "My God, now I remember it all." And I promised I'd never go back again.

FRED THOMAS, AGE 38
Washington, D.C.

: PRIDE FROM THE SOLES UP :

The story that's on my mind is on my mind because I just got word that my great-uncle Jim died. His name was Jim Cobb and this is a story he used to tell me about looking for work in the Depression. He'd been out of work like everybody else for months and months and pounded the pavement and wore out the soles of his shoes—his shoes were threadbare and so forth. And finally he got hired and the man who hired him, as he told the story, said, "I want you to know why you got this job, because there were twenty or thirty other applications. I hired you because you polished around the soles of your shoes, you polished the edges of your shoe soles." And the man said, "I think that's a sign of somebody who'll take pride in his work." And I polish the soles of my shoes to this day.

WARREN CORBETT, AGE 30
Washington, D.C.

: SCRAP METAL DAYS :

When I was growing up in St. Louis during World War II, the kids in the neighborhood would get together and go en masse to the neighborhood theater. We'd have our ten cents to get in and our five cents for popcorn, and we'd go, six or eight or ten or twelve of us, at ten in the morning and stay till six at night. During the war, there was such a shortage of gasoline, rubber, and metal. One way to encourage people to get scrap metal was to have kids bring it to the movies on Saturday. We'd each have to bring a piece of metal and that was our entrance fee. If you didn't have your piece of metal, you would have to pay a dime to get in. The metal would be piled up in a parking lot and then they would send it down to be melted down for airplanes and whatever else was needed. I once donated my pair of roller skates and then I cried afterwards, wishing I still had them. A couple of kids took their mothers' good pots and pans from the kitchen and some took their fathers' tools out of the tool chest. . . anything to get metal so that we could get into the movies.

SHARON BABER, AGE 42

Arlington, Virginia

: DOWN TO THE LAST DOLLAR :

There were times, you know, when we were right down to the last dollar. I remember once we had started off to travel around, sort of mixing vacation with my father's selling to keep the family together in the summer. I think they were down finally to about eight dollars, and before the end of the day they had about a dollar and a half left. My dad had gone into general delivery at the post office to pick up some things that would have come from his mother who was watching our home and supervising the business that was being run out of the basement. There was a letter asking for a dollar and a half as a refund for something. My dad said, "Well, if I send a dollar and a half, that's the last money we've got." And my mother said, "Well, just go ahead, Charles, the good Lord will take care of us some way." So he went in to make out a money order to pay the dollar and a half and got to talking with the woman who was making out the money order. And before they were through, she had asked to see some of his things. And he sold her about forty dollars worth, and she brought in some other friends. So before the day was out, we were back in business again and going. But I don't know how many kids today had their families down to the last dollar they have.

CHARLES BERGUN, AGE 46

Lafayette, California

INNOCENTS

Family stories are peopled with characters in conflict; heroes shoot outlaws, jokers play pranks, immigrants outsmart border guards. But there is a particular kind of family character who is not bent on getting the better of another, nor is he a victim or the butt of a joke. He simply gets the better of himself.

It's the innocent who, in a characteristic episode, gets into the wrong car, drives away with the wrong wife, talks to her all the way home, and doesn't notice the difference. William Humphrey writes about Giles Ordway who rode his horse and buggy to Knoxville on business. By accident he took the train home. About a week later he remembered the horse and buggy. He went to the depot to buy his ticket, and purchased a round trip![1]

These family stories are related to many traditional tales and jokes found around the world. "The Stupid Man" is even a category in folktale indexes. Oftentimes, they are told about children in the family. A child's solution to a problem often seems comical to us, yet forgiveable and charming because it makes perfect sense from the young person's point of view. In one family, a child gently sat on an egg, hoping to hatch it like a mother hen. In another, a child was told by her sister that they should split a diet soda which had only two calories, that way they would only consume one calorie apiece. The young child asked how her sister could be so sure that the two wouldn't end up in the same glass.

We spoke to one family which told about an incident which happened when the mother was pregnant, and her two children were suggesting names for the baby.

"Well, if it's a boy," said the oldest child, "can we name him John?"

"Maybe," said the mother.

"Well, if it's a girl," she went on, "can we name her Mary?"

"Maybe."

Finally, the youngest child, anxious to prove her intelligence, piped up, "Well, if it's a dog, Mom, can we name it Lassie?"[2]

Sometimes these stories are told to teach a lesson, to tease a child or an absent-minded adult into changing his behavior, and thus resemble moral or cautionary stories. But perhaps more often, the celebrated mistake is so much the product of a child's stage of life, or an adult's established way of thinking, that the tales are just playful and forgiving. We don't laugh at these innocents derisively, but gently. Perhaps we understand that the simple day-to-day tasks of going to work, keeping track of money, or finding our car in a parking lot aren't all that easy. We all do them, succeeding most of the time, but failure is inevitable. And if one person fails a little more often, a little more flagrantly than another, he deserves some affection along with our laughter; perhaps we're laughing at a small part of ourselves.

NANCY CHISUM

: THE FOGGY MUSICIAN :

We've always been a musical family. When my grandfather was old, he elapsed into a complete fog. He wouldn't say a sensible word, week in and week out. But his nurse would bring him to the dinner table and he'd sit there and he'd eat. The night boat to Norfolk from Baltimore would come by every night at eight o'clock and it would go "Booooooaaah" as it went by the house. One night, out of this total fog he had been in for months, grandfather stood up, went over to the piano, poked it, and said, "E Flat." Then he sat down and went right back into the fog.

: INNARDS I :

My mother's family are emigrants from Sweden and one of my great-uncles was well-known as a storyteller in the town that he came from. He used to declare that he had a next door neighbor named Henrik who was over seven feet tall. He was an enormously strong man. He only cut his hair and shaved once a year, and only bathed once a year. He was quite a character. People would just tell stories about how Henrik would just take a whole fish and gulp it down, bones and all. . . . One of the stories they tell is that Henrik always used to go to the butcher's and buy, or actually he was given, all of the innards of the animals, because he loved to eat them. He'd bicycle over and they'd be wrapped up in brown paper and he'd put the brown paper inside his coat and button it up to keep the sack next to his body and he'd bicycle home.

Well, one day when he was bicycling home, there was a drunk motorist coming the other way. He got very close to Henrik and Henrik swerved and he went down into a ditch and his bicycle crashed. The motorist stopped and he got very frightened because Henrik's jacket had come open and the bag had broken and all of the entrails were all over his chest. And the motorist, who was very drunk, said, "Oh, no! Get an ambulance!" And Henrik at that point stood up and said, "No, no!" And the motorist fainted and Henrik had to get help for him instead.

: INNARDS II :

I bought a secondhand bicycle with the money I had saved over a period of years and got a job in a meat shop delivering meat. The man I worked for had a big saloon business. In those days the saloons had what was called a free lunch counter. There would be a place in the back of the bar where you could go and eat whatever you wanted, included free when you paid for the price of the beer. My job was to deliver the liver. They always bought large quantities of it. If they'd buy fifty pounds of liver, I couldn't put that much on my bicycle, but I could make two twenty-five pound trips. The liver was always wet and messy so he always wrapped it in double thicknesses of butcher paper. Then I'd quickly put it in the carrier basket of my bicycle and I'd run down to the saloon. I'd carry it in and by that time the paper would be soaked.

Well one day when I had twenty-five pounds of liver in the basket, the fellow said, "Look. There's a delivery over on Orchard Lane. The woman's in a hurry. Go there first and then go to the saloon." So I did, but this was a slight delay and the moisture from the liver got into the paper a little deeper. Just as I turned to come up to the front door of the saloon a woman came along in a car and hit the front wheel of my bicycle. I was sent sprawling into the street. The liver had been in the paper just long enough to soak through so that when it spilled into the street, there was all this bloody liver laying in the street and me laying in the street. She looked at me and she said, "Oh, are you all right?" I guess she thought the liver was me spread all over the street.

TED F. SILVEY, AGE 71
Washington, D.C.

: FOUR TWENTY-FIVES :

My grandmother had a younger brother who was a funny guy. He had been living on the farm until it was time to go to college. When he was ready to leave home, his father gave him a one hundred dollar bill. And you know that was the most money he had ever seen. Before that he had never seen anything bigger than a five. So he went down to the bank to get it broken down. To the bank teller he said, "Can I have change for this one hundred dollar bill?" And the teller asked, "How would you like it?" He replied, "Just give me four twenty-fives."

: UP FROM THE DEAD :

The grandfather after whom I was named was David Herman. He was blind in one eye, and he was once hit by a hearse. The two drivers, two young gentlemen, figured they'd just pick him up and take him to the hospital. So they picked him up and put him in the back of the hearse. When he woke up, he found he was in the back of the hearse. So he decided that no one was going to bury him! He opened the door when they stopped at a traffic light, and he started to run, and they started to run after him, but they couldn't catch him. Eventually the whole story came out in the newspaper about how they ran after this man jumping from a hearse.

DAVID CAREY
New York, New York

WENDY WOLF

: On the Wings of a Turkey :

This is about my great-grandfather. He would have died around 1910, or so. His name was Frank, and he was supposed to have been a real small guy, very short, very slight. He was out in the woods running his turkey traps one day. He was very lucky that day, and he got something like eight or ten, maybe a dozen turkeys. Now a wild turkey's a pretty big animal. I don't know if you've ever seen one. He had all of them collected, and he was holding a half dozen in each hand by the feet, and he swung them over his shoulder to carry them. Then a wind came up and caught in the turkey's wings as he swung them over his shoulder, and supposedly carried him up in the air. He had to let go of a few turkeys before they let him down.

And this is my dad's addition to the story—that his grandfather, the son of the man this was supposed to have happened to, always said that if their grandpa had been smart, he wouldn't have let go of them, but would've held on until they flew him over the house and then let go of a few, and he would've been home, and he wouldn't have to carry them all.

DENNIS F. SIEVERS
Vincennes, Indiana

LOUISE TIRANOFF

: To Life! :

Well, my grandfather came from Poland, and he just died here about a year ago, at the age of ninety-five. I remember one thing he said. He was a very wise man, but he was kind of a boozer all his life. My grandmother was also from Poland, and she didn't approve of alcohol, and so they had kind of a going battle all their lives about him drinking. On his birthday or something like that I'd take him a bottle of bourbon. And he told me one day when I brought him a bottle of bourbon for his birthday—I think he was ninety-two at the time—he said that he had given up alcohol, that alcohol had killed two of his brothers and so he thought that it was time for him to quit, because he wasn't old enough to die yet. So I asked him about the brothers it had killed. And he told me it had killed his brothers Collin and Stanley. I checked up on it and found that Collin was ninety-two when he died and Stanley was eighty-nine.

ROBERT KOSMICKI, AGE 36
Washington, D.C.

: The Walrus Story :

This is a story about my younger sister Ann. She was probably about seven years old and I was probably about twelve. Her birthday happened to fall on Easter Sunday, and true to family tradition, you got to pick what you wanted to do on your birthday. She decided that she wanted to go to the Coney Island Aquarium, so after church on Sunday the family packed up to go. Everybody was still dressed in their Easter finery, including an old Easter hat that my mother had stayed up until the wee hours of the morning putting a new velvet ribbon and a new flower on, so it would look pretty and new for Ann to wear to church on Easter Sunday on her birthday.

So we went to Coney Island, walked around, looked, and then it was time to go home. And being a family of four women and one man, three of the women had to go to the bathroom, and I stayed with my father. We wandered around a little bit, and then it's time to meet at the walrus exhibit, which is an outdoor exhibit. We get there and all of a sudden there's this huge crowd around the exhibit, and we're wondering what's going on. So we nose our way up and look around and everyone is laughing hysterically. And we look at the walrus, and here's the walrus diving and jumping in the water wearing an Easter bonnet — my sister's Easter bonnet! Then we saw this one bright red, shrieking, hysterical little girl crying because her Easter bonnet is being worn by the walrus. The zoo keeper is yelling at my mother about how the animal is going to eat this hat and choke and die, and she will be responsible for this eight-hundred-dollar walrus.

Well, finally the zoo keeper got the hat away from the walrus and handed it back to my sister, who didn't look too pleased about getting it back at all. And we packed up in the family station wagon and went home. And that's the end of the walrus story. Every time the family gets together we tell it.

CAROL BIGELOW RIGGS, AGE 25

Arlington, Virginia

: HOW MOTHER LEFT HER MARK :

When we moved into our house in 1935, it still had an outhouse. Being a large house, it had two doors with two holes in each door so you could seat four comfortably. We had plumbing, too, but there were nine in our household and mother kept up the outhouses because there were times when everyone had to use the bathroom at the same time. She had shellacked the wooden seats one day and a week or more had gone by, and she went out and sat down and realized that she was not going to be able to get up. The shellac was still sticky. So she contemplated the various alternatives, one of which seemed to be to holler for help, and another one not to holler for help and she realized that the eventual outcome would be that one way or another she was going to have to get up and leave part of her attached. So she finally did it alone. The ring around her backside took several weeks to heal!

MIDGE HEIMER

Germantown, Maryland

: NAPOLEON :

One of my ancestors had once driven a carriage for Napoleon when he was fleeing Russia because the czar had made a bargain with Napoleon to provide transport through Germany, which is where my family came from. Later on, the family came to the United States to live.

This ancestor was a very old man. He was poor of eyesight, he was hard of hearing, and he had no sense of smell whatsoever. They lived out in the woods and he didn't recognize many of the animals here or how they lived.

So one day he was strolling there with his walking cane and his Sunday best, and he came upon a skunk. The skunk of course had a nice big stripe up his tail and a great plume and it reminded him of Napoleon whom he had driven in his carriage. And he said, "Well, Napoleon, what are you doing here?" He took his cane and gave the skunk a big smack and of course the skunk retaliated. The old gentleman was completely unaware of it because he had no sense of smell and he returned home but no one would let him in the house. They made him go to the barn where they burned the Sunday clothes which he had brought all the way from Germany.

CAROL MAAS, AGE 27
Greenbelt, Maryland

: A STUDENT TILL THE END :

My grandmother was married to a rabbi who apparently was not much of a worker. As a rabbi, he was a perpetual student, but he decided that what he really wanted to do of all the things in the world was to be a farmer—never having farmed in his life. He had about five or six children at that point, and off he went to a communal farm, my grandmother protesting all the way. They discovered that this was not for them, and they moved into another farm with a person who was an extremely shrewd businessman, and when he milked the cows he added a considerable amount of water to the milk. And my grandfather, who in addition to being a poor businessman, was also terribly honest, decided that that wasn't for him. So off they went to St. Louis, where my grandmother opened a small grocery store, and my grandfather spent all his time in synagogue praying. And it was there that my mother was born.

The early stories about my mother in St. Louis are mostly about the staunch bravery of my grandmother, and the flitting around of my grandfather from city to city. He never had any money. And he died in San Francisco when he was reading a book crossing the street. He was hit by a car. He was a student till the end.

HELEN ABRAMS
New York, New York

: THE VIEW FROM THE TRANSOM :

I had a dog named Shane. My niece and nephew called him Shame, but that's another story. When I went off to boarding school, my mother hired a neighborhood kid named Stevie to walk Shane. One February morning my mother had overslept when she heard Stevie knocking at the door. So she threw on a flimsy housecoat and rushed downstairs and grabbed the dog and there was Stevie happily retreating toward his house through the backyard. She called him back and he begrudgingly took the dog for a walk — and my mother found she was locked out.

It was lightly snowing, not real cold, but snowing, and there was my mother in her baby doll pajamas and a housecoat. She rang the doorbell, tried to wake my father, but nobody would awake. She pounded at the door, but nobody would awake. She decided, "Ah! The kids get in by going in the milk chute next to the back door." You could reach in through the outer door and unlock the inner door and get in. She tried that, but just about two months before we had put in a top latch because my grandmother, who was in her seventies and living with us, was afraid of rapists. My mother couldn't reach the top latch, so she went to the garage and got a log; she stood up on it, shimmied herself through, and reached up to get the top latch. And just as she was unlocking it, the log slipped out, and she went lurching forward and got herself wedged halfway in and halfway out of the milk chute! Her backside was sticking out and it was just about time for the milkman to come and try with some difficulty to deliver the milk or for Stevie to return and see Mrs. LaRiche in this precarious position.

So she decided to shout, and started screaming "Bill, Bill," but my father keeps the air conditioner on summer and winter to drown out bird sounds. My grandmother heard her and said, "Betty, Betty, what is the matter?"

And my mother said, "Get Bill, I'm stuck in the milk chute and I hurt!"

"The clothes chute," said my grandmother, "what the hell are you doing in the clothes chute?"

"Not the clothes chute, damn it, the milk chute!"

"Bill, Bill, Betty's stuck in the clothes chute"—by this time my grandmother is looking down the chute—"and I can't see her anywhere!"

"Not the clothes chute, damn it, the milk chute!"

"What the hell is she doing in the clothes chute?" said my father.

"Not the clothes chute, damn it, the milk chute!"

So my father comes down and sees her and says, "What the hell are you doing in there?"

"Never mind, just get me out." So he started fiddling with her legs and she says, "Stop fiddling with my legs, get me a chair!"

And my grandmother is saying, "Oh, I thought the house was on fire!"

So my father got her a chair and mother got herself out with some difficulty just moments before Stevie returned and the milkman came. Grandmother screamed again, "I thought the house was on fire. I think I'm going to have a heart attack."

"If you are going to have a heart attack," said my father, "go to your room and have it!" They forgot about my mother, they were so upset with one another!

But the clincher of the story is that friends of theirs told the local [Cleveland] **Plain Dealer** *gossip columnist about the incident and the columnist wrote about it with this poem appearing underneath:*

There was a lady quite handsome
Who got wedged in her bedroom transom.
Cry as she might, they ignored her plight
Reasoning the view was worth more than the ransom.

JEFFREY LARICHE, AGE 34
Cleveland, Ohio

MIGRATIONS

In nineteenth-century Norway a well-to-do governess fell in love with a poor farmer. The caste system discouraged marriage, but the governess was determined. In a burst of rebellious exuberance and a blue wedding dress, she married the farmer and sailed for America the same day, May 17, 1843. It was Norway's independence day.

Their ship, the *Tricolors*, arrived in New York harbor on July 4, America's Independence Day. Here, as their great-granddaughter Miriam Fors tells it, "they were free to love each other."

They moved from New York to Wisconsin where they built a log cabin. When the Civil War broke out, the farmer went to fight for the Union. His wife and young son longed for a flag to fly above their home, but American flags were scarce and there was little cloth to be had. So the mother and son took unbleached muslin flour sacks and made the white portions of the flag. Others were dyed red with Indian berries. But blue cloth was almost impossible to acquire.

When there seemed no alternative, she took her blue wedding dress out of the large wooden trunk she had brought from Norway. And with tears in her eyes, she cut out the blue background for the white stars. Her son cut down a sapling tree, and the Norwegian immigrant family had an American flag to fly above their home.[1]

Beyond the circumstances and coincidences of this crossing-over narrative lies one of the great human stories. It is, like the epic of Moses, a migration story. As Moses struggled against the pharaoh and escaped across the desert toward the promised land, so the family member escapes from a home riddled with hardship and oppression, making his way across ocean and land to establish himself in a new home. The only difference is, as William Humphreys was to put it in his novel, *The Ordways*, for the ordinary family "the waves were not to part."[2]

Like the story of Moses, the family migration story has three parts: a reason for departure, a journey, and a struggle for survival in a new home. Although there may be a dramatic narrative about only one of the three parts, all three are often touched on by the family storyteller. In the story of the Norwegian migration, for example, the oppression of the rigid Norwegian social system marks the first; the Independence Day journey, the second. Finally, the sewing of an American flag symbolizes their assimilation into a new home. The three-part structure helps to explain why the episode of the flag, taking place two decades after the actual migration, is still part of one continuous narrative. The assimilation of the family into its new home, however long that takes, is an integral part of the migration.

East coast dwellers, particularly those whose ancestors migrated to this country in the past three generations, frequently tell a crossing-over story as one of their most basic and furthest back family tales. Families who have been in this country longer often replace the immigration saga with a story about the westward migration as their oldest tale, their story of origins.

MARIAN PATTEN

The reasons for a family's departure from their old home are often depicted in a dramatic incident. In the slave experience this is the moment of capture. In Alex Haley's family, the story is told of the ancestor Kunta Kinte who went out to chop wood for a drum when he was captured and brought into slavery.[3] That single piece of detail—that Kunta Kinte was chopping wood—was not a random scrap of remembrance. It was passed down through the generations because it was part of the dramatic moment at which the destiny of a family was transformed. A number of family stories handed down in black families center on the moment of capture, and suggest that some Africans were lured by slave traders onto ships through the use of red cloth. This example was told by a college student, and had been passed down from "granny's grandmother":

She told granny that one day she and some other children were playing in Africa. They sighted a red flag flying at a distance from them. They became curious as to what the red flag was and ran to it. On approaching they were grabbed by some white men and put on a ship. This ship brought them to Virginia where they were sold. She always hated anything red because that was the color that attracted her from home and people whom she never saw or heard from. She is referred to as often saying, "Oh that red rag, that red rag brought me here."[4]

Westward journeys were often embarked on in episodes as dramatic and at times as violent as those of the immigrant or the slave. In "The Family Saga as a Form of Folklore," Mody Boatright offers this example:

In 1846 when Jim Dandy was a youth in Tennessee, there were in the community in which he lived two factions: the mountain boys and the valley boys, or the hill boys and the plantation boys. They crashed each other's parties and dances and had numerous fist fights. Then the valley boys brought knives into action, and the arms race was on. The mountain boys went to a valley boys' dance on a river boat with hickory clubs concealed in their pants legs. The fight began on signal. A valley boy drew a pistol and shot a mountain boy in the knee. But the clubs were more effective than the single pistol, and many a valley boy was knocked off into the river. Some climbed back in their wet clothes and reentered the fight, but when it was over, thirteen were missing. A mob formed and began rounding up the mountain boys. But not Jim and his brother Watt. They hid in a cave where an old fisherwoman brought them food. They eventually got to Texas after shooting two of their pursuers.[5]

Few families are driven to embark on such harrowing, difficult migrations on the basis of a single incident; these stories are often a dramatic summation of years of oppression.

On their journey across the ocean or the Great Plains, the perils Americans most remember come from human rather than natural forces—from Indians and border guards, not hurricanes and storms. We have, however, heard occasional stories of storms at sea, even of an ancestor who fell off the Mayflower.

At times, humorous incidents attach themselves to one of the parts of the migration story, incidents which would have been long buried had they not taken place in that sensitive period. On one family's migration to Iowa by train, for instance, the family horse and cow were on one end of the railroad car and the furniture on the other.

And I do remember my folks telling this, when my dad opened his office desk a very weak cat got out of the area where the typewriter ordinarily is put and I have no idea how long the cat had been en route. It came from St. Paul—just no idea how long it had been en route. That poor cat was pretty weak.[6]

As families journeyed westward they often kept diaries and journals in which were recorded items of interest as well as

PAUL REIMERS

their day-to-day routines. Yet Francis Haines, Sr., who studied travelers' accounts of journeys on the Oregon Trail, notes that these memoirs do not mention one episode which is frequently retold by their descendants. He calls this apocryphal story "Goldilocks on the Oregon Trail."[7] In these tales, Goldilocks, described as a three-year-old dimpled darling (or in some versions as a twelve-year-old redhead) is found to be unbearably attractive by a tribe of friendly Indians who stop the wagon train and offer to trade a number of ponies in return for this fair child. The white pioneers never surrender her, although in one version "Goldilocks'" father offers the chief her braid, and the Indians go on their way begrudgingly. In "Suny," the story from our collection, the woman is a red-haired beauty about to be married, and the chief offers forty horses (see p. 72). The historian Haines suggests that these stories are based on some Anglo-Saxon misconception that all other people on earth envy their children and their women. He also notes that similar stories were current in the folklore of England a century ago with the Gypsies as the dark-skinned people who wanted the blond English offspring.

The third part of the migration saga explains how an immigrant or a pioneer establishes a new home. The central thrust of many adjustment stories is the problem, comical to all but those involved, of having time-honored customs viewed as eccentric in a new place; oftentimes accents, outmoded beliefs, and a lack of familiarity with new lifestyles become a source of humor and of family stories. There is also a distinct group of tales about misunderstanding objects and customs in "modern America" (see pp. 79–82). A number of stories are also told about name changes (see pp. 78–9). For the immigrant arriving in America these changes were often the work of an inconsiderate, ignorant, or harried immigration inspector at Ellis Island; for the slave they were the deliberate work of a master imposing an American name in an effort to crush the slave's African identity; for the westward traveler they may have been an intentional effort to disguise his identity; a number of drifters west are said to have taken a new name off a tombstone.

Storyteller and ballad singer Maggie Hammons tells a good example of a family migration saga. The story goes that her great-grandfather was friendly with an old Indian who would visit him every day. They would swap tales and jokes. He liked the old Indian. One day the Indian came to him and said, "I had a dream last night." And he went on to say that an Indian's dreams always come true. Maggie's great-grandfather had a beautiful gun that was one of his most prized possessions, and the Indian told him that he had had a dream about owning that gun. So out of fear, her great-grandfather gave the Indian his weapon.

A few weeks later the great-grandfather came up with a plan to reclaim his possession. He went to the Indian and said, "I dreamed I had my gun back. Not only did I have my gun back, but I also had one of your ponies."

The Indian thought for a while. At last he said, "Take it, paleface, but dream no more."

Afraid that the Indians would kill him now, Maggie's great-grandfather rounded up his ponies, his family, and his possessions and left the area with the Indians in pursuit. They crossed the Newcon River, swimming across with the horses, escaped the Indians, and finally settled in a new home.

LOUISE TIRANOFF

The Hammons family originally came from Great Britain, and Maggie is a folksinger. Folklorists often stress the British origin of many of her ballads. But as far as she is concerned, her history begins with the story of her great-grandfather's journey across the river.[8]

Families often tell a migration saga as the first real narrative in the history of a family. One reason for this is practical. The great blank wall which separates an individual from his past before his ancestors arrived in America or before they journeyed west was, in part, intended to be that way. The poverty and hardship left behind was often painful and immigrants wanted to become Americans quickly. Those who moved west often did so for unsavory reasons, leaving behind broken hearts, unpaid debts, and dead men—and they were damned if they wanted those to come down in oral tradition.

Migrations also make ideal origin stories: they explain why the old world ended and how the new world began. The three-part origin sagas have a foot in both worlds, and suggest the way in which an ancestor steps out of the amorphous flow of European or American history and into the oral history of a particular family.

Family stories, of course, are not myths. The family is a social grouping but it is not a tribe. Family tales are peopled with ordinary men and women, not gods. The stories seldom go back more than a hundred years, and they do not begin, "In the beginning . . ." Still, there is often a migration saga which serves a mythological function for the family. It introduces a dramatic beginning, a dynamic sense of origins, and a patriarch or matriarch who brings future generations to a promised land.

: THE CZAR'S ARMY :

We're Jews and my grandfather was a Jew in Russia in the army under the Czar, which of course wasn't a good place for a Jew to be at all. But he had no choice being drafted. All I know is he had done something to aggravate his senior officer, or the officer wanted to make times difficult for him. So he was told that he was supposed to clean this officer's horse. The officer didn't like how he had done it, and he ordered my grandfather to lick the sweat off the backside of the horse. It's a double indignity because it violates Jewish laws. He was forced to do it, so he did it and that night he left, he just split from the army. I don't know the rest of the details except that was the point at which he left Russia. He made his way to the United States.

GERRY RUGEL, AGE 29
Washington, D.C.

: FISHBOK :

My father's side of the family came from Hessia, a little town called Fishbok, and they migrated to this country in about 1850. The basic story that runs along the line is that my great-great-grandfather was in Hessia, in the little town of Fishbok, going to a grocery store, and another young man came in the store after he did. At the same time, a Prussian officer also walked into the store. The young man who had followed him in didn't give him the proper respect, didn't salute him, or whatever he had to do, so the man, the Prussian officer, took out his saber and slashed him across the face, cut his [face] open. At which point my great-great-grandfather said, "Well that's enough, I've had it with this country," and decided to emigrate which he did.

ALAN LUDWIG, AGE 24
Erie, Pennsylvania

: THE CORN SQUEEZERS :

The Amish side of my family was named Blank, and they got kicked out of the [Amish country], according to the stories that have been told, because they had this bad habit of making "corn squeezings." The way the story goes is that in the Revolutionary War the Hessian soldiers were gotten drunk by drinking the "corn squeezings" of the Blanks, and the church never forgave the family for this. But, because they contributed to winning the war and securing American independence they were sort of forgiven for that particular piece of business.

Then when the Civil War came along, and they had all the troops going into the battle of Gettysburg, my great-grandfather was a little bit ticked off because he was a restless youth and kind of wanted to get involved in this but he wasn't allowed to. So he and his brothers went out and started selling their corn squeezings to the northern troops. And [when] the Union troops came in they found the corn squeezings — and they stayed a day too long, so they were unable to satisfy the need for replacements in Pickett's charge! So my great-grandpa's dad and mother were kicked out because that was the second time they'd been involved with physical violence, and war, and booze. As a result of that they were [strongly] encouraged to move west!

NANCY RIGG
Denver, Colorado

: THE LORD'S DAUGHTER :

SUSAN: *I guess the first story I would tell is the one about my great-great-grandfather, who was a very poor peasant on a farm in Ireland. His last name was McCarthy. I'm not sure of his first name. And he fell in love with Kathleen O'Brien, the daughter of the big lord of the neighborhood.*

CHRISTOPHER: *And the lord didn't like him; he didn't want her to marry him. So one night he put a ladder up to her window, and they both came down. And they went into her father's stable and got the fastest horses in almost the world. The next morning when the father woke up, he saw that his daughter was missing, and he got so furious, he said, "No matter how fast they run, I can sure catch them." And he went to the stable, and his horses were gone. So he had to run by foot, and by the time he got to the boat station, they were already to America.*

SUSAN: *They came to this country, and he became a landscape gardener, and evidently they did very well, because they made enough money to go back and snoot it up in Ireland for awhile.*

SUSAN MEEHAN, AGE 38, AND CHRISTOPHER MEEHAN
Washington, D.C.

: THE TRUNK BUSINESS :

My dad and my uncle had a leather store in Rumania where they made trunks and harnesses and saddles. Apparently they were pretty good artisans because the local dignitary, the prince or whatever, asked them to make him a special trunk with secret drawers and things of that nature. They finished the trunk, and when the prince and his men came to collect it, my father and my uncle only charged him for the labor, since they felt that it was quite an honor to have been asked to make the trunk. The prince's men slapped them and spat on them for having the affrontery to charge even for labor. A local ordinance was then passed that applied to my father and uncle only. They could no longer throw water into the street which was the only way to dispose of water in that community. So they had no way to operate their business and that's why they both decided they had to leave. In addition to religious oppression, they couldn't make a living.

My dad had a relative fairly near the border of Rumania who was a miller. He figured out a way to get my dad over the border. He went to the border guard with a wagon and a horse, my dad, and a large sack of flour. He called the guard out and asked him to help my father carry the sack of flour across the border. When he got it across the border my dad just kept walking.

In several of the other countries he got by because he had a birth certificate written in Rumanian which looked very official, rolled up in a metal tube. When anyone would challenge him for his credentials he would take this certificate out. Of course, no one could read it outside of Rumania, so he kept going.

When my father, and later my uncle, got to the United States they opened one of the first and largest trunk manufacturing businesses in Cleveland. They made trunks for people all over the world, shipping them as far away as India, and they actually made the first automobile trunk. Instead of a car having a trunk that you could lift up, it had a trunk that you strapped on to the back. It was made to fit the back of a Pierce Arrow body.

They also designed the first trunk made exclusively for clothing. You see, traveling salesmen didn't have automobiles and when they would have to sell clothes in another community, they would have to ship the clothes by train. In baggage handling, a regular rectangular trunk could be stowed upside down, which means that the clothing samples would arrive all disheveled. So my father and uncle designed a trunk which could only be stood on its end. Now you see clothing trunks with a hump on the top. They designed that so that hangers would go into that hump. You couldn't stand it any other way than on its bottom and that was the start of the clothing trunk.

MORTIMER L. FEIGENBAUM, AGE 57
Washington, D.C.

LORRAINE ARDEN

: SUNY :

This is the story as I heard it. My great-great-grandmother Suny was very young and very, very, very beautiful—and, as a matter of fact, she was. I have photographs of her. And she had beautiful bright red hair, and she was always dressed in the height of the latest fashion of that year. And she had some—not a great many—beautiful things, china and silverware, that she was very proud of.

Well my great-great-grandfather arrived in Boston to take her west with a group of other people, to make this very long, rigorous journey. Some place in Iowa or Nebraska they ran into a band of Indians who wanted to buy her because she had such beautiful red hair. I can remember very clearly my father's aunt, who is my great-aunt, telling me this story over and over again, about how horrified she was by those Indians and how marvelous they thought she was with this big pompadour sort of pile of red curls that she had and her bright blue dress. They offered my great-great-grandfather forty ponies for her, and somehow he got out of this difficult situation politely without offending anybody, and she made it out to Denver. My aunt Catherine always used to finish the story by saying that forever after she was deathly, deathly afraid of Indians.

SUSAN DAVIS, AGE 24
Philadelphia, Pennsylvania

: BORDER BALLAD :

My grandfather was a teacher in Russia and consequently, he was quite distinguished—had a mustache, spoke High Russian, and didn't have a Jewish accent or anything like that. One day he went out to teach, and two Russian soldiers attempted to rape my grandmother, who was a redhead of Dutch extraction, and somebody went and called my grandfather. He came back and he practically beat the two Russian soldiers to death.

Now this was unheard of in Russia and immediately there was a warrant out for his arrest. About the same time, his brother-in-law had been called to service. Jews never wanted to go into the Russian army, so the two of them decided to leave the country.

When they reached the border there was a guard with a rifle there, and my grandfather—who appeared like a Russian—

gave all his baggage to my grand-uncle and told him, "Now look. I'm going to distract the guard, you sneak across the border."

So what happened was this. He's busy talking with the guard, and they're talking about the large number of Jews who tried to get across the border. The guard says that if he sees them, he shoots them. My granddad says that that's absolutely the right thing to do. And they go on with it. Somehow or other, the guard realizes something's happening, and sees uncle, and starts to raise his rifle. My grandfather grabbed it—"Please, please! You're here all the time, let me have the gun and let me. . . ." The guard gave it to him, and he hit the guard over the head with his own gun, and that's how they crossed the border.

ROBERT FREED

Bethesda, Maryland

: THE LAST COVERED WAGON :

I had a relative who rode on the last covered wagon going west. She just died a year or so ago. Her father came from a very fancy family in England, who disinherited him because he had married an American woman. He became a Baptist preacher and a musician and had lots of children. His wife came down with tuberculosis and died, and he was told that he would have to go west to save the children, so they made and loaded a covered wagon, and in 1910 they rode west. They had a box with coals down below in which they would cook all their food, gently, as they went. By the way, they walked, they did not ride in their covered wagon.

At one point they were riding down in Kansas, and there was an awful snowstorm for three days and nights. The twelve-year-old walked barefoot with her ten-year-old sister for three days and nights, trying to get help for the rest of the family, and they lived to tell about it. They used to earn their money by playing music as they got into each town. There were about seven or eight sisters and brothers and the father; he would preach, and then afterwards they would all play music and take up a collection. And in that way they would earn their way to the next town. Eventually, they got to Oklahoma.

SUSAN MEEHAN, AGE 38

Washington, D.C.

: Crossing-over Melodrama :

My grandfather came to America in about 1906 or so. Apparently he came either on a freighter or in steerage on a passenger ship that came from Germany to New Orleans. There was a big storm at sea and he was washed overboard by one wave, but almost before he knew what was happening, another wave came and washed him back. That's what my grandmother says. I don't know if that actually happened or not.

FREDERICK L. KEPPLER
Washington, D.C.

: Tiny Feet :

There's just two stories I know about my great-great-grandmother, Nancy. She was Irish, and she came across during one of the potato famines. Apparently she cried so loud on the boat that the captain threatened to throw her overboard. The other story is that her feet were so tiny that she could do an Irish jig on a silver platter.

When I was about five or six I asked, "How did I get the name Nancy?" And this is what they told me. And that's all I know about her.

NANCY KILCZEWSKI, AGE 35
Herndon, Virginia

: One Last Goodbye :

My grandfather didn't tell stories, but my grandmother still does, and she tells them over and over so many times that you remember them. When she left Russia during the Russian Revolution, they had soldiers out after her and my grandfather. They had just gotten married, and most of his older brothers and sisters had been in this country for a while, so he wanted to come here.

They escaped one night with my grandfather's father. The way she explained it it's very hard to visualize, but they ran across the military lines, and they were shot at. And when they were at their destination, my grandmother decided that she didn't like the way she left. She wanted to go back to say goodbye to her family, because she knew she wouldn't be seeing them

JOAN BERNICK

again, so she ran back through these military lines, and they shot at her again. She said her goodbyes. Then she came back through, and they got on the boat, the three of them, and came over.

VICKI PERLER, AGE 29

Gaithersburg, Maryland

: TWIST OF FATE I :

My great-grandfather, Moses Erlich, was apparently a very important man in Springfield, Massachusetts. The story was that Moses had actually come to Hartford and set out as a very young man, about fifteen, to go to Boston to make his fortune. The train goes from Hartford to Springfield to Boston. He was an orthodox Jew, so I assume he must have been wearing a black long coat and a black hat, with long paiss on the side. At Springfield, a man got on the train dressed like him and sat down next to him. The train apparently had a twenty-minute stop or so, and [the man] said, "Where are you going?"

He said, "I am Moses Erlich. I am going to Boston to seek my fortune."

"Well, why don't you seek your fortune in Springfield?"

He said, "What would I do in Springfield?"

"The Jewish community has sent me to the train, because we're trying to get thirteen Jews to settle in Springfield so we can have a minyan. If you get off the train with me here, I'll get you a job."

So he said, "Fine!" and he got off, and he said, "What's the job going to be?"

"You meet all the trains from Hartford to Boston, try to get 'em to come off and settle in Springfield."

LYNN CHAITOWITZ, AGE 39

Kensington, Maryland

: TWIST OF FATE II :

Probably the oldest story that the parents on my mother's side passed on comes from the time they were settling Louisiana before the Civil War. Our family history extends back into Tennessee in the 1750s. And the stories that are told are mainly about the migration that they made apparently from there into northern Louisiana, before the land was settled and cultivated. There's one story about my great-grandparents, or their grandparents who were in northern Louisiana, just passing through. But the winter had [started] and she was very pregnant, so they were forced to stop. Since the weather was getting pretty bad they had to look for shelter, and they found this old hunter's cabin. There was no hunter but there was firewood and they had some provisions so they stopped with the idea they would just stay there until the storm ended and move on, and hoped that whoever built it and maintained it wouldn't mind too much. As it turned out, the guy never returned so they simply stayed there and decided to claim the land and built their own house right there at the cabin site. That's how they got their start in northern Louisiana.

ANDREW GRIFFIN
Washington, D.C.

: TWIST OF FATE III :

One of my forebears came as an eighteen-year-old farmboy from Brunswick, which was under the rule at that time of the Prince of Hesse who was selling mercenaries to George the Third to fight [with] the British. This poor kid didn't know anything about the war and was drafted off the farm and sent over here to America, down in Pennsylvania. The story was told that once he stopped to light his pipe. You had to use a flint, and oftentimes it took a while to light it. So, by the time he got his pipe lit his troop was a half mile off and he was all alone out there in Pennsylvania. And it looked like home, so he just took off into the woods and got a job on a farm. After a while he saved up enough to buy his own farm and that's how part of me got here.

S. ZIMMERMAN, AGE 44
Springfield, Ohio

: BREAKFAST WITH THE INDIANS :

I wanted to tell a story about my family—my aunt and uncle and their ranch. He went to Wyoming after the Civil War and started a ranch, my uncle did, in the late 1860s or early 1870s. This was on a river called the Cheyenne, and this was an incident that happened there.

The Indians used to travel between the Black Hills and the Bighorn Mountains in Wyoming, so they went through my uncle's ranch as they went back and forth. On this occasion, the cowboys were all out, everyone was away from the ranch except for my aunt and her son. This was just in the morning after everyone had left to go to work, and the door opened and three Indians came in. They didn't say anything. And my aunt's story of this is very movielandish—she just motioned to the table for them to sit down and she cooked pancakes for them—a lot of pancakes—and she gave them coffee. And they thanked her, they nodded, and left then.

And sometime after that these same Indians came by and gave her a really lovely buckskin dress, really fantastic, it is just beautiful and it's still in the family, for remembering.

ALBERT HERMAN, AGE 47
Bethesda, Maryland

: O Lucky Man! :

There's a story on my father's side of the family about how the family got its name, which is Glickman. Evidently when my great-grandfather, or a relative of his who came over to the States maybe a few years earlier, was passing through Ellis Island sometime around 1904, he was asked by some official what his name was. He was standing in the line there and he didn't understand what was being asked; he didn't have any English at all, just probably spoke Russian and Yiddish. And he said something like, "I'm licht man," which means "lucky man." His name was written down as Glickman.

RALPH GLICKMAN, AGE 28
Silver Spring, Maryland

: Miller :

I'd like to tell the story of how my last name got to be what it is. When my great-grandfather came to this country as a draft dodger from Russia, his last name was twenty-eight letters long with no English vowels in it. The story of how to pronounce it died with him. When he got here on the boat, right around the turn of the century, there was this man about five up in the line who was an American. His name was Miller. The customs of-

ficials asked him his name and he gave it. The customs man knew how to spell it, so he wrote it down and passed him right through. Most of these immigrants were going through a lot of trouble because they didn't know how to speak English. So when my great-grandfather got up there, he just said, "My name is Miller." And they passed him right through. He wrote back to the old country and told them that if any of them immigrated to this country, they should immediately change their name to Miller so that they could get through.

ROBERT MILLER
Charlotte, North Carolina

: ON THE JOB TRAINING I :

My family tells a story about a distant cousin who had been a rabbinical scholar in Europe. But you can't earn a living in America being a rabbinical scholar, so he decided he would be a tailor. He went to the first tailor's place, where they were doing some manufacturing, and the manufacturer said to him, "Well, where's your scissors?" He said, "I don't have any." He said, "You can't be a tailor if you don't have a scissors." So he said, "Well, what kind of scissors should I have?" And he told him. So the next day he went out and bought that kind of scis-

LOUISE TIRANOFF

E. MACMILLAN

sors, and he applied for another job. Well this time he brought the right kind of scissors. And the boss said, "Well, all right, cut this." And he said, "Well, how do you want me to do it?" So the first day he got the scissors, the second day the boss showed him how to cut it. But he said, "If you don't know that, you're not a tailor," and my cousin lost his job. Each day after he got a different job, until several months went by and he really had a job—and he was a tailor.

ELAINE GURALNICK, AGE 48
Baltimore, Maryland

: ON THE JOB TRAINING II :

My grandfather had been an apprentice shoemaker in Latvia. He sewed the upper part of the shoe to the soles and he decided that was the logical job for him to do after he got here. So he took a bag lunch and went out in search of work. The first place he went to was a walk-up where each flat was a different factory. He went to the first one and they said, "Have you any experience with electrical equipment?" And he said, "Sure, sure." He had never seen an electrical machine before. So he starts sewing with this thing and it goes wild. He ruins one shoe and he ruins two shoes and he ruins three and he stuffs them in his lunch bag and gets out of there in a hurry. Then he goes up to the second floor, another factory, and he pulls the trick again. And then the third floor. Each time he goes out on the street and dumps out his wasted shoes. By the time he got to the fourth floor he was an expert, and he got the job. I like the story because it says something about on the job training and about having a little bit of gall in getting a job.

BETTY-CHIA KARRO, AGE 35
Washington, D.C.

: ON THE JOB TRAINING III :

During the Depression, grandfather saw a job advertised for an elevator repairman. Really, they wanted two. So he and a good friend from college whom he had studied engineering with applied for the job. The man asked them if they knew anything about elevators. "Oh, yes," they said, "we know all about elevators." "Okay, you're hired." So as soon as they were hired, grandfather and his friend went up to the top, to the little house on the top of the building, and locked the door, took the whole thing apart and put the whole thing back together, and then they knew all about elevators. They didn't know a thing before, but they weren't going to tell him that. He's seventy-five now, and he'll still tackle anything.

MIDGE HEIMER
Germantown, Maryland

: BANANA I :

When he first came to America, my grandfather said he had heard of bananas but he didn't quite know what they were. So his cousins who had been here awhile—a grand total of about three months—and who were wise to the ways of the world, decided to pull a joke on him. They gave him a banana, and speaking in Yiddish they used the word that has kind of two meanings. It can either mean, "bend it" or "do you like it?" And they set him up by asking him to bend it gently because he didn't want to break it. And it snapped. Then he realized that they were playing a joke on the green cousin from the old

*country. And he said, "Oh, this is a banana, everybody knows
how you break them and you eat them." And then, he proceeded
to eat it—skin and all—saying every last bit was delicious.
Thinking back on it—every time my granddad saw bananas
he'd crack up.*

MARVIN SAKOLSKY, AGE 30
Riverdale, Maryland

: BANANA II :

*My grandfather was an émigré from Latvia and he came over
when he was a little older than thirteen. His first time out of
that area was this trip. When he got to London, there was a
layover between boats. He was stuck in the street and he bought
this banana which he had never seen before and wanted to eat
it. He ate the skin and threw the banana away—well, you eat a
peach that way!*

BETTY-CHIA KARRO, AGE 35
Washington, D.C.

: UNCLE SAM WANTS YOU :

*My great-grandfather had come from Poland, or right near
Poland, and he came to this country during the Spanish-
American War. There was one of those Uncle Sam posters say-
ing "We Want You" and he thought it meant him! "Why me?"
he wondered. "What's so special about me? I just came to
America." And he went and he joined the army!*

DAVID NACHAMANOFF, AGE 10½
Arlington, Virginia

Americans love to tell stories of how an ancestor, a grandparent, or a parent lost the fortune which would otherwise have gone to them. Often our forebears owned an insignificant plot of land—which they lost through a quirk of circumstance—and which now sits smack in the middle of a downtown city block, spilling its revenues to everyone it seems, except the storyteller and his family. As one professional genealogist told us, whatever city our ancestors were from, their farms always seemed to have graced what was soon to become the biggest intersection of the busiest section of town. Our nineteenth-century forebears, writes folklorist Mody Boatright, often missed their chance for untold wealth by failing to find a lost mine or buried treasure.[1] Nowadays, we lose our fortunes in the stock market, real estate ventures, or entrepreneurial gambles.

According to folklorist Stanley Brandes, who first wrote about this category, these kinds of stories are told almost exclusively by whites, particularly those from working and lower middle class backgrounds. In Europe and Latin America, he suggests, success is often considered to hinge on luck, and local stories often tell of winning the lottery or receiving an unexpected gift.[2] Americans, on the other hand, are imbued with the Protestant ethic. Failure or success is viewed as a direct reflection of our personal virtues or flaws. This is a terrible burden, Brandes writes, "the knowledge that we will be measured by our degree of success, a success over which we are supposed to have virtual control but over which in actuality we do not."[3] Confronted with failure, a family misfortune story somehow consoles us. We can absolve ourselves by blaming our ancestors, by telling often humorous stories of how our forebears lost their wealth by letting themselves be victimized by relatives, by failing to capitalize on a rare opportunity, or by losing their legitimate inheritance.

LOST FORTUNES

: CADILLAC SQUARE :

My father's great-grandfather ran a station of the underground railroad in what is now Cadillac Square in downtown Detroit, Michigan. When the Civil War came they were trying to carry supplies down into the southern areas to northern troops, and at one point the whole wagon train was captured. This destroyed

ALICE TAYLOR

my grandmother's father financially, and apparently they never recovered. They lost the farm in Cadillac Square, and so now we are poor Americans like everybody else and don't own Cadillac Square in Detroit.

GERTRUDE LEE AIKEN, AGE 37
Washington, D.C.

: AN EVEN SWAP :

My father's father left Farmington, Missouri, in 1893 heading for southwestern Oklahoma. At that time, land was being parceled out by lottery. He and his brother registered and eventually found some land in Indian territory and established a hog farm. There's an interesting story which is supposed to be true that when my grandfather owned the hog farm, a man who owned a hotel in a small, nearby town offered to trade him the hotel and four square blocks of downtown real estate for the hog farm—an even swap. Grandpa told him, "I can make a better living out of the hog farm. I know nothing about running a hotel. Besides that town will never amount to anything. I mean, who ever heard of a town named 'Tulsa'?"

DANIEL W. HUMPHREY, AGE 28
Holdenville, Oklahoma

: THE WAR OF THE WIVES :

The Cuttings were apparently very wealthy at one point. There's still a very prominent New York family called Cutting. That is one branch of it, very far removed. In order to justify the lack of money in my family, the story goes that my great-grandfather was married to a woman for twenty years, got itchy feet, divorced her, and then he decided he wanted to marry some more women. And, depending on who tells the story, it's six wives, seven wives, at one point it went up to twenty-four wives, that this gentleman had. On his death bed, he was in the process of divorcing one wife and marrying another one. His will had not yet been changed, and his divorce papers had not yet been filed, or maybe it was that the will had been changed, but the divorce papers had not been filed, but his last wife and his next wife fought over the money until it was all gone. Gobbled up in legal fees.

HEATHER CUTTING RAYL, AGE 24
Fall River, Massachusetts

: How About Vending Machines? :

My father and his friends were sitting around one night, and they came up with the idea to use vending machines for everything. They figured that the retail merchant of the future would be the vending machine. And for a long time they were thinking of things that could be sold in vending machines, like Coke and all. But they never got to do it, and now you know you see so many vending machines. They sell everything under the sun in them. He wishes he had done it.

JOSEPH DEMARIA, AGE 17
Lakewood, New Jersey

: The Stubborn New Englander :

My grandfather's grandfather was pretty stubborn, like your typical crusty New Englander. When the family came over from Ireland, some of them went to New England and some of them went to South America. And the part of the family that went down to South America apparently became quite wealthy. When the last relative in South America died, he left no heirs, and a lawyer from South America spent years trying to find someone who could inherit the property. Eventually, he came to my great-great-grandfather's farm in Chicopee and said, "You're the relative of so-and-so in South America, and you can inherit a lot of land. And I can set it up for you, but I spent a long time looking for you and I'm not going to tell you how to do it unless you give me half of it." At that point my great-great-grandfather said, "Half of it, you crook!" and got his gun and chased him off the farm and never inherited any of it. He'd rather have none of it than give half of it to that lawyer. He was just that stubborn.

GREGORY F. FARRELL, AGE 22
Rockville, Maryland

MARIAN PATTEN

: A BET ON DECATUR :

My grandmother was born in Germany, in Pomerania. It doesn't exist any longer. She came to this country at the age of three months. Her father was a soldier, of course; everyone in Prussia at that time was a soldier. Poor man, every time he got his little shoemaking business going, the kaiser would start another war and he'd have to pack up and off he'd go. So finally, after about the third war, he decided that was enough. He packed up mom and the kiddies and they came to this country and went out to the middle west and settled in Iowa. And at that time the railroad was driving west and the information was it was either going to go through Omaha or Decatur. He bet on Decatur. Right. He lost.

MARTHA L. SWARTWOUT
Wheaton, Maryland

: TUCKER AND FOX :

My father's uncle had a hotel right in the city called Tucker's Hotel. That was his name, Dan Tucker. He always played cards and one night he played with this guy named Fox — Fox by name and nature. He came down to the last thing he had left, which was the hotel. He said, "I'm on." And he signed it away. He lost the game. In the morning he nearly went crazy, but he was crazy for doing it. He lost everything. And to this very day it's called Fox's Hotel.

MARGARET TUCKER, AGE 35
Arlington, Virginia

: GREAT-UNCLE HORACE :

My great-uncle Horace died before I was born; he lived up in Maine where everybody worth legending about lived. He was very frugal and he was very attached to his mother, my great-grandmother. The story about him was that he was a drummer boy in the Civil War and he came back shell-shocked. He was never quite right in the head after that. After my great-grandmother died, he kept her house just the way it had been. He never threw anything away.

After he died they were clearing the house out and on the second floor they found hogshead after hogshead full of empty shredded wheat boxes which he had been unable to throw away. They started building a bonfire and threw them in and when they got about half way through they found money in some of them and realized that he hadn't trusted banks either! So they never knew what they had burned up.

Horace was a very queer coot. He used to repair watches for free, and it seems that he forgot to return them because there's a safe up in that house in Maine, full of neatly repaired watches. There are traces of him everywhere.

JOAN RADNER
Washington, D.C.

: MOUTHWASH :

About a year after my grandfather died I took a trip across the country and stopped in St. Louis to see my grandmother. It turned out that they had a lot of money tucked away here and there—money under the mattress, in different banks, fifties here and there. It all added up to close to one hundred thousand dollars.

When I stopped again on the way back, I went into the house and my grandmother says, "Oh Leslie, I have something for you, upstairs. I had thought about giving it to you on your way across country."

And here I was, old greedy me thinking that maybe she had found a hundred dollar bill under the mattress and was thinking of giving it to me. So I followed her upstairs, toward the bedroom when she all of a sudden makes a cut into the bathroom, and she opens the cabinet and pulls out these two huge bottles of mouthwash and she says, "Your grandfather was going to use these but he didn't get the chance."

LESLIE HALL, AGE 25
Washington, D.C.

: THE COMSTOCK LODE :

My great-grandfather was a great traveler. He'd go off for years for a time, and my great-grandmother would never see him. She'd just be suffering along trying to make do until one day he'd walk in and say, "I'm home!" "Yes, I see that," she'd *say. But he went out west with two other men, and they bought a small claim. And they didn't have enough money to try it out. So they had to sell it for fifty dollars. The man who bought it tried it out, and it later became very famous. It was known as the Comstock Lode. And now it's a great symbol of remorse in our family.*

SUZANNE MACKENZIE, AGE 17
Brewster, Massachusetts

: THE BIG ONE GOT AWAY :

Summitville was one of those turn-of-the-century boom towns where they found a couple of motherlodes and people became very wealthy. When the war came and the war effort demanded more attention, the town became a ghost town.

In 1955 my father, through some bit of business, acquired the lease [to mine for silver and copper]. My mother used to pan for gold in the water from our clothes after we'd go out there and roll around in the dirt. And she has three or four gold buttons from the gold that she got out of our clothes.

But anyway, what happened was, back in 1974 — yeah it was seventy-four, after we had released our lease on this particular

CAROL DANDY

part of the property—a man was bulldozing the roads. This guy wasn't a miner, he was just a bulldozer operator and a rock hound. And he was just tooling along the road there and all of a sudden he saw this little glimmer in the distance. He took a look, and it was about three feet by three feet and weighed eight to nine hundred pounds—not what you would call a dainty gold nugget! It had been there for years and years and years and it took several harsh, harsh winters to work its way up to the top and then roll out on to the road.

And he got back into his bulldozer and went back down to see the geologist and the foreman [and] they said, "Why don't you show us what you've got." And the guy said, "Bring your truck." They all almost had a heart attack.

It turned out that that particular sample of rock is the largest sample of high grade gold ore that's been found in North America! It's worth over a million dollars—and the rock now stands in the Museum of Natural History in Denver.

And when (we) heard about the rock everybody in the family had to go see it. We took pictures of my nephew on the rock, and sent them out to everybody in the family.

Boy! Talk about the one that got away!

NANCY RIGG
Denver, Colorado

MARTHA SWARTWOUT

Amerian family storytellers wax poetic over tales of courtship, and are especially enamored of the seemingly serendipitous first meetings of husbands and wives. Romance inevitably transforms reality. Two persons meet as a result of some meaningless combination of circumstances. If they died the next day the encounter would have little significance, but if they take to each other and finally marry, a sort of "alchemy of mind" transforms the incident into a rendezvous with destiny and the deepest sort of romance.

The family storyteller typically reshapes reality in a number of ways when narrating a courtship. To begin, any dramatic or memorable episode in the early stages of dating is likely to be remembered as a first encounter, "the first time I met your dad." Further, selective remembering and after-the-fact interpretation often add an element of love at first sight, as in this romantic Civil War story:

My great-grandfather, Alan Taylor Sherman, came to Washington with the Union army during the Civil War. He stopped at my great-grandmother's house to get some water and she was the one who handed him the glass of water. He put his hand over hers as he took the glass of water, and then he got off the horse, and after that, they got married.[1]

Is it plausible that General Alan Taylor Sherman fell in love with a woman because she brought him a glass of water? Probably not. After the fact, the storyteller imbues his courtship with romance by postulating instant attraction. Marriage bonds seem to be strengthened by the memory of a romantic, passionate courtship, of love at first sight. By the same token succeeding generations, exaggerating the romance still more, can look back at their progenitors as having been linked by mysterious and powerful passions.

First encounters are also made to seem predestined in families. In one story, for instance, two persons who had the same initials, M. A. B., accidentally took each other's luggage when they arrived in this country. They met when clearing up the confusion and went on to get married. If they had not wed, the incident would not have been worth remembering. Instead, the chance encounter is imbued with meaning. In this sense, Americans think in reverse, revising the

COURTSHIPS

past on the basis of what happened later, replacing coincidence with destiny.

In "Fifty Ways to Meet Your Lover," part of his "Heirs" series in *The Washington Post*, Michael Kernan retells a courtship story he collected from a couple married five years. It combines two chance encounters, and illustrates this metamorphosis once again.

A college radical leader, he had written an angry manifesto that was circulated around the campus. One day after a rally, as he was walking away in his uniform of jeans, blue plastic windbreaker, and uncombed hair, this girl accosted him.

"Did you write that crap?" she demanded. For twenty minutes they wrangled about politics there on the path while people walked around them. Finally she snapped, "Man, you are a bad trip" and stormed off in her jeans, blue plastic windbreaker, and uncombed hair.

The next summer which he spent with his wealthy parents on Long Island, he was a guest at a flossy wedding. He was milling around, champagne glass in hand, in the big striped tent overlooking the Sound. Suddenly he saw a big picture hat, with a face under it that he knew from somewhere.

"You!" he said.

"You!" she said.[2]

A second coincidental meeting introduces a variation on the destiny theme. The aura of predestination is doubled. A man and a woman are taken with each other but lose touch. Years later, against all odds they are brought together for a second chance. This time they have no choice but to blame fate.

Storytellers effect a final transmutation in their courtship romances by adding or emphasizing details from fiction. When snatches of popular love stories are suggested in the family tales, they take on some of the aura of romantic fiction. The story about General Sherman proposing to a young lady who brought him a glass of water suggests *Gone With The Wind* and a host of other romantic tales.

Storytellers are also familiar with fairy tales, and on different occasions will use them to establish the tone, to supply details, or to structure their courtship story. One lady quoted earlier even began by saying, "It's almost like a fairy tale the way it happened" as she told of a handsome son who married

ALICE TEMPLE

JAY BURG

a scrubwoman tyrannized by a drunken father. "But it's very interesting," she said, "because it's sort of like Cinderella and the prince."[3]

One of the oldest and most widespread themes in folktales from around the world concerns a suitor who must pass a test to win a true love's hand in marriage. He may be forced to climb a mountain, slay a dragon, start a princess laughing; perhaps she must detect a pea beneath a mattress. A number of family tales also tell how a grandmother or a mother chose between her suitors by putting her lovers to the test. They illustrate once again how folk and fairy tales influence family tradition. Here, novelist Maria Katzenbach tells an interviewer about a favorite family courtship story:

One [story] I like best is how my grandmother chose between the two finalists of all the men who were courting her. She had them to dinner, one Monday night, the other Tuesday night. She had the same dinner served both nights; she played the same songs on the piano; she told the same jokes. After dinner she asked each beau out into the garden behind her house in Georgetown. "What beautiful cherry blossoms," she said to the first beau. He nodded, "Yes, they are beautiful." The next night she said the same thing to her other suitor. He leapt up on the fence and broke off a twig from the cherry tree and brought it to her. Then and there she agreed to marry him. Now, I can't be sure that a story like this isn't just a tall tale. It's been told so many times. But then a little imagination is required to bring the past back to us.[4]

In still another example, a grandmother was said to have chosen among her suitors by taking them for a carriage ride. When she got the horses galloping at top speed she would drop the reins. She married the man who did not jump from the cab in fright.[5]

The family storyteller, then, takes the iron rod of reality and bends it a number of ways in the courtship story. Any early dating episode is likely to be recalled as a first encounter, mixed emotions are transformed into love at first sight, coincidence is changed to destiny, and motifs, themes, and details from fiction romanticize reality. The result is a sort of charter for the family's life together, the family romance.

: THE TEST I :

My mother was dating my father and another man, and she couldn't decide which one to marry. And she had dates with both of them two days apart. For the first one they went for a walk in the park and he wore a sweatsuit, only he called it his "perspiration trousers." And she decided that he wasn't for her. So the great test was she took my father for a walk in the same park. And she said, "Let's run down the hill." And he took her hand and they ran down the hill together. And that's how she decided that was going to be the one.

NANCY KILCZEWSKI, AGE 35
Herndon, Virginia

: THE TEST II :

My grandmother tells this story. So that her sons would be able to tell if the prospective bride would be industrious and diligent, they took a long string and tied it into many knots very tightly, and then they would give this tightly-knotted string to the prospective bride. If she was very careful and diligent about untying it and didn't go into tantrums or anything like that, then she would be a good, industrious wife. If she had tantrums and was impatient and didn't finish it, then she wouldn't be good enough for her son.

: ON THE BALCONY :

[During World War II] my mom was living in Thuringia, which is all the way east, up in the mountains [of Germany]. One summer's night at some very late hour she was walking with her girlfriend. Naturally the whole city was blacked out because of the attacks. Out of the darkness these two soldiers approached them. At first they were getting kind of scared because it was so black, and there was nobody around them. But these two young guys had lost their way and just wanted to know how to get back to the house where they were staying. And the two girls said, "OK, we know where that is, we'll walk you over."

So they walked them over to the house, and said, goodnight, and the two soldiers said, "Now we really can't let you go home by yourselves. We have to walk you back to where you live."

My father, I guess, liked my mother very much, and he said that she would hear from him and he said — he was a pilot — said that tomorrow morning she should stand out on her balcony and watch for him. She naturally said to herself, "What does he want, how can I see him, coming down in a plane?"

But, next morning she went out on her balcony, looked out, and she was brushing her hair — she had very long hair she told me — and suddenly out of the sky emerged two planes. They started circling around the city, like they always do before they start to climb. But then one of them stayed, I think, instead of circling around and banked its wings, yeah, and she knew that was my father, the young gentleman, and she waved.

Somehow my father, through all kinds of friends, found out where she lived, and started writing her, and on his next vacation from the front they were engaged. It was one of those quick war things; it took only a few hours. They got married in 1947.

They never had a honeymoon. The only luxury they had at the wedding was, my mother, somehow, found somebody who had a coach, a white coach — in that devastated city with hardly any houses standing, and nothing to eat, and nothing to wear except old clothes. No wedding dress, no flowers, nothing — and so that's what they had, they drove the horse-drawn carriage to the church. It was the only thing they had, it was something very romantic.

MARIAN BRAUNSHAUSEN, AGE 19
Washington, D.C.

: THE FERRIS WHEEL :

We have a story about a set of grandparents who got stuck on a ferris wheel at Coney Island way back when. It was their first date and they got stuck on the top of the wheel — that's pretty high up — and supposedly my grandfather proposed marriage to her. There was no way she could get out of it unless she jumped off or something.

: THE WALLET MAKER :

My grandfather was a wealthy wallet maker during the height of the Depression. In 1930 he advertised for a secretary, and since jobs were almost nonexistent, two hundred women lined

DONNA CHAPPELL

up outside his office for interviews. Many of these women had held jobs before the Depression, and had all of the secretarial skills they needed. My grandmother was nineteen, just out of high school, and could barely type. She was about the seventy-fifth person he saw, and it was love at first sight. When she told him that she couldn't take shorthand, he said, "Don't worry, I'll buy you a dictaphone." He spent more on a dictaphone than her salary would have been for two months.

Three weeks later they were married.

BARBARA LAUTMAN
Washington, D.C.

ANN HAWKINS

: DOWN TO THE WIRE :

There's some story about Arac, my great-great-grandfather. He had two wives. His first died as they often did in those days. He had been living alone for about seven years since she died, and he wanted to find himself a new wife. So he drove in a buckboard, a wagon, into Bedford, Indiana, the county seat. He went up to this widow's house that he knew, and he said, "I'm going into town to buy a few bales of wire, and when I come back, I want you to decide whether or not you'll marry me." She was stunned. And he went in and bought the wire, came back, and she had decided to marry him. That was their courtship.

PHILIP LINNEMEIER, AGE 23
Bloomington, Indiana

: ONLY YOU :

This is a love story. This is a gay love story. Kitty and I met in college and after we got together we started to go to this one gay bar in downtown Atlanta. They had a singer that used to come around and sing "Only You," the old 1950s song by the Platters. There weren't that many places to go, so we would keep going to the same bar and she would be there singing "Only You," and we adopted it as our song.

After we'd been together about a year I moved to Europe. We missed each other a lot so after about three months Kitty decided to come over and meet me, and we would go to Paris for Christmas. We fooled around like tourists for about a week and on Christmas day we woke up and didn't have anything to do. There was nobody on the streets, everybody was home doing their Christmas thing; we were just tourists. We were walking up and down the streets and finally came to an old kind of run down cafe. There wasn't anything to do but eat, so we went in and ordered omelets and sandwiches and everything else there was, and sat there and ate a lot. Then a group of teenage boys came in and they all sat down and started to get really rowdy. They put a couple of francs in the juke box and "Only You" came on right there in Paris.

: SURE OF HIMSELF :

My grandfather was a courier on the train, and he was sent up to Frederick with a message. While he was there he met a woman, and the next time he was sent up, he went to New York, went to Tiffany's, and had a diamond ring made, a cluster that I wear. Almost a year and a half later, he was sent up to Frederick again, and when he saw this woman, he went up to her and proposed to her, and she said, "Yes," so he opened a pocket and took out the ring. Later she said, "If I had known he was that sure of himself, I'd have never said, 'Yes.' "

MARGARET SAYLOR, AGE 69
Silver Spring, Maryland

: PEARL'S COURTSHIP :

My great-grandmother Rebecca had six daughters. Pearl was the most beautiful one: blonde hair, blue eyes, fair skin, and a beautiful figure. The rest of them got fat fairly early, but Pearl never did, and she was always very vain. Pearl went to work in a real estate firm, and one of the young fellows there was very attractive. She liked him a lot, but he was not Jewish, and the family was not very happy about this relationship. They went out together, taking one mother or the other with them. He knew they were traditional, and his parents were also. They tried to be as nice as they could about how the families felt, and they never really had any physical relationship. They had a platonic one. Finally, the family said, "Pearl is not getting any younger, and we must introduce her to a nice Jewish boy and get her married." So this was arranged, and she thought, well, she liked her friend John very much, even though he's not Jewish, but nothing would ever come of it. So she went ahead and entered into this marriage that was somewhat arranged by the family. And it turned out that this fellow was a drunk, and no one knew it. Not all Jewish boys are as nice as people think. Pearl couldn't put up with this, so she went ahead and had a nervous breakdown.

My great-grandmother Rebecca then called in the non-Jewish fellow, John, and said, "We don't know what to do with Pearl. For months and months, this is what she's been through." Well, he was very upset and said, "Of course I'll come and see if I can help." So he came to the hospital and gradually got her over the nervous breakdown. His visits and his attention were what brought her out of it.

Well, this marriage had never been consumated, so it was annulled, and my great-grandmother decided that part of Pearl's problem was that she was still a virgin. She was probably thrity-five or thirty-six by that time, so my great-grandmother, in her humanness, called John in and said, "You know how I always liked to travel. Well, I just decided I need to take about a six-week trip, and while I'm gone, I want you to take very good care of Pearl and help her in every way, because she has some needs that are not being met." He was obviously the only person she really loved, but she herself didn't realize how much she did. All the years he had never married another girl either so it was apparent they belonged together.

When my great-grandmother returned, John and Pearl had their physical relationship going strong, and they got married. And they had a very beautiful marriage with no children, because she was beyond the age where she could have children. And they were married thirty-two years, and she passed away this winter. This all came out after my great-aunt Pearl passed away last winter. My mother told me all these things that happened.

MITZI WERNICK

REBECCA COFMAN
Bethesda, Maryland

JAY BURG

: TAKE CARE OF NINA :

My aunt Nina—we called her Aunt Nina, even though she was my father's second cousin—used to speak about her first husband. There's a picture over the desk, and it was her husband and her first husband standing in front of a Model A Ford. She said, "That was my first husband Jack, and there's Louis." So I asked my mother, "Why does Aunt Nina talk about her first husband Jack in front of Uncle Louis like that?"

And she said, "Well, this is how they got together." Uncle Louis and Jack were best of friends, and they were in a bar one night in Mississippi, and one of the hands came in and shot Jack dead. And while he was dying, he said, "Louis, take care of Nina!" So he married her.

LESLIE BARDEN, AGE 32
Bethesda, Maryland

: ONE POINT TELLS YOU :

My mom's a practicing pharmacist, and my dad's a professor in pharmacy. They met in pharmacy school and got married right after school. When they both took the state board exam, he got a ninety-nine, and she got a ninety-eight out of a hundred, which are damn good scores. Whenever mother would come home from one of the drugstores saying, "Well, I gave him 500 milligrams of tetracycline," dad would jump on her saying, "No, it should have been 250 mils," and they'd argue back and forth. He'd say, "One point tells you that it's this way." And she'd whine.

About ten years ago, this old prof of theirs came down, a guy named Straley. At dinner he said, "Well, how long have you guys been married?" "Twenty-five years." And he says, "Well, I think we can tell you. You know we graded your exam up there, and, well, we knew you two were getting married, and we knew we didn't want any trouble. And to tell you the truth, Elizabeth here got the ninety-nine, and you got the ninety-eight." My mother had taken fifteen years of crap from my father. She was flabbergasted, and soon came a chance for her to bellow at the top of her lungs, "One point tells you."

RICHARD MILLER, AGE 32
Washington, D.C.

: DUMB CITY KID :

My mother grew up in Memphis, and my father says that the
way she managed to trap him was she told him that her father
owned a plantation. And when he asked what kind of planta-
tion it was, she said, "Well, it's a sardine plantation." And he
was such a dumb city kid that he believed her!

ELINOR ABRAMSON
Washington, D.C.

: LATE TO THE WEDDING :

When they got married, my dad, being a great mountain clim-
ber, was late to the wedding because he couldn't get off Mount
Rainier. Mount Rainier's about fourteen thousand feet tall,
with a nice steamboat prow glacier which had come apart, and
he had no way to get across the son of a gun. He marched up a
thousand feet and sat down on his big mountaineering pants
and just started sliding on this ice. He must have been going
about forty miles an hour. He went, "Wheoo," and sailed right
over this ten-foot crevasse. Finally he got off the mountain, ran
to his wedding, and got married.

RICHARD MILLER, AGE 32
Washington, D.C.

SUSAN DAWSON

: APHRODITE :

We didn't have a car when I was little, but my husband courted me in an automobile and that automobile was called Aphrodite. Aphrodite was fantastic. I remember every inch of it. It was a green Rambler, and it had a real personality — a very dynamic car, not static at all. When it was coming to pick me up, its blinkers went on and off and they were placed in such a way that it looked like it was smiling through the grill work.

That car wasn't sold; we would have never parted with it willingly. One day its brakes died when my husband was in it and it crashed into a pole because he averted hitting a group of school children. It wrapped itself around the pole and he got a fine of twenty dollars for destroying public property. He thought that it would be best to just leave the car, walk away from it, and never go back. That's what he did. It was beyond its time at that point and it had obviously let us down.

The second automobile we got was called Eusephelus. Things were breaking down already and it was not so exciting. The third one was called Demon. We skipped Cupid somewhere along the way. Demon is the contemporary, it's the car we've got now. But Aphrodite was the mythic automobile.

SUSANNE ROSCHWALB
Pittsburgh, Pennsylvania

Families enjoy gossiping about their relatives and many tell full-blown stories about squabbles and feuds. Recent family arguments and divorces, of course, are usually talked about in hushed tones, not with the dramatic flair reserved for stories. Only with time can the irony, the pathos, even the humor begin to emerge from the bitterness. As one woman said about her mother's broken marriage, "It's just looking back on something that's very, very far away. It just takes time, and then it's just history, and you can live with it and work with it."[1]

By the time families are telling stories about the young married lives of their grandparents and great-grandparents, much of the pain has dissipated. Once tragic stories like this odd tale sound humorous to later generations:

Notorious? Yes! This is a little strange, but one of my great-grandfathers lived in the bathroom. In Germany, the bathroom was large — it was more than just a bathroom. And he couldn't stand his wife. So he moved into the bathroom. He brought his bed in there and he lived there.[2]

Of course people also fight with relatives other than their spouses, and in the most surprising ways. Bill Howard told how his cousin Mr. Rick woke up early each morning to visit his sister's house where he would build a fire, put on water for hominy, and then wake her up. Once Mr. Rick was returning from his sister's, when he met Bill and breathed a long sigh. "I do my part," he said, "and speak to my sister on Monday, Wednesday, and Friday, but she won't do her part and speak to me on Tuesday and Thursday."[3]

Dividing up inheritances, as many of us know, often leads to bickering if not bitter disputes and, years later, to tales. In one, the death of a flamboyant, moderately wealthy aunt precipitated an argument among four nieces over who should inherit her mink coat. One claimed it fit her perfectly, another that she had often borrowed it in years past, one that she was most in need, and still another that it had once been promised her in conversation!

Some of the most elaborate family feud stories we collected are set in the Appalachian Mountains. In a distinctive storytelling style, they unfold pitched battles between two branches of a large extended family. Feuding families of this kind are part of our literature and lore. The Hatfields and McCoys are celebrated in song, and in the course of his adventures, Huckleberry Finn suddenly finds himself caught in the crossfire between clans of Shepherdsons and Grangerfords. He has never heard of such feuds before, and his friend Buck explains it to him this way:

. . . a feud is this way: A man has a quarrel with another man, and kills him; then that other man's brother kills him; then the other brothers, on both sides, goes for one another; then the cousins chip in—and by and by everybody's killed off, and there ain't no more feud. But it's kind of slow, and takes a long time.[4]

Our first story, "Die with It in You, Frankie," is a particularly striking example of a feud tale. It recounts an episode memorialized in the folksong "Frankie and Johnny," and is well known in the region. The narrative comes from a cultural setting where large, extended families comprise a community, and where the most dramatic episodes in the history of the area are likely to come down in the traditions of various branches of the family.

: "DIE WITH IT IN YOU, FRANKIE" :

Well, my great-great grandfather was a first cousin to Charlie Silvers that got his head cut off. Charlie's wife, Frankie, cut his head off, cut his body up, and burned it all night. Hid part of his remains in a log—his lights, the guts, the parts that won't burn, under a rock. He was buried in a little family cemetery up on the ridge above where she killed him, what was left of him, what they could find. And she was the first woman ever hanged in North Carolina, or legally anyway. My mother was raised just about a half a mile from where that happened. Oh Lordy, I've heard that all my life. Well, I tell you, it's even been put in books.

I tell it to you like my uncle At told me because he told it different than anybody else. He said it wasn't Frankie that started it, it was her daddy. I don't know what they had against Charlie, but he was a trapper. This was way back before the Civil War, a long time ago. It was nearly Christmas and

Charlie had been out cutting wood all that day to burn all during Christmas. There was a big snow on the ground. They lived in a little shantylike cabin that just had two rooms, a kitchen-livingroom where the fireplace was, and a back bedroom. And they had a daughter—she couldn't have been more than a year old; she was still crawling.

So anyway, my great-great-uncle At told me that her daddy was down to supper that night and Charlie had got through cutting that tree down. He had piled up the wood and come in and eaten supper. And they said that when Charlie got in, he said, "I'm beat, I think I'll lay down." And Frankie said, "Well, I fixed a pallet for you by the fireplace. I thought you might want to take a nap before you got ready to go to bed." [laughs] I don't know why he wanted to take a nap before he got ready to go to bed to sleep again. But anyway, he got the baby and laid down there in front of the fireplace and went to sleep. And when he got to sleep, my great-uncle said that her daddy said, "Now's your chance, Frankie."

And they said she went and laid the baby in the back room. Then she took the ax that Charlie had brought in and come back in there. Charlie was laying on his back, and they said everytime she'd come back to take a swing at him, he would smile at her in his sleep. And she swung about three times and her arm about give out. "Well," she said, "I just can't do it. I can't kill him like this." And her pap said, "If you don't kill him, I'll kill you and him both." So I reckon she figured she better go ahead. And they said that finally she come down and give one hit in the head. They claim that he jumped up and screamed, "God bless the child." And she run back there in the bedroom and jumped under the covers and hid. She was so scared. Well, according to my uncle At, when she went in there her daddy took the ax and he come back and cut Charlie's head square off. They said he hit him so hard that his head bounced against the rafters of the cabin.

And they said about that time the baby got up and was crawling, and they said it crawled in its own dad's blood. And they said it got over there to the table where it tried to stand itself up with its hands, and it left blood prints on the table. They said you couldn't wash them off or nothing. You couldn't get them off.

So Uncle At said Frankie's daddy cut him up and done all that dirty work hisself. And he used all that wood Charlie had

DOROTHY JACKSON

*cut up to last through Christmas and burned his body all night
long. And they said he took Charlie's head and put it under a
stump, an old hollow stump, and that he put on his boots to
carry the rest of him and put it under a rock. I've seen that rock
a hundred times. And then he went down to the river, the Toe
River that runs by the foot of that holler, about half a mile
down the road there. And he walked in the snow down there and
then backtracked up. And of course it was put out that Frankie
claimed that Charlie had went across the river for his
Christmas liquor and hadn't come back.*

*It got to be two or three days, and everybody was wondering
what had happened to him. They said this old man, I forget his
name — I think they called him Dickie Collins — lived over
cross the mountain somewhere and had been a' noticing Charlie's dog. It had always been with Charlie, and he said the dog
would go up to the house and holler and just bark and go on.
And Dickie just got suspicious, so one day when Frankie was
out he went down there to the house and got to looking around.
And he found some bloody chips and things around the fireplace, and he lifted up the floor boards and found blood down
under there. So word got out that he had been killed. I mean
that was evidence enough to know.*

*And they always told something about how his daddy had
went over to Tennessee where they had this New Guinea slave
that had what they called a conjure ball, or something. You'd
ask it a question and it would swing. And however it was that*

they was asking it, they said it would swing right toward the house. When they come back they arrested Frankie. I reckon they got her to confess to killing him.

At that time the county seat was in Morgan, North Carolina, almost fifty miles away on the east side of the Blue Ridge Mountains. You had to go plum over there to the courthouse. They took her over there where they had her trial and they found her guilty and sentenced her to be hung.

I don't know if she bribed the jailer or who it was, but anyway, her family slipped her out and was trying to get back over the mountains. They had her hair cut off short like a man's and she was wearing a big old hat and walking alongside a haywagon. Her uncle was up in the haywagon driving. The sheriff comes up and says, "Where are you going, Frankie?" And she turned around and tried to put on a man's voice and said, "Thank you, sir, but my name is Tom." And they said her uncle turned around and said, "Yes sir her *name is Tom." And so they knew right then who it was and took her back in to jail.*

Before they hung her she was supposed to have sung this song, an old ballad that they sing back up there now. They just call it "Frankie Silvers' Ballad." I don't know whether she did sing it or not. They claim up there that that's how the Frankie and Johnny story got started. Course the Frankie and Johnny song ain't nothing like the song that she sung. But I reckon it just rolled over.

According to the best I ever heard, when they were taking her body back across the mountains to bury her—you know, they didn't have no embalming in them days—that she just got to stinking so bad that finally they had to bury her on the way, somewhere close to where Lake James is now. And they got her husband Charlie's remains and buried him in the graveyard up on the hill with the Silvers family.

People never could figure out why she done it, unless it was jealousy. In the song there's a rhyme that says "the jealous thought that first gave strife." They don't know why she was jealous. One of [Charlie's] brothers who lived to be way up in his nineties told years and years later that there wasn't never nothing bad come out on him. And in communities like that nothing happened that wasn't found out and told, you know. My grandmammy's uncle was the only one that I ever heard say that her daddy was there eating supper with them that evening, and that he done it. He's way up in his eighties, or close to eighty anyway now, and its not been a year ago since he told me that.

But they did always say that before she hung she was about to tell something and her mother or her daddy either one hollered out, "Die with it in you, Frankie." They say she just didn't say anything.

Frankie's daughter, the little baby, I think her mother kept it for a while, but most of them moved off. But her girl married somebody from Madison County, I think. And then her daughter, Frankie's granddaughter, married my grandmother's uncle. Anyway that's about all I know about it.

ROBERT L. MCMILLAN, AGE 24
Lenoir, North Carolina

: DICEY'S MAN :

My family is from Scotch-Irish descent. They settled in South Carolina, in the mountains, and they were tenant farmers on southern plantations. James Horne had eleven children, ten daughters. The oldest one was Dicey, and the son was Ananias. They were tenant farmers on the Thorne plantation. And another tenant farmer was Peter Gosnell, who married Dicey.

One night they were having a corn husking party at Peter Gosnell and Dicey's house. They were drinking corn liquor and got too drunk, and Peter Gosnell slammed his fist down on the table to punctuate a point he was making, and he broke a plate. James Horne, being the father of the clan, reprimanded him for this, and Peter got very insulted and said, "I'll do whatever I want in my own house!" They got into a fight and were rolling around on the floor, but the family separated them, and everything seemed all right.

But that night when James Horne was walking home through the woods, Peter sneaked out and stabbed him eleven times and killed him. It started a family feud between Dicey and the rest of the family. They said, "That man's bad. You have to leave him. He killed your father." And she said, no, she's going to stick by her man.

Ananias and Rebecca Horne settled down in North Carolina, right across the line. They had nothing to do with Dicey and her family anymore. One of the sons of Ananias and Rebecca Horne was named Rome Horne, and he made journeys. He walked up into the mountains and finally located

Dicey's family. Dicey was about to turn one hundred—this was about in 1913—and he came back and tried to get Ananias and his descendants interested in going up into the mountains for Dicey's hundredth birthday party. And no one was interested in going. So Rome and his family went off in a horse-drawn wagon, and they drove past Ananias' home. As they drove past, they saw that Ananias was sitting out on the porch, chewing tobacco. My father was a little boy about ten years old then, and Rome said to my father, "Jump out of the wagon and go see if grandfather won't change his mind." My father ran up to the porch and asked Ananias, and Ananias said, "Son, I ain't seen Dicey in fifty years, and I ain't about to see her now." The whole family just split off.

AMY LOUISE HORNE, AGE 22
McLean, Virginia

: THE HOWARDS AND THE BAKERS :

I'm from Clay County, eastern Kentucky. I've been in D.C. for three years, but before that I lived in Kentucky all my life. There were two families in Clay County that held more power, more land than anyone else, the Bakers and the Howards. The land is really poor down there, very hilly. The Bakers had a lot of bottom land and were still trying to make a go of it by farming. And the Howards—this is my family—decided that timber was better, and they were getting quite wealthy. It was also pretty much a political dichotomy: the Howards were Republican and the Bakers were Democrats. The Howards were getting more and more political offices, because they had more financial control of the county. And the Bakers got teed off about this.

I guess the feud supposedly started about 1869. The incident that was handed down to me was that Tom Baker, the eldest son of the Baker clan, decided that he'd fix those Howards. He'd put a dent in their pocket and bulge his out a bit by going down to Crane Creek, which straddled both their farms, and taking their log rafts. He was going to sell them in Manchester, rather than in Baileyville, where everyone would know they were Howard logs because of the type of poplar they were.

So he went down to the creek where they had all their rafts tied up waiting for the water to rise a little more. He cut the ropes and jumped onto the back of one and went down the river leading all these rafts, just as pretty as you please. Well, it was about dusk and my grandfather Israel was on the hill, and he saw Tom Baker doing this. And he ran down the hill and jumped on the log raft right behind him and said, "Tom Baker, draw your pistol, because I aim for one of us to drop dead in this river tonight." And Tom Baker said, "Now Israel, a man can't shoot on the water. Let us get up onto the land." So my grandpa, being a fair man and not sure that Tom Baker was, told Tom to jump onto the bank first, which he did. And they went out, paced their ten steps, and aimed their irons at each other. Grandfather shot once, didn't hit, shot again, didn't hit, shot again, and didn't hit. It wasn't that the men were such bad shots; it was just that their artillery was so bad. All this time Tom Baker hadn't got a shot out once, and so he hollered out about that point. "Israel, my gun is jammed. My damn gun is jammed." My grandfather walked over and looked at the gun, and neither one of them could make it work right. So he supposedly told Tom Baker, says, "Now, Tom, I've given you one chance for a fair fight, but I cannot grant that either me or the Lord will grant you the same chance tomorrow night."

This started the whole hundred year history of shooting at each other, which ended up with the state militia coming in at one point. All the other families would take up allegiances with one side or the other. And the law, of course, or what stood for the law, was bought off appropriately. You see the Bakers—I guess the Howards did this too, but they never told me what the Howards did—the Bakers would come up at night and they'd get their shotguns and they'd take pot shots at the windows. And then by the time the Howards could get up and get their guns loaded and get to the windows, the Bakers had gone. They just did this to hassle them.

Well, one night they did this and they shot my great-grandfather, Ballard, the head of the Howard clan. And from that wound, Ballard ended up dying. So they charged George Baker, the head of the Baker clan with the death of Ballard Howard, the head of the Howard clan. And the state militia came in and arrested him and took him to jail. He was in jail and they had the state militia all around the exercise yard, but when he went out for his exercise period, all of a sudden from a second story window across the street there was a shot and he was shot clear through the heart.

So the militia and all the townspeople ran up to the second story window, and they saw a Colt pistol and a Stetson hat. And they hollered out, "Whose hat is this?" And my grandfather Israel calmly walked out of the crowd and said, "My hat, gentlemen," and walked out. And they wouldn't bother him because the town people would have gone crazy: as the oldest son, he had the right to avenge his father's death. My uncle Snowdy was a little boy, and he was there then. He won't admit that his father actually killed anyone, but everyone else in the family swears that that's true.

I guess this feud was one of the biggest ones in the area. The Bakers eventually went up to Round County, about a hundred miles north, and fought with the Underwoods. Now supposedly there aren't any Bakers in the county. I don't know anyone by that name. We, by trial and error or whatever, won the battle. It's such a violent history to inherit and yet the whole time that you're told it you get feelings of pride and identity without identifying the violence with yourself. I don't know how you filter that out. I just know you do.

BEVERLY LEE HOWARD, AGE 24

Washington, D.C.

SANDRA GROSS

: A TURN OF FORTUNE :

When my great-grandmother died, I guess it was in the mid–1800s. They were really wealthy, and they had a huge farm and a lot of slaves. You really measured your wealth by the slaves, so in the will they divided the slaves between three of the children and gave one child the land, because land was worth nothing compared to slaves. Nothing at all. At the end of the Civil War, the ones who got the slaves had nothing, and the guy with the land was really getting big. So they all came to him and expected him to share, and they just thought he stank because he wouldn't. He said, "If it had come out the other way around, you would not have shared your slaves with me."

One brother moved in on the boundary of his farmland, so that they had farms side by side, but they didn't talk to each other for their entire lives. One died, and they still hadn't talked to each other. That feud, conflict, has still kept two sides of the family apart. They just never see each other.

MARY LEE GEARY, AGE 17

Arlington, Virginia

: EXPENSES :

This story is about my father's grandparents. It was about the turn of the century right after a depression when they had all that inflation at the time. My great-grandmother was complaining because she felt she didn't have enough money to run the house. My great-grandfather took care of all the rest of the bills and everything, and apparently gave her a small sum for the week. So he said to her, "You make up a list and we'll go over the list at the end of the week, and then we'll see if you need more money." My great-grandmother apparently was a women's libber from way back and she said, "I make up a list nothing. You make up a list, too, on every penny you spend and we'll go over it at the end of the week." So my great-grandmother made up this extensive list where she put down everything, like two cents for candy for little Arthur, who was my grandfather, everything. Every single penny she spent was down there in this big list, three or four pages. So my great-grandfather comes home Friday night and says, "Okay, let's go over the list now." So they sit down and go over this whole list of things and he goes, "Uh hum, uh hum, this looks very reasonable." And she says, "Okay, now let's see your *list." So he takes it out and there was one thing written on the piece of paper—"miscellaneous."*

And that's a true story.

: HOW GRANDPA ALLEN DIED :

My great-grandpa Allen was a railroad man for years and years and years, maybe sixty years or so, and he knew the railroad schedules by heart. He kept a big stopwatch and he knew when the railroad trains would pass the house; the railroad track was right near the house where they lived. And he had a very unhappy marriage; he saw himself as henpecked. Through the years the tension rose and rose and rose in the marriage until one night Grandpa Allen took out his stopwatch and checked it, and he said goodnight to Grandma Allen just like he always did every night. And he walked out the door, went out to the railroad track, and he put his head on the railroad track. The train severed his head from his body. And that's how Grandpa Allen died.

PHIL HOOSE, AGE 27
Speedway, Indiana

Supernatural occurrences comprise the subject matter for many family tales. One story which we collected in different versions concerns a gambling grandfather with a nagging wife who pleaded with him to change his evil ways. Her cajoling had no effect on him until the occasion when he sat down and played poker with a distinguished gentleman who won all of the money. When the mysterious gambler stood up he had pig's hooves, and he disappeared in a puff of smoke. The grandfather cried, "The devil!" And his gambling days were through.[1] This motif is found in many parts of the world and in the United States.

Among the most common supernatural stories are those which tell of how a clock stops, a mirror cracks, or a favorite animal dies at the moment of a relative's death. Others are told about occurrences that seemed supernatural at first, but that later investigation revealed as quite ordinary, as in the final story in this section, "The Ghost in the Window." This tale is told as a children's story; others in this section are told almost tongue-in-cheek; and still others are told seriously, suggesting the different attitudes Americans take towards these supernatural occurrences.

SUPERNATURAL HAPPENINGS

: JOHN SIMMS :

My mother collected little toy boats or model boats I guess you'd call them. There was a little boy who helped her collect them named John Simms. Right after high school John was killed in a car accident. He was buried and she went to his funeral and it was over. In the course of the next twenty-five years he was forgotten.

She's an artist, and one night about six years ago she was working at her desk, and she just got the strangest feeling that if she looked up into the window John Simms would be standing there, after all these years. It made her so nervous—and my mother's not the nervous type—that she shut the blinds. Then she could hear him whistling—there was a little whistle that boys have when they call each other at night. She kept hearing the whistle over and over in the background. Finally she couldn't think, her hands were shaking and she had to go to bed. She went to bed and read a little bit, put her book down, and turned out the light and then she dreamed, very vividly, that the phone rang. She turned on the light, moved the book,

JOANNE MORELAND

she picked up the phone and the voice at the other end answered and said, "Hello Nancy, this is John Simms." She put the phone down, she woke up, and the feeling was gone, she wasn't scared.

John's been in the house ever since. The place he likes to stand is in her room over a heating grate, right next to the case with the little boats in it. It's the funniest thing—there can be heat roaring out of the grate and you can feel it, yet it's cold. It's like a wall, warm here and cold up there. It's the strangest thing in the world and we can't get anyone to explain it, except that we've got a ghost standing in the corner. Sometimes he rides in the car with us. He's very nice to have around, particularly if you're walking up from the garage alone at night—it's comforting.

ELLEN WILDS, AGE 23

: THE TABLE CRACKED :

I call my mother's whole family psychic. I don't know what you'd call them. When they die they leave a message to tell somebody they're leaving and goodbye. My aunt had this pretty, really pretty glass thing over the table. They were cleaning the dishes, and they heard a crack in the room. The whole table had just cracked in the middle. Then they received a telegram the next day saying that an uncle had died.

I don't know if you'd call them psychic. I just think that we love each other too much, so we have to come back and say, "Goodbye." That's my mother's family.

EDDITA OSBORNE, AGE 14
Takoma Park, Maryland

: THE SILENT COMPANION :

My father has a lot of Maine hunting stories, everyone in this area has Maine hunting stories. This is his sole ghost story. It was late in November, very cold, snowy, blustery. He was staying in a camp, and he went out north along this road. He had been walking along for about a quarter of a mile when suddenly he looked to his right and there was someone walking beside him, a very strange-looking fellow. He had a long black coat that came down to about here, mid-calf, and a leather hat, and he was carrying a long, long rifle about four feet long. And the man never said a word. My father said, "Catch anything?" And the man never said anything. So he tried again, maybe this guy is deaf. Nothing. So he started to get a little nervous, because he's out in the middle of nowhere and this man may be a lunatic or something. And so he turns to say something a third time, and the man is not there. He looks behind him, and there are his tracks in the snow and beside them, nothing. So he went back to his cabin tout de suite, *and he took a long sit in front of the fire before he decided to go back out again.*

SUZANNE MACKENZIE, AGE 17

Brewster, Massachusetts

: A GHOST IN THE FAMILY :

We've got a ghost standing in the corner. Mother and I just know he's there; my younger brother and sister don't. Sometimes we've had some funny things happen. Things will disappear and reappear in a room, or you're eating a bowl of soup, and you put the spoon down, and you reach for it, and it's not there; you look for it, and you know it couldn't have gone anywhere, and you look at it again, and suddenly it's there, and you know you didn't overlook it.

We've also got my great-grandmother. She's been dead for twenty-one years, and no one's had the heart to tell her. It's a hard thing. We've had people see her. I've had friends stay over and sleep in my mother's room while she's out of town, and they've woken up and seen my great-grandmother sitting next to the bed, and most of them have promptly gotten up and slept in the living room.

ELLEN WILDS, AGE 23

Arlington, Virginia

: THE GHOST IN THE WINDOW :

This actually happened to my mother, and it was in Good Thunder, Minnesota. My mother, Clara, was about twelve years old and her sister Alma about eleven. They lived on a rather isolated farm. One evening in the dead of winter their parents had to go somewhere and left the two girls in the farmhouse. Now they washed the supper dishes, and they decided that before they went to bed they would play a game of blindman's bluff. They went into the parlor and pushed the chairs back against the wall so there would be room in the center. And they had just sat down to take their shoes off so they could move quietly when they heard the sound of footsteps squeaking in the very cold snow. And so they decided not to take off their shoes since they expected to open the door. And they heard the footsteps going squeak, squeak, squeak, squeak, squeak. And someone fumbles at the doorknob but no one knocks. And they hear the footsteps going away.

Then they heard the footsteps going squeak, squeak, squeak towards the back door. They thought it was a neighbor because people in the country rarely use the front door. So they waited again for the knock, but no one knocked. Just a shuffling around the door, and then squeak, squeak, squeak towards the window of the parlor where they were.

This really frightened them, and suddenly in the window appeared two glowing balls of fire and between them a white star. And from below the fiery circles came two columns of smoke that came in silent puffs. And it all moved back and forth and up and down at the window. The girls were frightened, and it moved back and forth and up and down, and then squeak, squeak, squeak, it went away. They were terrified. They couldn't move. They sat petrified until their folks came home. But even their parents had no explanation.

The next morning they were helping their mother get breakfast when their father came in from doing the chores. He said, "Girls, I know what your ghost was last night. Our old cow Star got out of the barn." (Star was a completely black cow with a star between her eyes.) "I followed her tracks from the front door to the back and to the window. She was attracted by the light, and the reflection of the lamp in the window made her eyes glow and the star show up. And the column of vapor was her breath."

That's the story as told me by my mother. I've told it to kids so many times. It's a true ghost story.

ARTHUR MAAS, AGE 58
Greenbelt, Maryland

OTHER
STORIES

As we listened to thousands of American family stories, the similarities and shared themes were striking, but some tales were difficult to categorize. The stories in this final section remind us that although family members share many life experiences with other Americans, some of their tales are particular to a specific ethnic group or region; others are simply unique to an individual family. Our categories are open-ended; there may also be varieties of family stories which are not represented in our collection or which we have not yet discerned.

: LIFE IN THE BRONX :

I grew up in the east Bronx, a lovely section that's been destroyed now, around Crotona Park. The park was the center of the world basically. It was divided up in a curious way. There's a lake in the center called Indian Lake which was always full of rowboats in the summer and ice skaters in the winter. And this was where the anarchists argued. Different political groups argued in different places. If you wanted to argue or agree, you'd know where to go. I'd go with my father. There were anarchists, there were communists, there were miscellaneous socialists, there were Zionists. And if you weren't interested in politics, you might be interested in religion. There were a whole series of synagogues there. And if you weren't interested in either one, then you were probably interested in making money. Those were the basic distinctions.

I'll tell you a story that gives the flavor of the thing. I got a goldfish when I was around eight years old, and my father took me to buy a goldfish bowl. The Sino-Japanese war had started and the five and dime was being picketed because the detente with the Communists and China had just broken up; in the Bronx that meant you picketed the five and dime. We started into the store to get the goldfish bowl but meanwhile the goldfish were sitting in a cardboard container on the sink. And someone stopped my father and said, "Comrade, why are you crossing our picket line? Do you want to support the fascism of Japan?" And my father very carefully said, "Comrade, what am I to do? Do you want to be responsible for the death of a goldfish? Where else can I get a goldfish bowl?" He said, "Pass, Comrade."

: River Ride :

This is a story about the Johnstown flood in 1889. This story about my uncle Gomer has been handed down for many years. During the night the water rose and he went up on the roof of the house. There was also a board on the roof of the house and the waters were rising some more and a pig got on one end of the board and Uncle Gomer was on the other. And as the waters rose, the house was lifted off its foundation, and Uncle Gomer and the pig see-sawed down the river.

BECKY MAYER
Johnstown, Pennsylvania

: War of the Worlds I :

My mother's family settled in New Jersey, in a place called Matawan. In 1938, you recall that Orson Welles had his "War of the Worlds" broadcast. They had just built their first crystal set back then and everyone was excited because they had just picked up Pittsburgh, Pennsylvania, WKDA. Well, the following day came this "War of the Worlds" broadcast from CBS in New York City. So they listened to that and they were getting terribly upset. It turned out that on that day there

MIDGE HEIMER

was a terrible dust storm in western New Jersey. As this broad-cast was going on, they were looking out the windows and seeing these big clouds of dust. And they thought, my God, this must be the worst invasion in history. They didn't really believe the radio, but when they saw that dust coming. . . .

So they packed up the old Packard and decided to head down to Barnegat Bay where they had a house. They got about five miles before traffic was so bad that they just completely stopped—all from that broadcast. Hundreds of people just like them had packed up their cars and were going. Most of them didn't even know where they were going, but they were going as far away as they could go. They remembered that in the broad-cast it said that landings were made in Princeton and Trenton, and they figured the invaders would be headed to New York City. Since they were about fifty miles from New York City, they figured that if they went down south along the Jersey coast, then they wouldn't be in any trouble. Finally, they got about ten miles before the police started running around telling everybody that it was a hoax and they could go home. They fi-nally went home, but they never forgot that episode.

JOHN WHITMORE, AGE 28
Arlington, Virginia

: WAR OF THE WORLDS II :

I remember Orson Welles' "War of the Worlds" broadcast very vividly. I was playing at a cousin's house when my father came to the door and said to my uncle, "Neal, I have something very serious to talk to you about. Let's go down to the basement where no one can hear us." When they came up they both looked grave. My father said, "We have to go home immediately," and so we left in great haste. My father had congregated the rest of the family and the four of us—my mother, father, brother, and I—sat in the family room around the radio, listen-ing to the broadcast. As the Martians came closer people were jumping out of windows and we became more frightened. Fi-nally an old aunt came to the door and my mother said, "Tuddi, you can't guess what's happened. The world is coming to an end." And she threw up her packages and her pocketbook, "Oh, my God," and she ran into the room. We all listened to the radio until the end of the broadcast. We weren't embarrassed. There were so many people in the same boat. A general terror had spread over most of the listeners. People had jumped out of windows and had called the police for gas masks. I remember when we got to our house my father said, "Look, the sky has turned purple." And it had, but of course not from the Martians. We sat there ready to die together. My grandmother was upset because my father hadn't picked her up from where she was. I imagine the older people prayed, but I don't remember that. I was so intent on what the man was saying on the radio and watching the expressions on the faces and wondering what was going on. We never knew until the very end when they said, "This has been a presentation by Orson Welles."

PAT RITTERHOFF
Timonium, Maryland

ELISSA ICHIYASU

: POPCO THE RACEHORSE :

My grandfather lived up on a family farm near Holton, Michigan. And there was a pond out back which is still there, but back in the old days the gypsies used to camp there. And they used to go down and, you know, talk with them some. But my grandmother didn't like him cavorting with the gypsies at all. She thought the gypsies were not people to be hung around with. They were accused of stealing and doctoring up their horses and so on. Well, one time the gypsies left, and my grandfather came back with a pony he called Popco. It was just a regular old spotted pony, and my grandmother always put it down.

My grandfather, Oscar, used the pony to take the milk cans into Holton—which is about seven miles—every day, just about the time of the morning that Mr. Ryerson would be riding his beautiful grey trotting horse into Holton to work. And it got to be a thing with him to say, "Hey, Oscar, you want to race?" Oscar would say, "No," and Mr. Ryerson would go off in a cloud of dust with the milk cans clattering. As it happened Oscar got to be pretty damned pissed at this. I mean day after day, "Hey, Oscar, you want to race?"—then boom. So one day he thought, "Hell, I'll give him his race," you know. So he's trotting along on Popco, here comes Ryerson, "Morning, Oscar, you want to race?" And Oscar says, "Sure. [Whistles.] Get up Popco." And Popco goes tearing down the road into Holton; the little pony had beaten Mr. Ryerson's trotting horse.

He came to find out about a year later when the gypsies came back that that little pony was the starting horse they used for the gypsies' races every year. And that was the end of Mr. Ryerson and Oscar's rivalry. I remember that because my mother told me that a couple of times. I like to think of that little triumph with the pony.

CONNIE CRONENWETT, AGE 31
Ann Arbor, Michigan

: THE COST OF LIVING :

My husband's grandfather was a doctor in a small town in Ohio. He wrote this story in his journal. One night he was called out in the country where a man was choking to death. He held the man's mouth open with a spoon all night long while someone went to fetch the proper instruments so he could

LOUISE TIRANOFF

relieve this man's suffering. When it was all over and he had spent the night with this man and he had saved his life, he sent the family a bill. It amounted to about one hundred dollars, and the family protested the amount of the bill. So he said to them, "Well, give me what you think his life is worth."

MARILYN JONNES
Washington, D. C.

: UNREQUITED LOVE :

There was a woman in the family who was married and had children. She was just living there in a little pioneer home in Tennessee or Missouri, a log cabin, I guess. There was an Indian, a Cherokee Indian chief, from a camp or village nearby, and he had seen her. One of the versions told is that what he really got excited about was her hair; I believe she either had red hair or blond hair. This chief fell in love with her, and he would stand on this hill that overlooked her cabin and just stand there and watch her. And he sent some of his Indians in to try to bargain for her because he wanted her for a wife. Of course she wasn't interested. When he died—he was an older man—when he died he had his body wrapped around a tree that would overlook her forever.

CHARLENE SMITH, AGE 30
JUDITH SMITH, AGE 33
Panburn, Arkansas

: PLUCKED GEESE I :

My grandparents' geese were in the cellar where the wine was kept. The faucet on one of the wine kegs was open and the geese drank the wine. They got drunk, keeled over, and passed out! When my grandparents found the geese in the cellar, passed out, they thought they had died of something. They couldn't eat them because they might have died of something awful, so they plucked them all to use the feathers for feather beds. And then the geese woke up! They woke up and made a whole lot of noise. My grandparents had to keep them tied on a string to the house for the rest of the summer until their feathers grew back, so they wouldn't wander too far and get cold.

DEBORAH SAPERSTONE
Bennington, Vermont

: PLUCKED GEESE II :

It's about Aunt Sally Hill. She lived in Winston-Salem, and I'm not sure how she was kin to us, but you know us southerners, we're kin to just about everyone. They had a big backyard and lots of geese, and the geese were wandering around and they got into a sack of dried beans, and they kind of still wandered around. And you know how dried beans swell up. Well they swelled up, causing the geese to pass out. Aunt Sally Hill and her help, Kansas and Charlie Shaws, thought the geese had died. A bunch of dead geese aren't going to do you any good, so they thought they'd make some good down comforters or pillows or whatever else you make with geese feathers—so they plucked 'em. And the geese, well the dried beans shrunk up, and suddenly they had a bunch of naked geese running around the yard! And as my mother always ends the story, "They all lived happily ever after and it was a very funny thing."

ELOISE SILLS, AGE 28
Charleston, South Carolina

Stories
for
Children

Haven't you heard about the friend of Vicki's little boy who wanted to go swimming one night in the dark? He felt his way up the steps of the high diving board, stood on the edge, then died when he performed a marvelous swan dive into an empty pool." With a story like this a mother warned her children against a new favorite pastime, swimming at night. It was so effective that her children never again felt so much as the urge to swim after dark. Parents often tell *cautionary tales* of this kind. Many of them involve a ghost, goblin, or boogeyman who will "get" the children if they misbehave (only occasionally will they tell about jolly characters like Santa Claus who will reward children for good behavior).

Some of these characters and episodes are real though perhaps exaggerated; others are pulled out of thin air by an adult with a lesson to teach. "My mother had so many relatives," said Regina O'Toole Sokas, "that every time you wanted to do anything she didn't want you to do she had a relative who died a horrible death doing that. If you wanted to go ice skating on a pond that wasn't quite frozen she had a cousin who had done that. . . . I don't know if they were all true, but she had so many relatives you believed her." [1]

A second variety of stories invented for children are *fantasies*, fairy tales of a sort often told as bedtime stories. [2] Playing off their children's imaginations, parents weave stories around witches, giants, and their own fantastic figures, shaping the images into charming, sometimes beautiful narratives which teach their lessons with a little more subtlety.

Many of our most beloved children's books began as stories invented by parents for their children. During World War I, Hugh Lofting wrote a series of letters to his youngsters, Elizabeth and Colin. He didn't want to concentrate on the battles, so he wrote about another subject he felt would interest them more, the animals that were wounded or stranded at the front. The letters evolved into stories about a marvelous veterinarian, which became later the famous *Dr. Doolittle* series.

For every children's book published, there are a hundred thousand stories spun by parents in the privacy of the children's bedroom, imprinted nowhere but on a child's mind. In this intimate setting, parents become engaged in an artistic partnership with their children, each inspiring the other;

their lovely, imaginative, or fantastic tales often remain among the most creative efforts of their lifetimes.

Ironically, parents rarely give these yarns a second thought. More often than not, such tales were recalled for us by the children who, now grown, look back nostalgically at the inventions of their parents. We have even had a few opportunities to interview the original storyteller, only to have his eyes glaze over as he struggles with foggy recollections of his ephemeral meanderings.

A surprising number of these bedtime fantasies were the creation of fathers. Perhaps because they spent little time with their children during the day, they were charged with putting them to bed at night. The bedtime stories were then a way of rendering a small amount of shared time intimate and special. The episodic narratives became a way of providing a busy man with a regularly scheduled time with his children as the latest adventure of "Mahogany and Mack" or "Bunyan Bunny" was spun. As one young woman said, "If it wasn't for storytelling there really wouldn't have been much of a relationship between child and father."[3] Interestingly enough, a few of the tales we did collect from mothers were told by divorced, working women.

Of course, no clear-cut line divides made up bedtime fantasies from traditional fairy tales and written stories. One of the children's favorite episodes in the Great-grandfather Wog series told by Arthur Maas (p. 138) described how a prehistoric caveman and his wild, naked children (modeled, of course, on the teller's own offspring) discovered cooking. The discovery was accidental, coming when the pig was hurriedly thrown into a burning bush during a storm—an episode which, Arthur Maas freely admits, is borrowed from Charles Lamb's "A Dissertation Upon Roast Pig."

At bedtime a story might be read from a book, told from pure invention, or be an adaptation of any traditional story which suits the needs—and the whims—of particular storytellers and their children. In this next example, "Goldilocks and the Three Bears" is revamped by one mother for her daughter and her son:

My husband and I have been separated for two and a half years and I have two children, one is eight and one is four. About a year and a half ago, when my little boy was not quite

NAN GRAHAM

three, he really started liking the story of the three bears, and he wanted it told over and over and over again.

But at one point I realized that he was identifying very, very strongly when I would start and say, "papa bear, mama bear and baby bear." Immediately, he would say, "Daddy, mommy, and baby bear is me."

When we got to Goldilocks, immediately that was his sister, so his sister was almost the bad guy. And he was identifying very strongly with this idea of everybody being together, and I was trying to cope with the fact that we had separate families now.

So one day I just switched it around, and when everybody got up it was mama bear, sister bear, and brother bear; and his eyes got wide and he looked at this and thought about it for a minute. And then, when it got to be Goldilocks—instead it became Curlylocks, who was a little boy. Well, both kids absolutely loved that.

Sometimes sister bear and brother bear would get up and they would help with breakfast. And sometimes when mama bear and sister bear and brother bear would go out for a walk, they would go over to visit daddy at his house.

Now it's progressed to the point where they'll say, "Tell the 'Three Bears,' or tell the 'Special One'" because this is the "Special One." And now there's no more problem as far as his sister being the bad guy. It's their special story, and it's helped me. I felt like I was coping with something that I really hadn't expected.[4]

Other stories, like Martha Bays' "Princess Oliva and the Bravest Knight" in this section are not based on any particular children's tale, but borrow some of the form and content from many well-known stories. She makes use of numerous fairy tale features such as a dragon, a mountain of ice, a poor shepherd boy, a knight in shining armor, and the three tests, yet combines them into an original narrative which meets the particular needs of her family. Martha Bays was going through a divorce and a career change while raising two daughters by herself when she created the tale. She needed a story which featured a hardnosed, practical heroine, but to create the narrative she relied on models remembered from childhood.

Adapting traditional stories or inventing new ones is a way of rendering them more personal and relevant and giving them an added emotional charge. Characters can be molded in the image of one's own children, from the absolute everyday scene ("Saul woke up this morning and he had a glass of orange juice before he ventured onto the big yellow school bus") to a prehistoric landscape with naked children following behind Great-grandfather Wog. A parent's tales can wield a magical transformation, allowing their children to experience in a personalized way some of their deepest, most far-flung fantasies.

: PRINCESS OLIVA AND
THE BRAVEST KNIGHT :

I like the whole idea of fairy stories. I think they're fun, but I don't like most of the female characters in them—they're pretty dull. So, I've made up stories for the kids.

Once upon a time there was a princess who wanted to marry the bravest knight in the land. She decided that any knight who married her had to pass three tests of courage. He had to save her from the dragon, he had to save her from a seven-headed serpent, and he had to save her from a mountain of snow and ice that was guarded by three giants who would let no man pass. So, Sir Broiderick, who was the most elegant man in the land, decided to try for her hand. Oliva went out and sat under a tree and waited for the dragon to come down and attack her so she could be saved. And all of the townspeople came out to watch. There was a big celebration, and pretty soon the dragon came down the hill spouting fire and smoke, and everybody cheered. But, Sir Broiderick wasn't around. Sir Broiderick was at the other end of the mountain gathering flowers because he thought it would be very elegant to give her a bouquet of flowers after he saved her from the dragon. The dragon came closer and closer, and the townspeople started running away. A shepherd boy named Cuthbert decided he just couldn't bear to see Oliva eaten, just eaten by the dragon, so he ran up and handed her a shepherd's crook. The dragon came down and landed in front of Oliva and swooped her up in the air, and she speared the shepherd's crook up into the roof of his mouth, and he dropped her in a thicket of bushes. Just presently, Sir Broiderick came riding up and he slew the dragon that was lying on the ground just writhing in pain with the shepherd's crook stuck in his mouth. Then, he presented Oliva with the bouquet of flowers and very kindly overlooked the fact that she was a mess from having been dropped in the thicket of bushes. Oliva thanked him very nicely and made Cuthbert assistant head butler.

Next Sir Broiderick had to save Oliva from the seven-headed serpent. Everybody got up before dawn one morning and went up the mountain to the cave of the seven-headed serpent. All the townspeople came up; hawkers sold hot chestnuts, and everyone waited for the serpent to come out. Well, presently, the sun came up, and that warmed up the cave enough so that the seven-headed serpent came crawling out, this loathsome, horrible creature with all seven heads hissing. And Sir Broiderick wasn't around because he decided to wear his suit of silver armor that day and was back at the castle polishing it. Well, Cuthbert just couldn't stand it. The serpent was crawling closer and closer to Oliva. So, he took his butcher knife, which he had taken along just in case anything had happened, and he presented the butcher's knife to Oliva. He had to cut off two of the seven heads to get to her. He was very sorry about that. Well, Oliva said, "I can't kill off the serpent, because then I can't be saved, and I won't know if Sir Broiderick is the bravest knight in the land." So, he said, "Well, why don't you just blind it if it gets too close." And presently, Sir Broiderick came riding up the mountainside, looking absolutely magnificent in his silver armor. And he cut off the remaining five heads of the serpent which were sort of feebly waving around. They all had been blinded by Oliva while she was waiting to be saved. And Oliva thanked him very nicely and made Cuthbert the captain of the palace guard.

The last test of courage was, could Sir Broiderick save Oliva from the mountain of snow and ice, guarded by two giants? Oliva went to the top of the mountain wearing a nice sturdy pair of shoes and a heavy tweed skirt, and waited to be saved. [Virginia: Mommy, you forgot. In the two others she had been wearing those elegant dresses.] Oh yes. The first time she wore a seafoam chiffon, but that got all torn up in the bushes. And the second time she wore red velvet, but that got all splattered with blood. So the third time she decided she'd better dress sensibly.

So, she waits up on top of the mountain. Sir Broiderick does not show up. He's out picking out an engagement ring. Well, the townspeople are getting very upset, and the giants are having to do tricks to entertain the people because they're getting very restive. And Oliva's up on top of the mountain turning bluer and bluer. And finally Cuthbert can't stand it any longer, and he goes back to the castle, and he gets the bear skin rug from the floor of the great hall of the castle. And he sneaks up the mountain past the giants who are too dumb to realize that he's a man. And he places the bear skin rug around poor Oliva. Well, the giants realize they've been tricked. And they come roaring up the mountain, determined to tear Cuthbert from limb to limb. Whereupon Oliva and Cuthbert make a huge snowball and roll it down upon the giants. Well, Sir Broiderick rides up in a perfectly beautiful set of golden armor, cuts off the giants' heads (which are the only things that can be seen above the avalanche), and rides up to claim his prize. But, by this time, Oliva and Cuthbert are sitting cuddled in the bear skin rug and don't even notice that he's there. So, he rides away looking for a princess who is more appreciative and better dressed.

And Oliva goes back to the castle and has Cuthbert knighted and says now he can try for her hand by passing the three tests of courage. Well, Cuthbert refuses to do that. He says its ridiculous, and he's not going to put her through that. So he goes back off to his shepherd's cottage. And Oliva climbs to the top *of the tallest tower in the castle and looks out into the sea and thinks. She comes back and goes to the shepherd's cottage where Cuthbert is very sadly polishing his armor and says that she will marry him after all, if he'll polish his own armor and be the jolliest papa in the world. And he agrees to that. So they're married in great pomp and ceremony. And after a time, they had eleven red-haired princes, each one of which is more mischievous than the last. And the townspeople who know those princes say that Sir Cuthbert is the bravest knight in the land!*

MARTHA AND VIRGINIA BAYS
Reston, Virginia

: WHALE OF A TALE :

Every night when they were growing up, I told my children stories about whales: a red whale, a white whale, and a blue whale. I probably created more whale stories than anybody living in the United States. I taught them how to learn about the planets using the whale of a tale—how the whales traveled to all the nine different planets, whales that have communicated from Earth to Mars to Venus. I've taught them different birds, different animals, alphabetically, just by using the whale as a concept. The whale stories that the children liked the most had some type of moral to them, and the concept would be a current event that had taken place.

DALE BROWN

Let's see. There was a red whale, a white whale, and a blue whale, and they decided to go to Washington, D.C., but they didn't know how to get there. Should they take Route 1, should they take 95, or should they take a side road? They all decided to take different paths. The red whale took the side road, and he saw the mountains, and he saw the valleys, and it took him a long, long time. The white whale took Route 1, and he saw the different highways, and he used to stop and go on all the red lights, past all the small towns. He'd see the different types of stores and different types of people and different industries and different walks of life. The blue whale thought he was the smartest. He took Route 95 and went very, very quickly. And he arrived in Washington first.

The blue whale was so proud that he arrived first that when they all congregated—the red whale, the white whale, and the blue whale—he said, "Hey, how's your trip?" And the blue whale said, "I made it in three hours." "That's fantastic! What did you do the rest of the time?" "Nothing." The white whale took Route 1, and he saw people, all sorts of people, different working-class people, interesting people. He stopped to talk to them, and he learned different stories about life. The red whale took the scenic route. It took him four times as long as the blue whale and twice as long as the white whale. And the red whale said, "I saw the most beautiful sunrise; I saw the most beautiful sunset. I looked up in the sky at night and I saw the most beautiful stars and the most beautiful planets. It took me twelve hours, but I'll never forget it." Which route would you have taken? And which one would you have enjoyed the most?

STANLEY COHEN, AGE 45

Suffern, New York

: THE FIREMAN WHALE :

It all started a good many years ago when there was an old mansion located just north of Asbury Park (New Jersey) on the beach. One night this old house burst into flames and the flames were raging very fiercely. The local fireman companies responded to the alarm and they were trying to put the fire out, but it go so bad that they decided that they would have to give up.

Well, it just so happened that about this time there was a whale swimming along in the ocean about three or four miles off Asbury Park and he saw this red glow in the sky, so he decided that he would swim in close to see what was going on. And when he got in fairly close to the beach, he could see this house on fire and that the men were squirting water on it but that they weren't really able to do very much. Their water pressure was too low. So the whale swam to shore and went up to the fire chief and said, "Can I help you put this fire out? I've got a lot of water here." The chief said, "Oh yes, you could. We'd appreciate it very much." So the whale went back into the ocean and filled his nose with a lot of water and came back and spouted water all over the fire. He did that several times and finally he put out the fire. Well, everybody cheered of course and the firemen were very grateful and they asked the whale to come back to the firehouse with them and celebrate with coffee and doughnuts, which the whale enjoyed very much. Finally, he said, "Well, it's time I got back to the ocean, I think."

Before he left, the fire chief said that they were going to have a Christmas party at the firehouse in a few weeks, and asked the whale if he'd like to come. The whale said he certainly would. So the night of the Christmas party the whale appeared again with a nice holly wreath and presents for the firemen. They were all very pleased, and they sang Christmas carols and the whale had a wonderful time. When it came time for him to go back to the ocean, the fire chief said, "You have been so helpful to us in putting out that fire that I wonder if we could put a telephone line from the firehouse here along the bottom of the ocean where you live and connect it to an underwater telephone there. Then, if we have any more bad fires some time and need your help, we could call you on the telephone. Would you be willing to come and help us put out the fire?" And the whale said of course, he'd like to do that very much.

Soon after that, some divers came, put in a telephone, and connected it with the firehouse. Every time since then that they've had a very bad fire around Asbury Park that they can't put out with their own fire apparatus, they call the whale. If he is home, which he usually is, he gets up, puts on the fire helmet which the firemen gave him as a present, and swims back to shore to put out the fire. And every time, he goes back to the firehouse and has coffee and doughnuts with the firemen. And that's the story of the fireman whale.

GEOFFREY VELASQUEZ AZOY, AGE 8
Little Silver, New Jersey

: THE SANDBOX :

My father used to make up Mit and Mat stories; I was Mat and my brother was Mit. The one I remember best is the one my brother doesn't figure in at all. We used to go to the beach every day; it was a very short drive from Philadelphia. We had a sandbox in the backyard and I was trying to get sand for it. My father used to bring a few buckets of sand back from the beach.

Well, Mat goes to the beach with her parents and she wants to bring sand back and her father says no, it won't fit in the car. So while they're sleeping on the beach, Mat filled the trunk of the car up with sand and then covered it over with towels. They drove home and Mat's father was very upset because the car wasn't riding properly. He couldn't understand it. He said he'd have to take it to the garage and have them check it out. But as they got close to the Benjamin Franklin Bridge, the load became less and the car was all right by the time they got home. Well, Mat couldn't wait to get out and look in the trunk for the sand. But it was gone! It had come out in dribbles. She noticed little dabs of sand in the driveway and she started to following it with her bucket, scooping it up. She ended up all the way back at the beach, at which point her parents were very upset and they called the police and there was this big search for this lost little girl. It made all the newspapers and they got her back and punished her for being such a silly little girl. But they were glad to get her back home.

The upshot was that everybody read about this poor little girl who didn't have any sand in her sandbox. And they started sending sand. She got sand from Arabia, sand from North Africa, and sand from everywhere, all over the world, all different colors of sand. The yard was full of it. It became ridiculous. There was too much sand. So she got this wonderful idea. She made the sand into bricks, beautifully colored bricks, different layers, and sold them for a quarter a piece. Pretty soon, she was back to having no sand in her sandbox and stealing it from the beach.

PAM MATLOCK
Washington, D.C.

: PEPPER AND SUCCOTASH :

When I was little my father used to make up stories to tell me and my brother about two twin red-headed boys named Pepper and Succotash. This was purely an individual art form. He would never know when he started out how the story was going to end up. He would just spin these yarns.

One time he told us the story of Pepper and Succotash going to Mars. I don't remember how they got there but all the people would have some kind of bubble gum and they would chew it and blow bubbles out of their ears and go floating around. The bubbles were something like helium. There were witches and the boys would chew this bubble gum and float away from the witches.

Another time Pepper and Succotash went down to the river on a picnic. There was no way to get across so they took a whole string of hot dogs and they made it into a lasso and threw it across the river to a stump. And then they monkey-walked across, you know, they had to hang. When they got across they ate all of the hot dogs and then after they had finished the picnic they didn't know how to get back over the stream. So one of them pulled out the plug and they walked across.

BRIAN R. GAY, AGE 11
Washington, D.C.

: Mahogany and Mac :

My husband used to make up the most wonderful stories for the kids. He invented two characters called Mahogany and Mac. One was a credenza, and one was a trailer truck. And Mahogany lived in Mac, you see, and they would go traveling all around the world and all around the globe. I even remember Mahogany and Mac going off into space and having adventures there. And they had very strong personalities. Mac was the strong male thing, and Mahogany was the woman. She was just a great big credenza—the kids loved that word, credenza. They thought it was great!

TAMARA DEFRIES, AGE 47
Falls Church, Virginia

: Bunyan Bunny :

My father and I used to have a rabbit club. We made up our own legends about Bunyan Bunny, the greatest rabbit of them all. He was really big, a superbunny. One of the stories that we made up together was about Niagara Falls. The reason that Niagara Falls was formed was that Bunyan Bunny was hopping along one day and he hopped all the way from New York to Niagara Falls. He was really thirsty and he saw a spring there. He bent over and he slipped in the mud and sat down. And he was so big that he formed the space where Niagara Falls is.

Dad also tried to weave history into the stories. He told how Bunyan Bunny helped to get the first pioneers out west. He used to tell me about the pioneers crossing in Conestoga wagons. Bunyan Bunny would perch on the mountaintop and see the dis-

tressed travelers. So he would hop out and pull their Conestoga
wagons to a spring. This rabbit club was just between the two
of us. We were the inner circle, just dad and me. And then there
was the outer circle, my sister, my brother, and my mother.

Providence, Rhode Island

: THE BREAD FACTORY TOUR :

Well, when I was younger we had sort of a little childhood
tradition. Almost every night my parents would tell my
younger brother and me a story about our stuffed animals. We
had two separate villages. One was Kittyville because my main
stuffed animal was a little cat that I got when I was two
months old. Eric had a little teddy bear, and there was Jungle-
ville, because in addition to the teddy bear he had this little
monkey. And we had a sequence of stories that developed about
kitty scouts and teddy scouts. Eric's little teddy bear also had a
yellow dog friend. They would have box-derby races. There
would be characterizations of morals that I guess they wanted
to instill in us. Yellow dog had square wheels, and even though
he lost in the end everybody gave him a prize for being the most
creative soap box car. And kitty scouts were always doing good
things.

One story involved a visit to the bread factory. All the kitty
scouts decided, "Hey, we ought to do something constructive
and go see how bread is made." Mr. Winsey, another cat, was
presiding over this meeting and he said, "Okay, I suggest a mo-
tion that we go visit the bread factory." And Pooh and Piglet
said that they'd second the motion. So, they all got on a train in
Kittyville station, and they went in the mountain to the bread
factory. When they got there, the bread factory people were
very nice and showed them how to make the bread and gave
them samples.

Well, during this time, Piglet noticed little trash cans around
and he strayed from the rest of the kitty-cat troop. After awhile
the rest of the kitty scouts had gone way far into the factory,
and they didn't notice that Piglet was gone. And what Piglet
had done was to go to the side of this one counter; he saw this
little hole, and it smelled kind of like trash, and he got inter-
ested in it. But he couldn't read, so he couldn't read that the

137 STORIES FOR CHILDREN

words on top of it said "trash chute." So, the next thing he knew, he stuck his head in, dove in, and was going miles and miles screaming, but nobody could hear him.

In the meantime, the rest of the kitty scouts finished their tour and were ready to get back on the train. And they couldn't understand why Piglet didn't come when they called for him, why he didn't answer. Eventually Pooh said, "I think I saw him looking in the trash bin. Oh my gosh, I wonder where he went." So, they got all of the staff of the bread factory to help them. Mr. Wimsey took his own initiative to go out and try to look for him in the back rooms. And he heard this noise in this huge bin at the end of a long tube. It was kind of a squealing noise. He opened it, and he saw Piglet, all wrapped up in rotten bread. And he said, "Piglet, what in the world got you into this mess?" And Piglet said, "It's only my nature. I can't help it." They finally got him out, but the kitty scouts would not let Piglet inside the train. He had to ride on top of the train all the way back to Kittyville. And for miles around the next day, there were reports of the most awful stench going through the village. When they got home they had to dunk him inside the bathtub, and give him a bath.

KIRSTEN STROMBERG, AGE 18
Silver Spring, Maryland

: GRANDFATHER WOG :

Great-great-great-great-great-great-great-great-great-great-great-great-grandfather Wog went hunting one day, and he took along his two daughters, Jog and Cog. Before long, they killed a pig, and they were bringing it home when a great big storm came up. The lightning flashed and the thunder rolled, and all of a sudden a lightning bolt hit a tree right beside them, and Grandfather Wog was so scared that he threw the pig over his shoulder and he and the girls went and hid in the rocks. And the lightning set the pile of brush on fire and they thought that their pig was all burned up, cause the flames licked around it.

Well when the fire died down, they came out and saw the pig was all black and charred. But something smelled awfully good. And Grandfather Wog stuck out his finger and he touched the pig. But it burned, oh! [Mr. Maas at this point puts his finger in his mouth as a gesture.] But it tasted so good. And

SUSAN SHAPIRO

he reached out and touched the pig again [again he puts his fingers in his mouth as if trying to ease the pain of a burn], but my that tasted good. And they decided that burnt pig was the best thing they ever tasted. And that was the beginning of cooking.

ARTHUR MAAS, AGE 58
Greenbelt, Maryland

: MAGIC CLOTHESPINS :

One story that has come down on my side of the family is what we call clothespin stories. The clothespins themselves were Grandma Gillis' great-grandmother's, a magic bag of clothespins that really went across the plains with her, in the wagon.

During the day they did ordinary clothespin work, but at night they became individuals. They always seemed to get themselves into trouble and make a horrible mess and then get themselves out of it. In one story the kids always liked, the clothespins would fall off on the ground and someone would pick them up and they'd see something important and try to tell it to the human people, and not being able to really relate the information to them they'd have to do it in some tricky way, like falling down right beside them and waking them up to make them see the Indians coming.

Of course these stories were made up on the spot in all generations including ours. Our children of course didn't know this and they'd say, "Daddy, tell me the clothespin story about such and such" and we wouldn't remember it and we'd try to get them to tell a little of it, and then we'd remember somewhat what it was like and go on with it.

RAYMOND AND NYLA WEBBER, AGES 38 AND 27
Page, Arizona

: THE CATS :

My grandmother was born in the middle of the Black Forest in 1858. I still remember the hair-raising witch stories she would tell us when we were little children. The old witch woman in the village would capture children and turn them into cats to do the laundry. One of her [my grandmother's] little girlfriends finally followed her back into the forest and put her eye to the keyhole. And she saw this huge tub with about a dozen cats around it that were as large as children. They were wearing little children's clothes and she could recognize little Heidi's dress— and there's little Jacob's shoes! And my grandmother would stand at the end of the table, going like this, pretending to be the witch, "Ein, zwei, drei!" counting out for the cats to do the laundry!

STEVEN SCHENK, AGE 28
Arlington, Virginia

: THE WAILING WOMAN :

The most interesting stories that came from my childhood were the stories that the parents and grandparents would tell you to keep you in line and were passed on to my father from his grandfather. They had to do with when they wanted to emphasize certain points, when they didn't want you out at certain times of the month, specifically on the dangerous nights of the week, like Friday night and Saturday night. They had these stories about the wailing woman, a woman who was condemned to walk the streets late on Friday and Saturday nights, wailing because she had killed her two children. The grandparents would tell these stories with all the children around them. And, I mean, you just don't question your grandmother. So they really sunk in.

Here's the most vivid example of this. I guess I was about ten or eleven, and I'd heard these stories over and over again, so naturally on Friday and Saturday nights I really seldom went out. But in my hometown—this was before indoor plumbing came in—we had the old family chamber pot. Every morning you had to go dump it. But something had happened that we didn't have it in the house. And it happened to be about midnight this one Friday night, and I had to go to the privy. I got about halfway to the outhouse and all of a sudden I heard this loud wail. I was so scared to death that I forgot I had to go to the bathroom. I went back to the house and just completely covered my head up. And it was many, many years that I would not go outside, especially on Friday nights. Any other night, it was fine. But those were the nights, Friday nights.

I guess it was when I was in my twenties that I happened to be out one night and I heard the same sound. What it was, was a

JAY BURG

cat. *But to this day when I hear this sound, it's still in the back of my mind. These are the things just rich in tradition that the old people had to keep you in line.*

GEORGE VALDEZ, JR., AGE 35
Wheaton, Maryland

: THE BINGO :

I remember my mother used to tell me about a boogeyman kind of thing. I must have been somewhere around two or three years old. You'd hear a train whistle every so often. I don't know where the train was in relation to where we lived, but some times you could sort of hear this eerie sound, particularly at night. And she would tell us that was the Bingo. She didn't describe it, but I'd gotten the idea that the Bingo was something awful. Then at other times she would refer to the Bingo, like when some of my toys would disappear every so often. I later learned that with most kids there are too many toys around, so you clear them out occasionally or put some away, and then get them out again at another time. So if I missed something and asked where it was, oh, the Bingo had taken it. And then I'd get threatened occasionally with other things the Bingo would do if I didn't behave.

CORINNE BLUM LEBOVIT, AGE 58
Silver Spring, Maryland

: UNCLE VESPER :

The only ghost I can remember is Uncle Vesper. I really think he was used to stop children in the family from doing things that they shouldn't do. That included coming downstairs Christmas Eve or going into the attic or playing in the basement or going outside in the yard, or whatever the particular situation was in growing up. Uncle Vesper was kind of the guardian or the implied threat; if you did something, Uncle Vesper would get you.

He supposedly lived in a shoebox in the attic and each time the family moved, they would make sort of a display of moving the shoebox to let the kids know that Uncle Vesper was not being left behind, that he was going to run the next household too.

When my older brother got married, they gave him a shoebox with Uncle Vesper in it. My other brother, when he got married, got Uncle Vesper too! So, in a way, Uncle Vesper kind of subdivides and takes responsibility for branches of the family.

ROBERT BACHMAN, AGE 27
Radnor, Pennsylvania

: USING THE BLARNEY :

My grandfather was Irish through and through. He was a big man, over six feet tall and about 220 pounds as I recall him. My aunt told me the story about how when they were all growing up and they didn't want to go to school for some reason, my grandfather would say, "Oh, I never missed a day of school in me life. Not for rain or snow, and I always walked to school." Many years later my aunt took a trip to Ireland and she went to my grandfather's old homestead. When she came back she said, "No wonder he went to school every day. His house was right next to the school." That was typical of him, to use the old blarney to get you to do something.

WILLIAM F. DELANEY, AGE 44
Burke, Virginia

RUTH COYNE

: ELBOWS AND HANDS :

"Don't stick your elbow out too far, it might go home in another car." My mother had a great story about this violinist she once knew who was riding with his hand out the window. This truck came along and took it off. He couldn't play the violin and he lost his livelihood. So, don't stick your hand out of the car!

ELIZABETH LANG, AGE 24
Larchmont, New York

: LIMA BEANS :

We hated lima beans and we were Catholic. And my father said that he hated them too, but my mother made them about two times a week. She said they were good for us. My father claimed that he had written to the Pope and that he had declared them a mortal sin, and we never had to eat them again.

JAMES MCEVOY, AGE 34
Omaha, Nebraska

: A DIRTY STORY :

Can I tell you a dirty story about my father? When my brother was about six or seven years old, he found a prophylactic in the pocket of Bessie the Buick. And so he asked my father what it was for. As my brother remembers it, my father was very much flustered by the question.

Then my father said, "Well, men who go to war need those." And my brother was stumped, so he asked for more explanation. My father said, "Well, a man puts that on" — and I'm sure he didn't use the word penis — but, "the man puts that on his penis and if he has to urinate while he's in the middle of battle, he does it in that little rubber thing. And then when he gets back and the battle is over, he takes it off and he can throw it away." My brother believed that for years.

ELINOR ABRAMSON
Washington, D.C.

: SNAKES IN CHURCH :

I had an experience on the Irish side. My grandmother found out that I was friends with a Protestant boy. Being a New Yorker we were friends with everyone. I had Jewish friends, I had Irish friends, I had Italian friends. I brought this one boy home, and my grandmother asked me what nationality he was. I didn't know. As a child you don't ask a kid what nationality he is or where he's from. You get your prejudice after many years. She says, "Well, what church does he go to?" And I say, "I don't know." So she asked him. He happened to be Lutheran and said that he went to the Lutheran church.

Well, my grandmother gave me a funny look and then that night she called me up to the house—we lived next door—and she says, "I don't want you to play with that boy anymore." And I say, "Why? I happen to like him." His name was Jack. She says, "Well, because the Lutherans in their services, before they go in, each one is handed a snake. And what they'd like to do is get little Catholic boys into the back and get them converted to Lutheran services. If they don't convert them, they sic the snakes on them." Now, whether this was something my grandmother made up at the time or whether it was in reality something that was handed down to her, I don't know. But this is just another example of what we got.

It didn't affect my behavior towards him, because I had known the boy for quite some time. And I just couldn't visualize him taking me in back of a church and sicking snakes on me. I broached the subject with him. He did just what you're doing; he laughed. So he took me to his church. I met his pastor, Reverend Black. He showed me all around the church, and I couldn't find a snake in it. Not a snake in the whole church.

JOSEPH COPPOLA, JR., AGE 46
Central Islip, New York

Family Expressions

Bubbling over with high spirits, Bettie, a seven-year-old girl from Attleboro, Massachusetts, had been entertaining the family for some time when her mother said laughingly, "What *does* make you do and say those things?" "Oh, I don't know," Bettie said, "I guess I'm just feeling agnipocus!"[1] From that moment forward whenever a member of the Weatherbee family was describing a good mood all of the vast resources and infinite subtleties of the English language paled before the nonsensical utterance of a seven-year-old girl.

In vain we look through Webster's unabridged third edition for euphonious words like "hudge," "Samuel Widgens," "squiblums." For it would take, after all, a member of the Sackett family to know that "hudge" means to pick up a child and hug him.[2] The Starr family alone would interpret "Samuel Widgens" as a sandwich.[3] And only at the door of the Woodville family might we be asked for "Squiblums, squiblums,"[4] a joking family reference to identification papers or other credentials. Expressions like these illustrate, perhaps better than any other form, how ingenious families can be.

Yet these terms and phrases are more than just a family's way of coming up with better words than the English language affords. They serve as passwords which affirm the ties of shared experience. They are also filled with meaning because the expression often carries a humorous piece of family history along with it. Hearing it, we can often remember the riotous situation which gave birth to the phrase.

"My family," said Stephen Tauber, "has numerous expressions which are elliptical allusions to a tale. In German this is called '*gefluketas wort*,' a winged word. . . ." He went on to give an example from his family:

My great-grandfather, that is to say my mother's mother's father, was a general storekeeper in the town of Littenz, in Czechoslovakia. One of the tales which is famous in our family was about the time that a farmer came to the store. His wife was cooking and had run out of sugar. So he came to the store to buy a cone of sugar—that's how it was sold in those days, a solid cone of sugar.

But of course you don't go into a store, buy what you want, and leave again, not in a small village. You chat and you talk, you talk about the crops, about the weather, about what you're doing, about the weather, and some more about the weather. My great-grandfather said, "Yes, it is looking very much like rain. Tell me, do you have an umbrella?" The farmer said, "No, I never had an umbrella, don't really need one." My great-grandfather said, "You know, it's really very handy. You're going to be walking home for four kilometers, you'll get wet. Why don't you buy an umbrella?"

"Eh"—they talk back and forth some more. Finally the farmer said, "All right, all right, I'll buy an umbrella from you."

So he bought an umbrella and went home—but with no sugar. And ever since in our family, whenever somebody goes shopping and comes back with something other than what he went out to buy, whatever he comes home with is called an umbrella.[5]

In the Tauber family, "umbrella" is indeed a winged word; it carries an episode in a general store in Littenz, Czechoslovakia, across nearly a hundred years to tease a child who brings the wrong item home from the supermarket.

Kim Garrett's grandfather Stevenson used a saying which dated from a perilous storm in 1886 when the whole family sought shelter in his large stone house. "The family at the time," Garrett writes, "included Telegraph, Uncle Alley's big white horse. Uncle Alley was badly crippled (a fact that Telegraph seemed to understand) and looked on his horse as a beloved companion as well as safe transportation. Telegraph was stabled on the porch at first, but as the storm grew worse, Uncle Alley grew more restless. No one thought it too strange when he asked that Telegraph be brought into the house. The parlor was the only room not crowded with kin, so Telegraph spent the rest of the night surrounded by family daguerreotypes. . . ."[6]

Since then, "Weather to bring the stock into the parlor" became one of Grandfather Stevenson's family expressions. The phrase evokes that dramatic and comical episode to charge and embellish a discussion about the weather. The family expression often enables us to bring a dramatic episode to bear on a similar but less dramatic episode in everyday life, imbuing the ordinary with vibrant associations from the past.

When outsiders are present a story like the stock in the parlor might be repeated in full. But family members have usually heard the tales, and they become part of the shared past, the storehouse of memories that can be drawn upon in the richly textured conversation of persons who know each other well. "Someone in my family had three children, one of whom was named Shields," Mrs. Slemp told us. "The old man was quite a drunk and often would beat up on his family when in liquor. One day he started in on Shields who by then was a grown teenager, and Shields licked the tar out of him. Finally the old man was down, and Shields was sitting on his chest. The old man looked up and said ruefully, 'Get up Shields, you beat your daddy.'"[7] This line, "Get up Shields, you beat your daddy," the most dramatic and quotable, became a traditional family expression.[8]

At times, however, a family phrase will emerge not from a story but from a memorable chance remark easily adapted to new situations. "How could any non-initiate guess," wrote R.A. Stewart Macalister,

that "to sing the hundredth psalm" meant "to fetch a glass of water" — as it does in a family known to me? If he be admitted to the domestic arcana so far as to learn the phrase and its meaning, how could he guess the nexus between the two ideas — a chance remark made upon a midsummer day — that to allow the heated water to run off from the cold-water tap took about as long a time as it would take to perform the act of piety specified?[9]

Some episodes in a family's past may be alluded to over and over again without becoming codified in a specific expression. If, for instance, in the Slemp family a child has beaten his father in checkers, rather than saying, "Get up Shields, you beat your daddy," someone could have said, "It's just like the time Shields beat up his old man." It would not have been as poetic, but it would have served the same purpose. When extended this way, the idea of the family expression or allusion plays an important part in every human relationship.

Oftentimes these expressions are hilarious solutions to the kinds of similar problems which crop up in families. In our collection, the phrases "two thousand monkeys" and "horses are falling left and right" are both used to tease a family

HELEN MACKEY GREY

member for exaggeration. A number are also told to correct behavior at the dinner table. Back in the 1860s, wrote Kim Garrett, "Sister Rhoda had a pet pig that died from overeating or 'busted from too much buttermilk. . . .' [And] for nearly a hundred years 'Strodie's pig' had been a specter hovering over any Stevenson-Baylor child who is inclined to overeat. 'Remember Strodie's pig!' is always fair warning that third helpings are out."[10] In another family, recalling the "Lefant kid" was all that was necessary to assure proper behavior at the table; the Lefant child once threw mashed potatoes while the visiting preacher was saying grace.[11]

Some of the most touching expressions serve to soothe and console. They are a way of defusing tense situations, telling members of the family that everything is all right. Maybe a humorous figure can be blamed if an object is lost or misplaced. In one family, for instance, "Mr. Rompback took it." The younger generation of another family drove down to a river where the boys were beginning a boat trip. Just as they were leaving, one of the boys got out of the boat, kissed his sister on the cheek, and said, "Goodbye, sis. Tell ma the boat floats." Now, when a family member calls or writes home from a trip, "Tell ma the boat floats" means that everything is all right.[12]

Family expressions are the poetry of everyday life. They are packed with alliteration, rhythm, and hyperbole. "Thank God for guts and gristle" is the rousing battle cry in one family whenever a dirty, difficult job need be done; "Too tired to tuck" is a phrase in another when a task simply seems too exhausting.[13] Expressions often take the form of a metaphor; an example in this section compares eating too much gum (or any excessive behavior) to "jumping off the fifteenth-story window for a breeze on a hot day."

Perhaps as we become more intimate with one another, our conversation moves from prose towards poetry. We compact our experiences and relate them not as long explanatory narratives but as terse exclamations. We begin to use catchwords and allusions and much of our conversation becomes laden with associations. At the same time our talk becomes more patterned and rhythmical. Linguists have shown that "when people speak to each other they keep a rhythm, a meter of regular beats, and time their entrances and exits to the rhythm of these beats."[14] Close families often seem particularly in sync with one another. They enjoy conversations which outsiders might consider repetitive but which they experience as comfortable and smooth. They develop a sense of timing and occasionally inject a family expression which teases and brings back a rush of memories, without missing a beat. As one young woman said about her relationship to her sister, "We refined our communication into a work of art."[15]

: Horses Are Falling Left and Right :

When my mother was a little girl from Kansas City, and was here in Washington with her family, she looked out the window of the Mayflower Hotel and said, "Oh mummy, it's so icy, horses are falling left and right!" And her mother rushed to the window and said, "What are you talking about?" And she said, "Well, one slipped." So over-exaggeration in our family is always, "Horses are falling left and right." This is a seventy-year-old saying, but they all say it.

: Two Thousand Monkeys :

My sister had a tendency to exaggerate and apparently she had heard some story at school about some monkeys getting loose in New York City from some show. She came home and told us this story about these two thousand monkeys that were loose in New York City. The next month there was a story in Reader's

Digest on the same subject and it was twelve monkeys. So every time she would rev up and begin to exaggerate, everybody would turn to her and say, "two thousand monkeys" and she would slow down.

: ABEDIAH :

My father grew up in Missouri in the Ozarks. There used to be a lot of traveling salesmen and peddlers, and there was this one man named Abediah who I think sold pots and pans and also hand organs and things like that. He would go through about once every six months and they would always invite him in for dinner. Abediah liked to talk an incredible amount. He would talk forever and interrupt everyone at the table, and the expression came about in my family that whenever you interrupted anyone, the others would call out "Abediah!" That expression came about in my grandfather's family and was passed down to us.

MARJORIE HUNT
McLean, Virginia

NAN GRAHAM

: TOMBSTONES:

When we were little and Williamsburg had just been restored, my family took us down there. Somewhere along the way, my brother needed a bathroom, and my mother didn't know where one was. But we were right near a very ancient cemetery, and she said, "Well, just run right in there behind a tombstone," which he did. After that, whenever our family traveled and the problem came up, it was always, "Hey Mom, I need a tombstone."

MIDGE HEIMER
Germantown, Maryland

: HOUDINI :

When I was young I bought my brother a book for his birthday, a biography of Houdini. He had barely unwrapped it when I grabbed it back from him and ran away and hid for the rest of the birthday party and read the book. It was a big joke that I had bought him a book which I had obviously wanted. So ever after that, anytime anyone gave a gift that was clearly something that the giver wanted perhaps more than the givee, it was called a Houdini.

MARGARET CLARK, AGE 26
Washington, D.C.

: DOWN TO THE RAG :

My grandmother was born in 1832. A neighbor of hers was inviting the minister to dinner, so she invited my grandmother too. Well, in those days, sugar was very expensive, so she didn't have very much at hand. It seems that in those days, the sugar bowls were quite large. So she took a piece of green muslin and put it down in the bottom of the sugar bowl and then put some sugar on top. Well, it was passed around, and when it got around to a little boy at the table, he looked in, and he said, "Ma, down to the rag." So that's been an expression in our family. If anything's down low, we say, "Down to the rag."

BLANCHE M. BOTTO, AGE 87
Kensington, Maryland

WENDY WOLF

: EASY HANDS :

My son, well, he gets into things. He's a real live wire. He was about two when I asked him, "Bryan, how come you're always getting into things?" And he said, "Mother, I've just got easy hands." It's become part of the family's sayings. It means getting into mischief and doing little things you shouldn't do. It's gone through the whole family; my sister uses it with her kids.

NANCY KILCZEWSKI, AGE 35
Herndon, Virginia

: MY SHOES ARE TOO BIG! :

This expression started when my brother came in drunk one night, and my mother asked him why he was walking funny. It's an excuse for anything now.

CINDY MACKAY
Ridgewood, New Jersey

: I HAVE TO GO OUT AND PICK BLUEBERRIES :

I had a younger sister who never liked to do dishes. We have a summer place in Maine where we spent many summers and when she didn't want to do the dishes she would always say that she had to go out and pick blueberries. That was a job that nobody wanted to do but when it came time to do the dishes, all of a sudden that looked pretty good. So now when any of us have something that we don't want to do, we "have to go out and pick blueberries," which means that we don't want to do that job.

LUCY PHINNEY
Woodbridge, Virginia

: THE RIGHT ONE DID IT :

We have a family expression for placing the blame on someone. It started a long time ago when we were little kids. If my mother broke something, we'd say, "Wow! The right one did it." Because if we had done it, we'd get in trouble. And that's gone through all our family. We still say it now. What would be a good example? The cherry dining-room table. My husband was sitting there and his cigarette fell out of his ashtray and he burned a hole in this beautiful table which he adores. That is a perfect example of the right one did it, because if I had burned the table there'd be hell to pay.

NOEL SCHWERDTFEGER, AGE 46
Alton, Illinois

: KESL GARTN! :

Each summer during the 1920s, my parents, my four sisters, and I escaped from our steamy flat in Hartford and went to Ocean Beach on Long Island Sound. In those days, none of the immigrant families could afford to rent a whole house, so we rented two rooms in a large cottage with three or four other families. I remember bringing our own pots, pans, and food and splitting the cost of ice with the other families. You can imagine the scene as four women, all used to their own kitchens, tried to fix three meals a day for their large families in one tiny kitchen. "My husband's coming home at four. I must have dinner ready!" "Thief! You used our milk." "That's my chopped liver!"

Finally, my mother had had enough. She threw up her hands, exclaiming, "I don't need this kesl gartn." This, undoubtedly, was a reference to the confusion that characterized Castle Garden, the immigrant processing station that preceded Ellis Island. "Kesl gartn" became an expression used to connote chaos in the family.

DAVID KOTKIN, AGE 68
Hartford, Connecticut

CAROLYN MITCHELL

DAN BERGER

: MRS. BURGUNDA :

When we were kids and one of us wanted one thing and one of us wanted another, particularly in the way of food for dinner, my mother would say, "I won't be a Mrs. Burgunda. I won't go crazy trying to satisfy all of you." There was a story her mother had told about a woman who did just that, who tried to accommodate the tastes of each child separately. And one very hot day she was just worn to a frazzle and she jumped out a window and committed suicide. So when my sister would be fighting for one thing and I'd want something else, she'd say, "I won't be a Mrs. Burgunda." And that would settle the whole situation.

: A WILMA CLEANING :

I remember a young girl used to come in and clean house for my mother occasionally. She lived across the street, and her name was Wilma. Because she was a young kid, she would kind of dust things off real quickly and that kind of stuff. After Wilma left and got married, my mother would say, when she was just giving the house a real quick cleaning, "I'm giving the house a Wilma cleaning." Well, I didn't think there was anything wrong with that, and so the next time Wilma was home to visit her family, she said, "What's your mom doing today?" I said, "Oh, she's giving the house a Wilma cleaning." "Now, what's that?" "Oh, you know, just a light brushover." And my mother, of course, had to go apologize.

PATRICIA JORGENSON

: CHARLOTTE'S PURPLE WIG :

To show how elegant she is, my cousin Charlotte's furniture is the most elegant, and Charlotte's food is the most elegant. There's no question about it.

We never know what kind of a wig she's going to have. One time she's a blonde; one time she's a redhead. One day she had come from Europe and she showed up in a purple wig — no one here had one. And as a sign of elegance, we now say, "Charlotte's purple wig." And we all know now that it's put-on elegance.

: CUT IT, HELEN :

When you felt that someone was putting you on, you'd say, "Cut it, Helen." There was nobody in our family named Helen, but it came about when one day the phone rang and somebody said to my mother, "Helen?" And my mother said, "No, I'm sorry, you must have the wrong number." And she said, "Helen, I know it's you." And she kept insisting, and my mother said, "No, you must have the wrong number." And finally she said, "Cut it, Helen!" My mother told us about it at dinner that night. From then on, it became an expression in the family. It's continued in my own family, though they probably don't realize why I say it or where it came from.

ILENE SHELTON
Takoma Park, Maryland

: MOVE THE BED :

We frequently say to each other, "Now, move that bed." That comes from my godmother who had a bed that needed to be moved. And we went Sunday after Sunday to move the bed and every time we got there, she had changed her mind, she didn't want the bed moved after all. It must have gone on for at least five or six weeks until finally my mother said, "We're not coming back again. Today we will move that bed." *So anytime in our family that you've really got to put your foot down and really go whole hog it means you're going to move that bed.*

JUDITH BRESSLER, AGE 34
Bluefield, West Virginia

: I KNOW A LITTLE GIRL WHO DIED FROM IT :

When my sister or I would complain about some minor ailment and my mother wanted to let us know that she didn't really think it was anything serious, she would sarcastically say, "I know a little girl who died from it." After a while all she had to say was, "I know a little girl who . . ." and we knew what she meant. Oddly enough, although what she said sounds depressing or frightening, I found it comforting; I couldn't really be very sick if she made a joke of it.

ISABEL GOLDSTEIN, AGE 38
New York, New York

LORRAINE ARDEN

: JUMPING OFF THE FIFTEENTH STORY WINDOW FOR A BREEZE ON A HOT DAY :

Our family has an apartment at the beach on the first floor of a fifteen-story building. One day my brother was passing out Chiclets, and rather than take one I took three. And when he saw that he said, "Well, why don't you just jump off the fifteenth story window for a breeze on a hot day!" And ever since then, whenever I overdo anything, my brother will call it, "jumping off the fifteenth story window for a breeze on a hot day." Sometimes I'll turn it around and say, "I think I'll jump off the fifteenth story window for a breeze on a hot day—and have a second dessert."

STEVEN ZEITLIN, AGE 28
Philadelphia, Pennsylvania

: PUTTING ON DOWN TO GOURDA :

I was thinking of a story that my family used to tell. Somewhere down in south Georgia there's a little town called Gourda, or something like that. One time when I was young, my great-uncle and my father and my mother and several other aunts and uncles and cousins were driving along together. And I kept asking Uncle Holt, "Where are we going? When are we going to get there? Where are we going? What's this all about?" And he kept saying, "Well, we're just putting on down to Gourda. We're putting on down to Gourda." And in my family that expression, "Putting on down to Gourda" means "We're not quite sure where we're going yet, but we're just keeping on, keeping on."

BETH HUNTER, AGE 29
Manchester, Georgia

: GONE, GARFIELD, GONE :

My grandfather was fishing, and he had a salmon on his line for twenty minutes and suddenly he lost it. He muttered to the guide because he was so despaired and said—the guide's name was Garfield—"Gone, Garfield, gone." And he just stared there at the water and at the line and at the salmon that was gone. And you know it's funny we've always said that if something's bad, "Geez, gone, Garfield, gone." It's kind of an expression that keeps on going.

PETE LUCKEY

: SHOOT FOR THE TOP :

Talk about expressions. There's one in my family. It's really not typical of a Jewish family because I read somewhere that Rose Kennedy used the same expression for her children. The expression as my father uses it is, "Shoot for the top, second best you can always get." With that kind of expression in the back of our minds, it was very difficult to think of anything but success or perfection. If I came back from a high school test and told my parents at the dinner table that I got a ninety-nine, instead of saying, "Gee, that's fantastic, an A+," my father would say, "Ninety-nine, Judy, why didn't you get a hundred?" So we grew up with that. It gave us a sense of confidence, not to mention arrogance, that's very hard to learn to cut out.

But now whenever things happen and the situation warrants it, we'll say, "Well, shoot for the top, second best you can always get." It has lots of different meanings. For example, if I

FAMILY EXPRESSIONS 160

want a lemon pie at a restaurant, and they only had chocolate cake, I would say, "Well, second best you can always get." If my mother wants to talk with me on the phone and only my husband is home, she might tease him by saying, "Well, Gary, second best you can always get." It means if you can't get your first choice, second best you can always get. It also means that you're so good you can always get second best, so you might as well try for achieving for the top.

JUDY GLECKLEN KOPFF, AGE 29
Washington, D.C.

: T'AINT YOUR CAT :

PATRICIA: *We have dozens of family expressions. "T'aint your cat," which meant, "It's none of your business."*

PRISCILLA: *And, "Do you think it will rain tomorrow?" If somebody in the family said, "Do you think it'll rain tomorrow?" you knew there was something going on around you that you should pay attention to. It meant, "There's something going on; I can't tell you what it is, but look around and you'll see."*

PATRICIA: *Another one was, "Remember that position is everything in life." This meant that one of the girls was sitting in an unlady-like manner, she better change immediately. And oh, "To heck with poverty, give the cat another herring." That meant that there was something you really wanted to do but couldn't afford it, but you wanted to do it, so "To heck with poverty, give the cat another herring."*

PATRICIA ANNABLE, AGE 50
PRISCILLA WULF, AGE 56
Slippery Rock, Pennsylvania

Family Customs

Anyone who takes the family for a drive on a Sunday afternoon, or goes on a camping trip on Memorial Day, or devises a particular whistle to call the family to dinner may soon find that these practices and events become established family customs. They can be as commonplace as the evening meal with its ceremony of carving the meat and tossing the salad, or as ritualized and sanctified as a wedding, funeral, or Christmas celebration. In an outstanding work on this subject, *Ritual in Family Living,* sociologists James Bossard and Eleanor Boll suggest that these customs, or "rituals" as they call them, constitute "much of the behavior of which a family is proud and of which its members definitely approve. As a phase of family life, it is what the family sees about itself that it likes and wants formally to continue."[1]

Families spend large amounts of time together and certain kinds of activities are bound to recur time and again. Many are just ordinary household necessities—washing dishes, cleaning house, eating breakfast. The shared activities we call customs generally extend beyond these everyday necessities to more expressive practices where there is more joking, laughter, storytelling, sport, celebration, and sensual pleasures like eating and drinking. But even day-to-day housework can become "ritualized" when adorned with expressive activities. Ellen Kurzman, for instance, was a working mother who often did not have time to cook for her children. One night, when the evening meal looked to be made up largely of leftovers, she came up with the idea for a restaurant. The children would dress up as waiters and chefs, and put together a menu from the miscellaneous portions lying in the corners of the refrigerator—one leftover baked potato, a chicken breast, a popover, and so on. Ellen and her husband would then order their portions from the menu. The tradition caught on, and she dubbed it "Ellen's Greasy Spoon."[2] Customs like these are often repeated not only because the children need to be fed or the house needs to be cleaned but because of the emotional satisfaction these practices afford. They come to embody repetition without boredom.

Many families seem to enjoy the idea that they have certain well-established traditions, even when they are in fact enacted only on rare occasions. Adults will often look back on their childhood outings, perhaps a trip to a swimming hole, as a longstanding custom of their younger years, when they actually went there maybe two or three times. Even current traditions can be more concept than custom. One young married couple think of themselves as having a tradition of reading some poetry or philosophy together on Sunday afternoons. "Whenever we miss a Sunday," one of them said, "we just think that, well we haven't fit in our tradition today. In fact, we seem to miss most Sundays." Yet they still think of this as one of their ongoing traditions—that idea is more important than the real participation.

In their volume, Bossard and Boll make a number of striking observations about the role of ritual in American family life. They note that the key to family rituals is leisure time. For this reason modern families, particularly those whose middle and upper class backgrounds afford them a more leisurely lifestyle, often have an abundance of rituals and traditions. Writing in 1950, they also suggest that the "larger the family the more numerous and rich the rituals, whether the family was large by number of children or was made large by the inclusion of relatives and family servants."[3] They observe a number of changes in family tradition over the years. Modern rituals tend to be adapted to smaller, nuclear family groups. They are often more personalized, more child-oriented, more secular, simpler, and of shorter duration—though according to their impression more numerous than ever before.

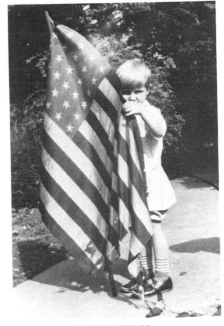

MIDGE HEIMER

Whereas stories encapsulate experience in a set verbal piece and photographs record shared events on Kodachrome, family celebrations capture the past by reenacting it. Oftentimes American cultural and religious holidays are symbolic representations of an historical event. Jews partake of the bitter herb on Passover to relive in some way the trials of Moses in the desert. The manger scene on Christian mantels at Christmas suggests a recreation of the birth of Christ. In the Dreschler family, the Christmas ritual also commemorates an era in the family's history:

My grandmother and grandfather went to Kansas in a covered wagon. My grandfather took out a section of land, I think that's 640 acres. There are almost no trees in that central section of Kansas. It's the rolling prairie. He planted a big grove of maple trees, and those trees were so sacred to him that he would never cut one, not even for Christmas. So presents were always put at each person's place at the dining-room table.

Even later on, when different branches of the family would have Christmas, they still use the table for their presents. We do now have a little tree, but the presents are always on the table. Trees are not for gifts. Trees are sacred in my family.[4]

Family celebrations symbolically recreate not only the original episode, but all of the subsequent occasions on which it was celebrated, the present continually recalling the past. Each Christmas recalls past Christmases. In fact, many families take home movies or snapshots on Christmas day each year, and spend part of the day reviewing their memories.

Families often call their traditions pastimes, yet they are doing much more than passing time. It is here, in religious celebrations and secular rituals, that the real emotional business of the family is often transacted. Stories are told, nicknames bantered, photos taken and perused. For some families these may be their only way of expressing kinship. For others it is here, over the dinner or the picnic table, that family members renew a dedication to one another which may affect where they reside, how they conduct their business, and the way they choose to live.

: A Little Bit of Home :

I'm in the foreign service and have served in many places in the Far East. I was in the Philippines for a while and having grown up in a temperate climate with hot summers and cold winters, I wasn't used to the constant heat. In November, my internal clock told me that Christmas was approaching but it was still 110° outside. So with the Christmas tree upstairs in what I called the den, I turned the air conditioner up very, very high, put on a long fleecy robe that I had in my trunk; I fixed some hot chocolate, and I sat out by the Christmas tree and pretended it was winter in St. Louis. Then I went out and it was 120° in the sunshine, but at least I had my taste of a typical hometown Christmas!

SHARON BABER, AGE 42
Arlington, Virginia

: APPLE SECTIONS :

On Christmas Eve the family—which included grandparents, seven children, their spouses, and children—had a family dinner. Grandfather would divide an apple into as many sections as were the number of family members. Each would eat his section and this would ensure the family's remaining together for the coming year.

KIT DECKER

: THE CHRISTMAS CAKE :

I tell you one thing . . . every year since we were children, my mother used to bake a large cake, and after she got so she couldn't bake it, she'd have it baked up there at a bakery. But she baked this cake and one Christmas we all stood around this cake and sang, "Happy Birthday, dear Jesus. We are so glad you were born today. Happy Birthday, dear Jesus . . ." My mother is still alive and we still do that every year.

HATTIE DAVIS, AGE 68
Washington, D.C.

: MEXICAN-AMERICAN CHRISTMAS :

The biggest thing at Christmas is having tamales Christmas Eve. We go to mass and come back and have hot tamales and coffee. Like I say, we didn't have many gifts; the food was really the thing that brought everybody together. It wasn't so much a religious holiday as it was just rejoicing that we'd had another good year of being together.

STELLA FRASER

: RUSSIAN-AMERICAN CHRISTMAS :

I think the only contact I had with the Slovak culture was through my grandparents. We had certain religious traditions, pretty much at Christmas time. You see, Russian Christmas is celebrated January sixth, a week after our New Year's. They had a two-week difference in their calendar. It has since changed in the Greek Orthodox Church, but when we were children we were lucky because we had two Christmases. On January sixth we would go to my grandparents' house and we

TOM KAVANAUGH

GEORGE COHEN

CAROL DANDY

would have Christmas Eve dinner, and we'd have to kneel down for an hour and pray. They prayed in Slovak, and we just knelt there and thought about how hungry we were. Then, the youngest child in the family—and for a while I was the youngest until my cousin was born, thank God—had to sit in a basket filled with straw. It signified the Christ child, sitting in this straw basket, and it was placed next to the table. Everybody else had to kneel down and pray and pray and pray. I can remember the straw pricking my legs terribly. Then we ate garlic before we could start eating the meal, because that meant we'd be healthy all year. What it meant, too, was that we had bad breath for the rest of the night. It was raw garlic, but I loved it.

KATHY KUNDLA CROSBY, AGE 32
Moscow, Pennsylvania

: ITALIAN-AMERICAN CHRISTMAS :

We always had a big celebration at our home on Christmas Eve. My mother was the second daughter, but the only one that was living in Pittsburgh, so everybody came to our house. We had all kinds of fish, smelts and anchovies, and what we call zeppolli, which is bread fried in deep fat and then sometimes sugared. We had a fish dinner called a calamari, which is squid that had been cooked in tomato sauce, which was the meat substitute for the spaghetti sauce. And we had bacala salad, which is codfish. They were all traditional dishes that were eaten on the day before Christmas.

MARY LOUISE ORTENZO
Columbia, Maryland

: HAMBURGER ON CHRISTMAS EVE :

We have hamburgers on Christmas Eve traditionally. Why? I think because mothers were trying to prepare a massive Christmas dinner and it was always such a hassle that all they could muster for Christmas Eve were hamburgers, potato chips, and a coke.

NANCY REDENBAUGH
Fort Collins, Colorado
ANN M. FLEMING
Pittsburgh, Pennsylvania

: Gag Present I :

We have an album, "Twenty Irish Tunes," that my mother or uncle got twelve years ago. It is the worst album on the face of the earth and every year it's passed back and forth as a gag present. Every year somebody gets "Twenty Irish Tunes" and if you have an album under the tree you pray like hell that it isn't you.

NANCY REDENBAUGH
Fort Collins, Colorado

: Gag Present II :

My cousin Keith came to visit me when I was living in New-foundland, Canada, and he brought some seal meat back to South Carolina with him—canned seal meat, which nobody in his family wanted to even try. So for a joke he wrapped it up and put it under the Christmas tree for his sister, Isabel. He did that to her two years in a row and the second year she recog-nized it, didn't even open it, and gave it to me as a present. Then when Keith got married I gave it to his wife as a Christmas present, she gave it back to me the next Christmas, and I gave it to Isabel as a wedding present! That's as far as it's gotten so far, but I'm sure one of us will get it back this Christmas!

AMANDA DARGAN, AGE 31
Darlington, South Carolina

: Traditions Lost, Traditions Created :

We didn't have any ritual ways of celebrating Christmas. For some reason they didn't carry over. I would try in the beginning when the children were small to read the message from the Gos-pel, from St. Luke, and The Night Before Christmas. *They weren't really interested, though. Somehow it didn't come across. We've started a new tradition now. At least one thing that you give has to be homemade. We started that just a few years ago. To really give something of yourself means so much more than going to a store. Even if it's a batch of brownies, it's something you've made.*

HELEN MACKEY GRAY, AGE 51
McLean, Virginia

: Waiting for Santa :

At Christmas, grandpa would sit with his shotgun across his knees in the library, saying that he was going to shoot Santa Claus when he came down the chimney, because he didn't want any old man walking through his house in the middle of the night! We didn't take him seriously but I guess we did go to bed with a little trepidation, hoping he wouldn't really shoot Santa Claus. In the morning he would put bootprints in the dust, take a bite out of the apple, and drink some of the water that we had left for Santa Claus.

NORA HUMPHREY, AGE 25
New York, New York

: Leaving Out the Trains :

Our family history comes in two parts. The first part comes when my brother and I, the oldest two, were little, and my parents were pretty happy together. We were sort of an ordinary suburban kind of family. The second part comes when my father started to leave our family some several months before my youngest brother was born. It took him a couple of years to accomplish the process of leaving completely. He left on the Christmas holidays. I was twelve or thirteen.

The next year, I don't know whether my mother did this on purpose, but we all sort of concurred in changing everything we had usually done. We had always decorated the house in a very certain way. We'd always had a certain kind of Christmas tree—a very tall Christmas tree—maybe because my father is six feet tall and we decorated it in a certain way. But when it came time for us to get together and to decide what to do, it dawned on all of us at once, I think, that we should buy a short, fat Christmas tree, a Scotch pine, kind of blue. So we bought a tree that was about as wide as it was tall, and we went through all the decorations and threw out about half of them and got a lot of new ones, and we fixed the house differently. We left out the trains . . . my father was the only one who ever played with the trains anyway. They went around the bottom of the Christmas tree. We just generally set everything up very, very differently. This was thirteen years ago. I was kind of dreading it, but it was a surprisingly good Christmas. We were all together and it was very pleasant. And we've done it that way ever since. We've bought that exact kind of tree and put the same decorations on it. It's never been the way it was when I was little. Of course, that's what my younger sister and brother remember, as our way of doing things.

: A MODERN SEDER :

In our house, we still hold the seder the first night. And when we're supposed to read the story of the going out from Egypt, my dad has every year—it's not a sermon—but he tells about more modern times, of the going out of his family from Russia and the going out of my mom's family from Germany, which is also very exciting. When my mom left, it wasn't so pleasant; it was late when they escaped. He reminds us that we should be very grateful. And he tells exactly what did happen and how really fantastic everything is in these days, and how we should really appreciate this. He brings in the religion a lot, how the religion really is very modern in its use. And you go through the Haggadah, and you look at modern applications. And it works. It makes me very appreciative.

ROBERT HORLICK, AGE 20
Riverdale, Maryland

: AN ECUMENICAL SEDER :

When my mother started giving the seder, we used the Haggadah that she had written, and we had a tradition of inviting our non-Jewish friends and teaching it to them the second night, so they could see what this ceremony was that they had heard about. I'm the only one in the family now who keeps kosher, so the seder is at my house because I won't go to anyone else's seder. Our seders now are very ecumenical. The best singer at ours now is my brother-in-law, Jim, who was raised as a Methodist. He's a complete atheist now, but he has a beautiful voice. We sing songs for everyone's tradition at the end of the seder. We usually end up with a rousing rendition of "Onward Christian Soldiers." We sing, "We Shall Overcome" and whatever is topical. One year, ecology was the whole theme, and all the younger people who came to the seder were into ecology. Our seders are usually with at least nineteen people, whoever in the family is in the area, and then my mother always feels that whoever doesn't have a place to come should come to us. So we've had very interesting seders through the years with people from all over the world, and all different Jewish traditions.

REBECCA COFMAN
Bethesda, Maryland

: SEASONAL EXCURSIONS :

In my family we had things we did at the turning of the seasons. In springtime we'd go up in the mountains and pick violets and honeysuckle. You just knew that springtime was officially here when you could go up in the mountains and pick your violets. Violets in the springtime, and then wild blackberries and plums in the summertime, and pecans and chestnuts up in the mountains in the fall time—and the leaves would just be magnificent. We'd always bring home colored leaves. And in the wintertime we'd go out and get a Christmas tree from the woods. You knew that when certain seasons were coming about that this was part of what you do. You do things the same way you have turkey for Thanksgiving.

BETH HUNTER, AGE 29
Manchester, Georgia

: THE FIRST SNOW OF THE YEAR :

During the first snow of the year, we would always run barefoot around the outside of the house. This was a lot of fun until my younger sister was in college and her home was a dormitory. It's a very long way to run around the whole dormitory with your shoes off.

DOUG AND LAURA MCDOWELL, AGES 40, 39
Annandale, Virginia

: HOME FOR DINNER :

In my family the meal ritual was important. I've never had a meal in my house when the entire family didn't sit down. Everything is passed until everyone's plates are filled, grace is said—Catholic grace, out loud—my mother takes her first bite,

*and everyone starts eating their cold dinner. Candles were lit,
every single night of my life. And there's no such thing as, "Oh,
I won't be home for dinner." You plan a month in advance if
you're going to miss a dinner for some reason. You bring your
friends to dinner; you don't go out very much. There's no such
thing as jumping up from the dinner table, at all. Dinner in my
house lasts very frequently until two o'clock in the morning.
Everyone sits and talks. All my life.*

KATHERINE BRODERICK, AGE 24
Washington, D.C.

: YOUR NAME IN PEANUT BUTTER :

*Every time we came home from the store with a new jar of pea-
nut butter, my dad, when we would go out of the room, would
write the initials of the one he thought had been the best that
week. And then the next morning, or whenever we'd go to open
the peanut butter to put on our toast or something, he'd call the
person, and they'd come running around, and he'd say, "Oh,
look what's here!" And he would tell us that it was the little
fairy that lived in the light downstairs, whose name was Ma-
tilda and that she had done it. That used to make you be good
so you could get your name in the peanut butter.*

EMILY SARDONIA, AGE 17
Fairfax, Virginia

: LIFE IN THE HOUSING PROJECT :

*When I was growing up before my family moved to another
kind of neighborhood, we lived in a public housing project. It's
a special something I think only black people can really relate
to. Projects were a part of every middle income black person's
background at one point or another. My brother and I made
very good friends with the family upstairs, with the children.
During the summer, we would spend a lot of time in the bedroom singing, and the kids upstairs would be singing, too. We
did four-part harmony through the ceilings, which were real
thin. When our parents weren't there, we used the radiators for
instrumentation. We used the radiators and spoons and the
wooden beds and we'd sing and do harmony and have some
background.*

: THE GOOD NIGHTS :

I remember a ritual that we had that was really neat: "the good nights." It went, "Good night, sleep tight, pleasant dreams, see you in the morning." My father would say, "good," and we would say "night," and he would say "sleep," and we would say "tight" and it went on that way. When we got older he started teaching us how to do it in other languages. We said it in German and we said it in French and we said it in Hungarian. His family had spoken Hungarian when he was a kid. We didn't know any Hungarian but we said "the good nights" in Hungarian. You couldn't go to bed without saying "the good nights" — it was just a really important thing.

SUSAN M. STRASSER, AGE 26
Pittsburgh, Pennsylvania

: AFTERNOON TEA :

When we were little we would have a tea party every afternoon. I was Mrs. Kratched and my sister was Mrs. Jones and we would dress up in our dressy clothes. I have no idea where the names came from, absolutely no idea, but I can see it just as plain as day, near the big jutting windows in the livingroom. We had a little wooden table and chairs that we had gotten for Christmas and a little cupboard in which we kept all our tea things — and every afternoon Mrs. Kratched and Mrs. Jones had tea.

NANCY REDENBAUGH
Fort Collins, Colorado

: THE ELEPHANT'S GRAVE :

Oh, this is my grandmother's favorite story. She grew up in Keene, New Hampshire. She was the oldest of like eight children, and her mother and father were hard pressed to make a living. They used to try to get the kids out from underfoot, and the favorite thing was to put flowers on the elephant's grave. Apparently when the circus train went through this town, an elephant dropped dead and it was buried there. And so that's all the kids had to do in Keene, New Hampshire, was go put flowers on the elephant's grave.

NANCY KILCZEWSKI, AGE 35
Herndon, Virginia

JULIE HAIFLEY

: Crossing of the Fathers :

Speaking of family traditions, there's one that's been operant in our family. It's a large family with five sons. My father since the early, early fifties has had sort of a rite of passage for his sons. When they are sixteen, he always takes them on a river trip, usually a boat trip down the Colorado River. He goes every year and is a boatman. We usually started out at the "Crossing of the Fathers" at the Grand Canyon, ran down through Phantom Branch and Lake Meade, and got off. It marked sort of your acceptance as a grownup, I guess. That's the first time you get to drink beer and get snuck into bars, that kind of thing, at the end of the river trip. Took about three weeks of pretty hard, hot, sweaty work.

RICHARD MILLER, AGE 32
Washington, D.C.

: The Jewish Matriarch :

Every Friday night, my grandmother would hold court. It was a Friday night tradition. After we had our Sabbath meal, my mother and father would say, "We're going to grandma's house." To me this was accepted procedure, standard order of things. Until the age of ninety-six, she had all her faculties. But

HELEN ALBANESE

even as she got older and went blind, she used to recognize everybody. She used to identify them by their voices and she would say, "You're the son of my daughter so-and-so. I'm glad to see you. Sit down and have a glass of tea, and have a homemade cake." She had no teeth, and she would drink tea according to the Russian style, in a glass with a piece of sugar in her mouth. She'd sip tea through the sugar.

But you talk about family life. It was amazing how this one old woman could keep a family together. She lived to the age of 103 and there were five generations alive at the time that she died. There's still a certain amount of togetherness. We've separated some as people moved in different directions and the old dynasty died off. But we had a cousins club named after my grandmother, because we realized that the only time we were seeing each other was at somebody's death and we decided we wanted to see each other at the good times, too.

ABE WORKMAN
Staten Island, New York

: THE TERRIFIC TRIO :

After my separation, when we first started being concerned about a sense of family, we decided that we were "the terrific trio," because there had been four of us, and now there were three of us. My daughter, being a little older, was more concerned because she was aware that there had been a distinct change in the family situation. She likes to draw and do all sorts of crafts things, so on her own she drew a picture of me and a picture of herself and a picture of her brother, each on a separate page, all colored, with a fancy cover that said, "The Terrific Trio," and a fancy back cover. She stapled them together and presented it to me as a book.

The two of them have hats alike—they are denim patchwork—and they asked for their names to be embroidered on them, so I did that, and then they wanted me to get a hat. Well, I didn't want one quite the same, but I have one that's just a floppy blue faded denim one, so I put my name on it, and we have been putting patches on them this year, flags and bicentennial special things. And they call them "our terrific trio hats." Sometimes they don't want to wear theirs unless I wear mine. I've had comments from people when I've gone places and they've said, "Well, aren't you identifying a little bit much with them?" And my reaction has always been, "When you *have switched from four to three you want to establish a certain amount of solidarity." Of course there's a loss. They know there's a loss.*

: SAINT GRUNE'S DAY :

At the dinner table someone was once saying, "Oranges and lemons say the bells of Saint Clements," and someone added, "Raisins and prunes say the bells of Saint Grunes." The next day became Saint Grune's day. Now, the holiday always falls in March when there are no other celebrations. Suddenly my mother will declare, "Tomorrow is Saint Grune's Day." Raisins and prunes are bought, but not eaten at dinner. It is a big dinner, however, served on good china. A lamb's head mask, left over from some Halloween party, always makes an appearance. Sometimes it is worn, or it appears as a centerpiece decorated with flowers. The holiday brightens up March.

KATHERINE THAMSIN JANNEY
Bethesda, Maryland

: BUTTER-NOSED BIRTHDAY I :

I'm twenty-nine years old. I'm actually twenty-nine and three quarters years old, which is very significant, because in my family birthdays are very important. We celebrate half birthdays, three-quarter birthdays. My seven-twelfths birthday is coming up in a couple of days.

Whenever it's someone's birthday, the other members of the family wake up that person by putting butter, or margarine, on that person's nose. The rationale, supposedly, is to make that person have a shiny day. But I recently found out from one of my sisters that it's not just so that we will have a shiny day. It's so that when we walk to work, or to school, or whatever, we keep the butter or margarine on our nose and people will say to us, "Why do you have butter on your nose?" and we'll say, "Glad you asked, you know, it's my birthday." I don't know if it's a New England tradition, but it's a tradition in my family. And that's because, you know, birthdays are very important to us.

JUDY GLECKLEN KOPFF, AGE 29
Washington, D.C.

: Butter-Nosed Birthday II :

In my family whenever it was someone's birthday you would get up before they got up and put butter on their nose when they were still asleep. My mother always thought this was a really fun tradition, but it led to a lot of fights. There was nothing you could do about it because it was traditional. It's true, it's true, there was nothing you could do. It was the tyranny of tradition!

CATHY CONDON
St. Louis, Missouri

: Birthday Tape :

I do tape a lot, every birthday. We tape "Happy Birthday," and then we interview. Everyone in the family gets a chance to say how they feel and what the year was like. And we also tape when we have a religious holiday or something like that. And just every once in a while when the family seems to be in the right mood, we'll bring the tape recorder out, and we'll have interviews, and we'll sing. Then we'll listen to tapes from previous years. And you can hear the kids voices change. The kids love it.

OSCAR GOLDFARB, AGE 39
Silver Spring, Maryland

: Day of Birth :

We had a tradition just in our immediate family that I really liked. On my brother's birthday and on my birthday, the family always has dinner together. And dad used to sit down with a drink and recount the day of our birth: what happened, how he felt, how my mother felt, what was going on that day. He did it every year. My father died about five years ago but my brother and I have kind of carried that on. On my birthday, my brother will say, "Well, twenty-seven years ago at this time," or I'll say, "Twenty-nine years ago at this time . . ."

VIRGINIA A. HEASLEY, AGE 27
Philadelphia, Pennsylvania

ARLENE GIBBS

: Happy Unbirthday! :

When I was little — I was one of six — my mother would come up with some day out of the year that was really far away from Christmas and your birthday, you know, that endless stretch. You'd come home from school and she'd tell you it was your unbirthday. She'd cook your favorite dinner, whatever it was — even hot dogs. And you could watch all your favorite television programs. Nobody could argue with you about it. People sang happy unbirthday to you. There was a cake sometimes and presents, but it wasn't like a birthday when you got real presents. It wasn't every year that everybody had one. It was just kind of spontaneous. It came from Alice in Wonderland. *Remember the Madhatter's teaparty? "Have a happy unbirthday!"*

WENDY ROGES, AGE 23
Washington, D.C.

: The Family Reunion :

ROBERTA: *It's like every member of the family . . .*

JERRY: *. . . has a special thing.*

ROBERTA: *Each one of my mother's brothers and sisters and my mother also has got their own traits and peculiarities. And all put together it makes for a unique affair. My uncle Jimmy is always screaming about the dirty rotten stinking cards, whenever he's playing cards.*

JERRY: *And there's always a pitch game going. The women play poker, and the men play pitch. Then there's the election every year, that's one of those things. . . .*

THERESA: *Oh, it's all in fun, we elect a president of the family every year.*

ROBERTA: *Well, there's kind of a tradition here. The elder is the head of the family anyway, he's the don. He always has been and he always will be. But every year, he's got to get elected! And every year a couple of the brothers will put up a fight, and they'll mount a campaign to get themselves elected president. They will go through all kinds of contortions and slogans and campaign songs and everything to get themselves elected. Then comes the day of an election and everybody will listen to their slogans and appeal and promptly vote Uncle John president again.*

THERESA: *And every year they raise our salaries.*

JERRY: *Every year they double the salaries.*

THERESA: *Cause we get nothing. And so they double it every year.*

JERRY: *You got to picture this family. Most of them are elderly, in their eighties.*

THERESA: *Not most of them, Jerry, there's only a few.*

JERRY: *All right, many of them. And they're—no not very square—they're the most energetic people you've ever seen for their ages. That's basically it.*

ROBERTA: *They are people who enjoy themselves and they have a spirit of fun about them and a spirit of nonsense. And the thing is that it never seems to surface until they get together—if you talk to one of them by himself he is a pillar of the church, as Ma says, just as square as the day is long!*

ROBERTA AND JERRY WILSON, AGES 38 AND 36

THERESA ROACH, AGE 64

Wilbraham, Massachusetts

ARLENE GIBBS

Family Photography

Standing proudly in gilt-edged frames or tacked hastily on refrigerator doors, photographs—breezy vacation snapshots, formal portraits, and bashful images of cowlicked schoolchildren—bear witness to a family's shared experiences. Today, photography has become so popular a domestic art that "amid the clutter of material culture to be found . . . in an average American household," writes historian Thomas Schlereth, "the ubiquitous snapshot must surely rank among the most commonplace."[1]

Photographs not only document family life; they have become an important form of family lore as well. To explore the role of photography in family life, we collected albums, trunks, and shoeboxes stuffed with photographs from more than two hundred families in the Washington, D.C., area. Among these six thousand images, we began to see that just as certain categories of stories recur from family to family, similar kinds of photos are enshrined in the home archives. Scenes of holiday celebrations, birthdays, picnics, and vacations dominate these collections, and children, from infancy through high school graduation, are favorite subjects for the home photographer. When we exhibited a typical selection of babies pictured on fuzzy rugs and in frothy bathtubs at the 1975 Festival of American Folklife, a visitor was moved to pull a dog-eared snapshot from her wallet and exclaim, "I have the same photo, only it's a different kid!" To be sure, there are a limited number of poses an infant can strike. But even so, the similarities among these baby photos and among other photos depicting smiling, intertwined families gathered around the hearth, on the front porch, or even around the family car, suggest that picture-taking creates as much as it records ritual scenes of domestic life.

Susan Sontag, in her remarkable collection of essays, *On Photography*, notes that the camera has the unique ability to "freeze moments in a life or a society" so that they are salvaged from "the relentless melt of time."[2] Families use this image-freezing magic of the camera to isolate, record, and confer importance on certain events in their lives. Rescued from the flow of time, rites of passage, sentimental reunions, trips, and outings are preserved on film, providing families with a visual history of their lives together. While we are free to photograph anything we want, we don't really do so, in fact. The commonalities in family photos suggest that home photographers and their subjects share certain notions about appropriate behavior in the face of a camera, and appropriate moments to photograph. Consciously or not, we tend to take photos according to the way we want to preserve, remember, and be remembered. In depicting certain kinds of events in certain ways, family photos, like other genres of folklore, are a creative transformation of selected experience into fixed images that can be shared in the years to come. They are a stylized reality; an expression of our values and ideals.

Family celebrations, prime moments for picture-taking, are now so influenced by the presence of the camera that the act of photography has itself become a holiday tradition. When asked about their favorite holiday customs, several informants jokingly recalled stumbling down the staircase each Christmas morning, into the glare of dad's movie lights. "Christmas, birthdays," moaned Carol Maas, "you hate to see the camera come out. You know it's going to be a picture of the Christmas tree. It's going to be a picture of everyone gathered behind the birthday cake . . . . You know how it is. Standard family pictures."[3]

Family photos adorn the piano and end table in Elmer and
Louisa Keck's livingroom, Pottstown, Pennsylvania.
Photograph by Margaret Yocom.

MYRA NOVOGRODSKY

NANCY SMITH

"I have the same photo, only it's a different kid."
MARCE POLLAN

JUDITH RUTTENBERG

NICHOLAS CARROLL

MILLY DANIEL

JOAN BERNICK

MARTHA SWARTWOUT

JENNIFER ROTHWELL

Photos of the family car recur with striking frequency in
family photo collections.

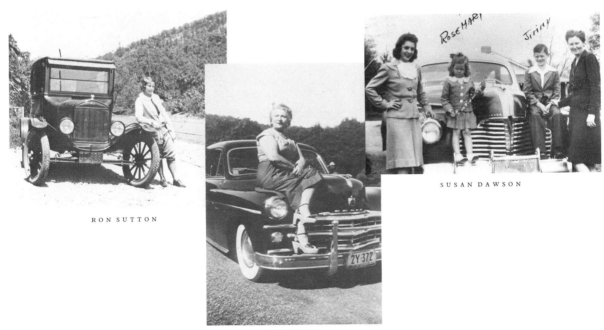

RON SUTTON

JAY BURG

SUSAN DAWSON

SANDRA GROSS

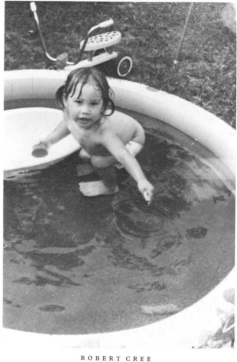

ROBERT CREE

"Cameras go with family life. Not to take pictures of one's children, particularly when they are young, is a sign of parental indifference. . . ."

SUSAN SONTAG

MARTHA ROSS

MRS. JEFFERSON PATTERSON

MYRA NOVOGRODSKY

*"Christmas, birthdays—you hate to see the camera come out.
You know it's going to be a picture of the Christmas tree. It's
going to be a picture of everyone gathered behind the birthday
cake. You know how it is, standard family pictures."*

CAROL MAAS

JEAN AND LIEN-SHENG YANG

Never a passive observer, the camera records selectively and often seems to direct the performance on which it intrudes. Bridal couples hold their embrace at the altar to afford the photographer ample time to record "the moment." Families pause at their annual reunions to hug and smile, creating a portrait of unity and affection for posterity. Photographer Tod Papageorge recalls the use of the camera in his own family.

On Christmas mornings my father was a photographer. My sister and I, called to attention, stared ferociously at those awful bulbs, not understanding that even as we sat there, blooming from the ribbons and wrapping paper, we were part of a ceremony; that we were, in fact, its motive.[4]

The ritual of photography extends beyond the picture-taking situation itself to form a vital link with other kinds of family traditions. Peggy Yocom, whose account of her family's folklore begins on p. 250, noted the relationship between images and narratives while reflecting on a visit to her grandparents, Elmer and Louisa Keck.

I was always aware of the many photographs that filled every livingroom end table, sat on each radiator, and spilled over onto the mantelpiece, television set, piano, and sometimes, the dining-room table . . . . As I trained my camera on Elmer and Louisa's home, I realized why the Kecks set out so many photographs and why, even though dusting had become a major chore, they kept them out. The photographs of their children and grandchildren and great-grandchildren, their sisters, brothers, parents, and friends — both living and dead — recreate for them the sense of the large Pottstown-based family they once had. Like a museum, the livingroom photographs preserve a cherished view of the past, recreate it in the present, and serve as a focal point for family storytelling.[5]

Photos serve as mnemonic devices, helping families to recall stories and preserve knowledge of past experiences.[6] Often, we tend to form glowing memories around the idyllic images we have taken, yet there are remarkable and everchanging differences between what Americans choose to preserve on film, and the stories and reminiscences their photos evoke. On a hot July day, Nancy Smith brought a huge photo album to share with us on Washington's National Mall. Her mother had made it for her as a wedding present and it contained a rich visual record of Nancy's life, as well as images of her parents, grandparents, and great-grandparents. As we leafed through the album, the invariably smiling images were dimmed by the poignant tales they evoked from Nancy. A seemingly contented photo of her aunt Rose on an American beach prompted Nancy to recount Rose's harrowing escape from Russia. A proud photo of her father in his World War II army uniform was counterpointed with tragic tales of his experiences in the war.

This story from another informant further illustrates the fact that stories and photos can actually record wholly different versions of "the truth."

The first summer after my father left us we went down to the seashore for a vacation . . . and we went out to eat in one of those places where a person comes around to take your picture at your table and then sells it to you. It's hanging in our upstairs hall now. I looked at it this past Christmas . . . . We looked kind of helpless in the picture. Here was my mother surrounded by all these kids, like what's she going to do? I called my mother out of the bedroom and said, "Remember that summer? Look at that. Don't we look sort of pathetic?" And she stood there and looked at it and she said, "Well, we did OK."[7]

We were curious about this photograph of the "pathetic" and "helpless" family. But when we tracked it down we saw only the standard family vacation picture, people eating well and having a good time. The photograph stood in marked emotional contrast to the story it elicited. (See above.)

Perhaps Jan and her family *were* feeling happy that summer evening. But while the photo itself remains fixed, its interpretation, like stories about our ancestors, can undergo radical change, depending on the vantage point of the viewer, or the teller. Some of our informants remarked that they rarely look at their images because they preferred not to relive the past. Caroline McDonald's mother, for instance, never looks at her extensive collection from the 1920s, because it forces her to recall that the camera, one of the family's most cherished possessions, had to be sold to feed the family during the Depression.[8]

*Nancy Smith's Aunt Rose, an immigrant from
Russia, is shown here on an American beach.*

The painful losses which photographs can bring to mind explain why Catherine Noren never saw her family's photos until 1972, almost forty years after the Holocaust forced her prosperous Jewish family to flee from Germany. Born in 1938, a few months before their departure, Catherine grew up in Australia and America only dimly aware of her roots. "People have various ways of dealing with loss," she said. "The way my family dealt with their enormous loss, of homeland, lifestyle, root-room, comfort was, I believe, to deny what they had lost ever existed, or had validity; to create determinedly a new set for themselves."[9] Like the stories and reminiscences of their prewar lives, the photos which documented their comfortable existence were secreted away, part of an unspoken agreement between family members to leave the past behind. Yet, the albums and studio shots were among the few possessions which they insisted on bringing from Germany, and while they effectively denied their ordeal, no one had thrown the photos out. When she discovered this vast treasury of images in her grandmother's home, Catherine used them as keys to unlock her relatives' memories, and although she didn't realize it at the time, to come to know her own family. The result of her search is *The Camera of My Family,* a book of photos, diaries, stories, and memories all of which, after decades of silence, her family members willingly shared.

In the absence of living memories which give meaning to these images, a photo itself can occasionally give birth to a family legend. A young woman from New Jersey recalled a photo of her great-uncle Max who, as a young man, had briefly joined Buffalo Bill's Wild West Show. His cowboy days were short-lived, but the only photo of Max that survives in the family shows him dressed in his western hat and chaps. Max's image fascinated his great-niece, who dubbed him "One-Gun Blum — The Jewish Cowboy." Though Max Blum spent most of his life as a tailor in Newark, New Jersey, his descendant, who knew him only through a single photograph, spun tales for her own children about "One Gun Blum's" alleged adventures out west. The photo, which for Max might have originally been a means of recording a proud yet ephemeral experience, became the symbol of his whole life and the base on which a family folk hero was molded.[10]

DAMON CORDON

Over time, a single photograph, like a dramatic family story, may come to symbolize an ancestor's personality and life history.

FAMILY ALBUMS

"Through photography," Sontag writes, "each family constructs a portrait of itself, a kit of images that bears witness to its connectedness." Nowhere is this more evident than in the album, which brings together the highlights of family life into a single form with its own story to tell. Now that snapshots are relatively inexpensive and many are taken to document each special occasion, the conventional wisdom suggests, "Your album does not have to contain every picture; you should select only the best or most important."[12] Thus, the making of an album involves a second stage of creativity — editing and juxtaposing images — possibly from a diverse range of scenes and circumstances. Nancy Smith's wedding-present album is a good example of a deliberate selection process, used to celebrate a fundamental personal transition by reminding Nancy of her ties with past generations.

Albums often center on particular units of time: babyhood, adolescence, or a memorable vacation. Joan Bernick encapsulated her romantic European courtship in an album containing snapshots, cryptic notes from her husband-to-be, long letters to her parents, and assorted ticket stubs, postcards, and other mementos from places she and Frank had visited. "My life falls into eras," Joan told us, "anyone's does.

Joan Bernick and her husband-to-be, Frank, open presents at their engagement party.

I have my high school period, courtship, and marriage. You enjoyed those things as you did them and you enjoy them again as you organize the album and again as you look through them."[13] The choice is usually deeply personal and may even reflect secrets kept by the individual owner. Anne Cohen also organized her photos by eras, but although all are important to her, not every image is intended to be shared with the family. In college, she had dated a young man whom she knew her parents would find objectionable. Even now, a decade later, Anne carefully hides those pages which contain his photos when her parents come to visit. "I call it," she laughed, "my removable past."

Perhaps because women so often serve as family historians, many of the albums we viewed were made by young wives and mothers to document their own families. The three pictured here vary in style, but each lender affirmed that picture-taking and viewing the albums later on were important parts of family life. Often, the album served as a catalyst for storytelling among intimate family members, or as an introduction to the family for new friends visiting for the first time.

Nancy Hallsted added her own pages to a commercial baby book as her children, John and Sheila, grew beyond infancy. After filling in each printed page with "Baby's first photo" and "Baby's first step," each successive page celebrates a particular day in her children's lives: birthdays, Christmases, and outings to the park or a beach. Many of the photos are cropped meticulously to eliminate what Nancy deemed inessential: distracting scenery, passersby, and even friends. The albums focus clearly on the children, and their relationship to their parents and grandparents.

"Cameras go with family life," Sontag reminds us. "Not to take pictures of one's children, especially when they are young, is a sign of parental indifference."[14] The albums are part of Nancy's avowed effort to create the strong family bonds she herself had missed as a child. Shuttled from aunts to cousins, she had few pleasant memories and, predictably, few youthful photos to share with John and Sheila. She regrets this lack of images, feeling that her legacy to her offspring is somehow incomplete. The albums, then, fill Nancy's need for family stability while also providing a loving record of her children's early lives.[15]

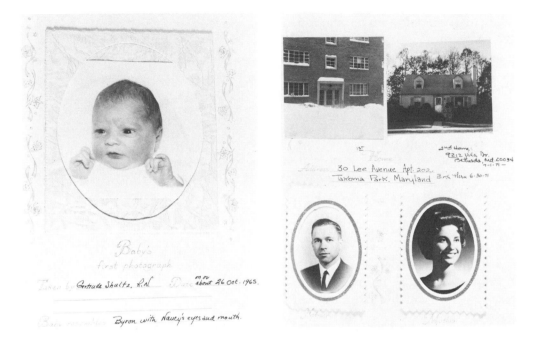

Nancy Hallsted added pages of photos to a conventional baby book to record the lives of her children as they grew up. Shown here are pages from the book she created for her daughter Sheila.

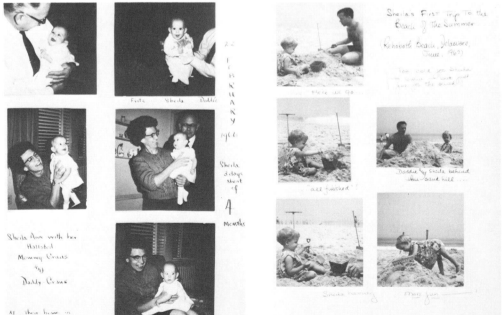

Martha Ross, an oral historian, is aware of our tendency to photograph only the highlights and never the ordinary events of family life. In her album, "Little Visits with the Rosses," Martha and her husband Don consciously broke with this tradition. They photographed each other setting the table, reading, washing dishes, and even sweeping dirt under the rug. Twenty-five years later, Martha shared her thoughts on "Little Visits" with us.

The occasion for putting this book together was the first Christmas after we were married. We made several copies: one went to my husband's parents, one went to my parents, and we also sent copies to two of my aunts. The purpose of the book was to illustrate our lives and the beginning of our marriage. My husband is a photographer and I do some art work, so the album was a collaborative effort. But the whole plan, including what shots were to be taken, was my idea. I wanted to give a balanced picture of our early relationship.[16]

Life in a rural commune was beautifully chronicled by Laduska Adriance, a commercial artist who lived in California during the late 1960s. Each page of her album from that time is an elaborate collage of photos, magazine cutouts, memorabilia, and handwritten text. She combined these forms to convey not only a sense of the chaotic household, but of the other events, trends, and personalities that were significant to that period of her life. Interspersed with photos and mementos were pictures of John Lennon and Bob Dylan, whom she considered part of her extended family.

In 1973 Laduska married and moved east. Her second album chronicles this passage to adulthood and the birth of her daughter. Where the first album pulsates with images and symbols of the youth culture, the more recent assemblage is simpler and more traditional in style, focusing clearly on the intimate relationships of the nuclear family. Still, Laduska feels that even the first album was created for her future offspring. "Looking back," she says, "I think that even then I wanted my children to know what my life was like."

Martha Ross created "Little Visits with the Rosses" to document the day-to-day activities of her early married life.

Chapter One . . .

On Oak Ridge's "G" Road
May, 1946

Courtship and

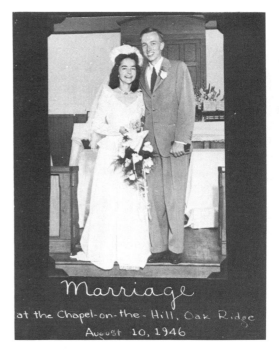

Marriage
at the Chapel-on-the-Hill, Oak Ridge
August 10, 1946

Chapter Two . . .

Housekeeping at 109 W. Madison

Washing the Dishes

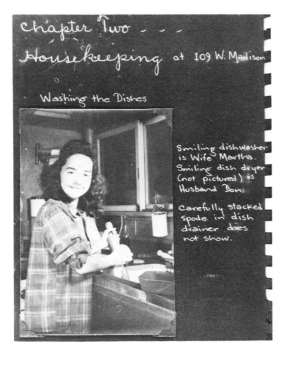

Smiling dishwasher is Wife Martha. Smiling dish dryer (not pictured) is Husband Don.

Carefully stacked spode in dish drainer does not show.

"In Oak Ridge, we immediately moved into our own tiny house. There were houses of various sizes and you qualified for a house by the size of your family. So we got one of the smallest houses. By the way, the peaked expression comes from the fact that I was pregnant by then and not feeling so well. So my creativity was not limited to the book!"

"This picture of my husband sweeping dirt under the rug is a joke but it characterizes our entire married relationship. He's really a very clean person, comes from a very neat family; I'm from a family of collectors and general household slobs. Even now when we entertain, he cleans the house, so this photo is a reversal of things. I was a southern belle, never taught how to sweep."

No sample of Husband Don's housekeeping, this is just a gag shot, since the sweet boy actually does all the sweeping and does it well.

Cleaning

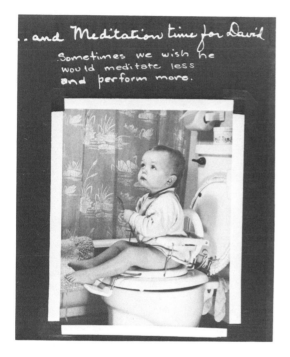

..and Meditation time for David
Sometimes we wish he would meditate less and perform more.

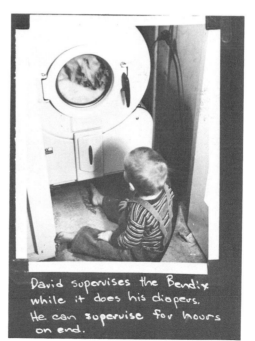

David supervises the Bendix while it does his diapers. He can supervise for hours on end.

Martha and Don added pages to "Little Visits" when their sons, David and Michael, were born.

"The Bendix was David's entertainment before television, watching the laundry slosh around. It was a very common pose, but who could imagine at that time that technology was going to move so fast that the Bendix would now be an historical object?"

Each page in Laduska Adriance's first album is a collage of photos, magazine cutouts, and written text which reflect her life in a California commune in the late 1960s.

THIS WAS ALL A PART
OF THE LOG
CABIN...
DYLAN
ROBIN
BILL
JOHN
DICKS
WHY
GO
TO
THE
WHY?

The photos in Laduska Adriance's second album begin with her wedding in 1973 and record the birth of her daughter.

We're rarely trying, in our photos and albums, to offer a balanced view of family life. Nancy Hallsted crops or discards those images that are extraneous to her vision of family bonds. The Adriance album does not reflect the conflicts of communal living, or those of the youth culture, but only its collective freedom and joy. Martha Ross, even in her attempt to depict day-to-day life, does not document the awkward adjustments to a new marital life, but rather domestic tranquility. What photos *do* signal is a creative expression of certain aspects of family life. In this way, family photography parallels other forms of folklore. Like our stories of heroes, rogues, and innocents, the photo of "One-Gun Blum" compresses the entirety of a personality into a single image. Like a migration story, the photo of the "pathetic" and "helpless" family assumes importance because it now seems to symbolize a turning point in that family's life. Just as Grace McDonald used anecdotes about each of her grandchildren as keys to their identities, Catherine Noren used her family photos to elicit stories and memories from her relatives. Picture-taking and sharing albums at holiday celebrations, like storytelling itself, have become an enjoyable and deeply-rooted family tradition.

While these images often cause us to remember the not-so-good times, either by association or by contrast, we seldom stop and say, "No, it didn't happen this way." Like the courtship story which becomes embellished over time, photos assume an aesthetic character of their own, one which focuses on the most positive and uncomplicated aspects of family life. We strut and smile, clown and cavort in the face of the camera because the resulting images affirm what we believe most worthy of preserving from the flow of family life.

Other Ways of Preserving the Past

I had a great-aunt who apparently was arrested by the czar and sentenced to Siberia for holding Jewish Sabbath services in her home. So she disguised herself as a man, so as not to be attacked, bundled up her belongings, which included incredibly heavy copper pots, on her back, and walked across Russia to the Turkish straits to get a boat to come to this country. We have the pots, which is why the children have the story.[1]

While storytelling, picture-taking, and the celebration of other rituals occur on specific occasions, families go about their daily lives surrounded by many objects, besides photographs, which stand as silent reminders of their heritage. A close connection exists between a family's stories and its memorabilia; for tangible articles often serve as reference points for stories, and explain the persistence of certain episodes in tradition. Some of these objects like the Ludwig's copper pots in the story above connect to a single incident; others serve as more general reminders of the past, its events and participants.

Often, the most significant material objects are those which evoke a feeling of "home":

There was one thing which we recognized very early as being very important in a traveling life. That was to bring along with you as many objects as you can with which you have an emotional attachment: the pictures on your wall, the family albums, the things that mean home to you no matter where you are. Furniture is nothing. You know you can buy or borrow it, but the things which mean home to you are extremely important . . . Churchill once said, "Necessities you can live without, but luxuries, never."[2]

In her book, *Coming of Age,* Simone de Beauvoir wrote, "My objects are myself . . . . The proprietor maintains a magic relationship with his property."[3] She suggests an interesting connection between our traditions and our possessions: "The possession of a garden means being able to take one's walk in it every afternoon. This armchair is waiting for me to sit in it every evening."[4] Taking her idea a little further, as objects of great emotional value, heirlooms can enhance and even motivate family rituals. For four generations the Heimer family, for instance, treasured an old doll they named Cinderella which was given to a child in the family as a Christmas present a little over a hundred years ago. Now, the doll is brought out and photographed with the family each year at Christmas and for her hundredth birthday the family threw a special Christmas party which included a cake with a hundred candles.

Possessions are also an interesting part of family tradition because they enable us to experience what some scholars have termed simultaneity:[5] by gathering around ourselves treasured objects from different times of our lives and our histories, we experience different eras at the same moment and in some way bring the totality of the past to bear upon the present. Many families have a "memory wall" or a particular alcove in which their most precious keepsakes and memorabilia are arranged to create this effect.

Some family artifacts have intrinsic or historical value and automatically assume the status of family heirlooms, as in this family story:

After the Civil War my great-grandfather was running a blockade outside of New Orleans. Around that time he was approached by an emissary from the Emperor Maximilian of Mexico to try to get his wife out of the country because things were looking a little nasty. The emperor was asked to go but he said, "No, no, my people love me . . . but send my wife out." And so they took the empress, and my great-grandfather and another man got her out of the country to France. And he was given a ring that had three diamonds in a square setting. And so all my brothers have used diamonds from that ring in their wedding rings, so they're just being passed on.[6]

Of course, the vast majority of objects which are passed from generation to generation are more modest: a lock of hair, a set of teacups, a yard of wedding lace, or a packet of love letters. The same object, without a history or a context, may elude a stranger's eye, but its association with relatives or shared events can make it special or set apart. One person's junk becomes another's keepsake.

The tangible nature of these objects does not necessarily fix their meaning, which may be as ephemeral as in any other form of folklore. Just as stories, expressions, and anecdotes are constantly being invented, remembered, and forgotten, objects too, pass in and out of family tradition. Once the association with the family is forgotten, the item may simply become a hand-me-down and may eventually be discarded. But when even the most worthless of objects becomes imbued with memories, it seems to defy any effort to get rid of it. A good example is Nancy Smith's kitchen chairs:

I have this kitchen set still. It's funny, the things you grow up with. Here it is in this picture before I was born [see below]— this is when we lived on Riverside Drive in New York. This set was in every house I've ever lived in. I have it in my kitchen. They're ugly chairs but they're sitting there. I keep thinking I ought to get rid of them. BUT I CAN'T GET RID OF THOSE CHAIRS! *I've seen them white, I've seen them brown, I've seen them green—they're my chairs and somehow they go with me.*[7]

Artifacts, like photographs, function as family folklore on several levels. First, the item can be an integral part of a tradition, such as Christmas tree ornaments that must appear each year before family members are convinced that the holiday has truly arrived. Artifacts can also be a direct record of family heritage, such as a letter, a diary, or even the yardstick used to measure and chart the children's growth. Perhaps most important, objects like the copper pots function as cues, eliciting a wealth of stories and reminiscences.

NANCY SMITH

While artifacts are a common means by which different families celebrate their heritage, they, more than other folkloric genres, tend to be exclusive to individuals or particular segments of the family. Many relatives might tell the same story or carry copies of the same family photo, but only one family member or unit can possess grandfather's rocking chair and, most likely, the stories which surround it. The uniqueness of objects renders them delicate as carriers of tradition. If a story is forgotten by one relative, it may be remembered and passed on by another. But when an artifact is lost, destroyed, or discarded, neither it nor the associations that make it precious can be replaced.

The family bible is the quintessential example of a written family record; surprisingly, though, it is often the least complete, having only a list of names and birthdates. Robert Rhode related a story to us to illustrate the use of the family bible by one of his ancestors. In this case, the bible serves two functions, as proof of age for the great-grandfather and as a cue for his descendant's story.

My aunt told me this story about my grandfather's father, I suppose. He wanted to join the Confederate army so he went to Tennessee. They told him he was too young. This must have been early in the war before they were taking everybody. He was seventeen and they said, "No, you look fifteen. We have to have proof of your age." So he rode back to Texas which took him several days and got a big family bible in which was recorded his birthday. He got the bible and rode back to Tennessee with his bible in his saddlebag to prove his age and they let him join. He kept the bible all during the war, and after it was over he returned it to Texas and the family still has it.[8]

Other material objects besides bibles can reveal valuable family folklore and history. In this age of instant communication, we frequently forget that letter writing was once an art. In addition to casual correspondence which by chance contains information of importance to the family historian and folklorist, there exists a genre of correspondence which deliberately records contemporary events or recreates times past. For example, the Civil War letters of John Brandon to his family give a soldier's eye view of that war. On October 6, 1861, he wrote his father:

We have no officers in this company worth a cent, except the captain. The others are all boys who got their offices through the influence of rich relatives, and not fit to command a squad of geese. I have not been on drill but twice since we have been here. Half of us have no horses. If things do not get better I will try and get transferred to Overton's company, if it comes here. I have not been out of camp but two hours since I have been here, except to drill.

Eight days later, a second letter followed:

We have not drilled any yet, we have been loafing ever since we have been here. I suppose we will have to go into the field unprepared. I do not see any other show now. If Frank or Albert get into a fever about going to war, tell them to mind their own business. If they want to live like dogs and be treated like dogs, the army is a very good place, but if not, they better stay out of it. Give my love to all, Your Son, John Brandon.[9]

Some rare individuals have recognized the possibilities of this vanishing form, and seized upon it deliberately. In 1972, at the age of eighty-two, Andrew Nicholas Conrady composed a twenty-six-page letter to introduce his newborn great-grandson to a part of the Conrady tradition that might otherwise be lost. Mr. Conrady explained his intentions at the beginning of the letter.

Dear Great-grandson: Greetings —
"Grace be with you, mercy and peace from God the Father, and from Christ Jesus the Son of the Father, in truth and charity." (John 2:3)
You being fifteen [15] days old and me being $82\frac{1}{4}$ years plus some twenty leap year days makes me some days over [30,000] thirty thousand days old. That makes me [2000] two thousand times as old as you. In truth that is what could be called a BIG generation gap. By the time you are old enough to read and understand this letter, great grandmother and me will likely have long since passed on to our eternal reward.
This letter will NOT be a scholarly masterpiece; rather, it will be some thoughts, some facts, some hopes, some plain fancy and others plain nonsense, but I trust you will enjoy reading all of it. . . .[10]

Letters have an inherent drawback as a record of family tradition: often written to be thrown away when read, they must have been saved in some way, either by chance or foresight. In addition, information usually must be culled from a number of letters or from other sources if they are to recreate a time of life.

A more concise means of recordkeeping is the memoir, a reminiscence of the past which focuses on personal or family history. Memoirs (as opposed to diaries) are intended for a wider audience than are letters, and for this reason are often more polished and literary in format and tone.

E. S. Goodwin used her memory of the floorplan of her childhood home as a basis for her memoir. As she takes the reader from room to room, she recounts the incidents and describes the persons she associates with each part of "the house on M Street."

It is too bad that I cannot show you the kitchen with its big woodburning range, its large table, and the muted light coming in through the windows on the areaway. And the pantry!, with shelves filled with wood, its capacious sink and its dumbwaiter for carrying food to the dining room above. We loved the dumbwaiter. It was such fun to give kittens a ride on it. Then, too, Lucetta and I found a closet under the back stairway that was littered with elegant fashion magazines. We had two colored pencils, red and blue, and we crept in there secretly and, by the light of a candle stub, we colored the pictures of pretty ladies. Lucetta's favorite color was blue, so I took red because my mother had taught me never to insist on first choice. We could have burnt the house down with that candle.[11]

Family history and needlework have long been linked together. Samplers embroidered by young girls frequently have the names and ages of family members stitched into them. Various types of presentation and commemorative quilts have been made and given to mark rites of passage: birth, the attainment of adulthood, marriage, moving into a new place of residence, even death. Often, the clothing of family members is stitched into a quilt, either intentionally or for the sake of frugality. In the best examples of these family artifacts, the makers have adopted needle and thread, yarn, and yard goods, as their medium of expression instead of the family historian's more usual tools of pen, ink, and paper.

Mrs. Ethel Mohamed, of Belzoni, Mississippi, began to embroider scenes from her family history at the age of sixty, after the death of her husband, Hassan. He was a Lebanese immigrant who first traveled to Mississippi as a peddler of household goods, and then became a successful dry-goods store owner. Many of her intricately stitched and appliqued works were inspired by particular memories of Hassan and their children. One showed the family with a new baby (see photograph on p. 207); another depicted her husband with his pushcart. Some of her works are drawn from the history of the community and some are more symbolic, depicting her children as the fruit of a sturdy tree of life, or herself and her husband riding in the beak of the bluebird of happiness.

Sophia Fairfield Wheat called upon genealogical research, family tradition, and her own memories and experiences to create her masterwork, the Fairfield Family History Quilt. The eighty-eight embroidered blocks of this quilt trace the history of the Fairfield family in America from 1631 to the present. The stories to accompany each incident are included with each block.

Ethel Mohamed explains the imagery in her embroidered pictures depicting the activities of a pioneer ancestor in her native Mississippi and the birth of a new baby in the family.

BETSY KEENEY

Betsy Keeney followed the tradition of commemorative needlework when she designed this quilt for the fiftieth wedding anniversary of her parents, Mary and Joseph Donovan. Since Mr. and Mrs. Donovan emigrated from County Cork, Mrs. Keeney included several Irish symbols such as the Claddagh ring and shamrock. Family-related symbols include images of Cape Cod (the scene of many vacations), a railway engine (to symbolize her father's occupation), and the ever-present pot of tea of which Mrs. Keeney said, "Through the years both happy and sometimes troubled there was something almost healing about sharing a cup of tea with someone loved."

One of the most unusual examples we found of preserving and artistically reinterpreting a family's past was a three-dimensional tableau of dolls created by artist Esther Luttikhuizen for Charlene James. The photograph on which the tableau is based depicts Charlene as a child standing outside St. Josephat's Basilica in Milwaukee, Wisconsin, with her mother, grandmother, and Aunt Vickie. The dolls, made in 1980, almost thirty years after the photo was taken, recreate for Charlene an almost mythological rendering of her past. "I had always shared a strong personal affinity with these women," she told us, "but only after I'd seen the dolls did I feel part of a continuous bloodline as well. My aunt Vickie was excluded because I wanted three dolls to reflect the three generations."

Most memorabilia are not so self-consciously created. But just about everybody has a drawer or shoebox filled with objects collected, or at least kept, because of their associations with certain persons, places, or events. These keepsakes, souvenirs, and mementos are preserved because they have developed their own histories and meanings. A ticket stub or dance card might recall a particular meeting, but a found rock or piece of an old toy might be less obvious (even to its owner). It is often unclear just why these objects are not discarded. They seldom have any intrinsic monetary value; their chief contribution appears to the uninitiated to be the perpetuation of clutter. But to their owners, these bits and pieces of the past represent significant aspects of their lives, although the exact significance may be difficult to articulate, even to themselves.

CHARLENE JAMES

In 1951, eight-year-old Nancy Davis wrote a letter to Albert Einstein. Her mother saved the first draft of the letter and included it in a photo album compiled for Nancy as a wedding present.

This ticket to Disneyland was included in an album made by Mrs. Mary Goodwin for her daughter Linda on the occasion of Linda's' twenty-first birthday.

A page from the 1903 baby book of Ida Elizabeth Sabin. (Contributed by her descendant, Mary Goodwin.)

We often seem caught in the tension between not quite knowing why we are saving something, and yet not quite wanting to throw it out. We feel that if we do discard some keepsake, we are somehow denying the meaning of the past. So we end up shifting it from box to box, and carrying it from old residence to new. "It's funny, my life has been a series of moves," Ron Sutton told us, "and I would suspect that every time I've moved, I've replaced the boxes. I've taken them out of wherever I've had them and as I put them away, I frequently will open them and for that moment kind of relive, you know, those moments."[12]

Andrew Conrady expressed his opinion of memorabilia quite emphatically in his letter to his great-grandson:

One more thing and then I am finished. Keepsakes. Keepsakes usually are junk of little value except sentiment, and something your kids or grandchildren turn into a holy war and refuse to speak to each other ever afterward. Mine are of little money value, but I want you to have them. If inflation keeps up its pace, I think by the time you are sixteen years old, you could take the whole kaboodle to a pawn broker. If he happens to be in good humor he might give you three bucks for the lot, about enough to buy you and your girlfriend two cokes and straws. Then again, you may only get enough for one coke and two straws.[13]

From copper pots to pressed flowers, the objects that decorate our homes and underscore the meanings of our lives become yet another vehicle for the transmission of folklore across the generations. Some are unlikely icons—common household objects which assume importance because of their associations—while others, like the family history quilt, are deliberate records of family life, and examples of folk artistry in their own right. But whether proudly displayed on a wall or consigned to the netherworld of a rarely opened drawer, our memorabilia remains a vital part of our family tradition for as long as its many meanings live in our memories.

Five American Families

The stories, expressions, traditions, and photographs in this book were shared with us by hundreds of American families. Presented here by form and theme, they delineate some of the recurring patterns in American family lore and suggest the many ways in which families encapsulate cherished parts of their past. Yet in this book Americans talk about their folklore in bits and snatches, leaving us to answer still the question: how and when and why are all the forms of folklore blended and shared in an individual family?

For this reason we invited five folklorists to think and comment about the folklore in their own families. Their essays present a more in-depth look at some specific American families who vary widely in their geographic locales and in the ways folklore plays a role in their lives.

Steven Zeitlin, whose grandparents immigrated from a Russian Jewish village at the turn of the century and settled in Philadelphia, highlights a traditional Russian dance still performed in the family; Amanda Dargan, who comes from an extended, rural South Carolina family, treats the subject of characterization in her family's folklore, demonstrating the ways in which stories, nicknames, descriptions, and imitations are used to pinpoint the idiosyncracies of her family members; Dennis Folly, an Afro-American folklorist, describes his family background in central Virginia, focusing on his great-grandmother and her use of proverbs as instructional devices. Anne Warner, well-known for the treasury of folksongs and vignettes of rural life in Appalachia and the northeast which she and her husband Frank collected in the thirties, forties, and fifties turns her attention to her "other folklore journal," in which she recorded her children's perceptive utterances as they grew up in Greenwich Village in New York. Finally, Margaret Yocom looks at the function of family tales as a unifying device which characterizes her Pennsylvania German family's ritual gatherings: weddings, anniversaries, and funerals.

These five essays offer us another way of looking at the stories, traditions, and photos in this book. A family story may seem funny to us, but it is far more so to the family who knows all the characters, and whose history is untangled in the telling. These essays remind us that family traditions are richest in meaning in the context of an individual family where the characters in the stories and the places pictured in the photographs reverberate with myriad associations.

At every wedding and every bar mitzvah in my family, when the sobriety of the ritual has at last given way to festive celebration, the band breaks into "Havah Nagilah," and the crowd comes to its feet. The family forms a circle, holds hands, the circle starts to turn, first right, then to the left, yielding a wide wedding ring of guests clapping joyously in time. Into the circle goes a disco dancing teenage cousin; a sixties flower child follows with the frug; my mother does the Charleston; and some cousins surface for the Philadelphia Mummer's Strut, holding the edges of their jackets, swaying side to side.

Then comes the highlight of the dance. My uncle Oscar, sixty-five years old, his arms crossed, struts towards the center of the ring. The audience holds its breath. He squats, leaps upward, kicks out a leg. The clapping intensifies. His knees bend again—another leg! Smiles and cheers burst along the circle of faces. He's down, then up, his heels barely touching the floor.

His three sons join him in the center, each performing the dance he learned from his father. Facing one another they vault upwards, downwards in unison, their legs shooting forward, suggesting together the spokes of a wheel. Richie with a crew cut and a wide smile dances and clowns; Marc, the tallest, struggles to make his long legs bend and stretch. Eddie, stocky but limber, goes low on his haunches. "*Havah nagilah, Hava nagilah, Havah nagilah, venismekha.*" One leg bends, the other extends, he leaps high in the air, the legs change places. "*Uru, uru akhim, Uru akhim b'-lev sa-may-ach.*" He vaults upwards, his legs rising even with his waist, and astonishingly, his fingers touch his toes. "*Uru akhim b'lev sa-may-ach.*"

The band moves into the final verse. Oscar begins to improvise and clown, as the instruments drag out the final line. "*Uru akhim, uru akhim b'-lev sa-m— — ay — — ach!*" The song ends and the clapping becomes applause.

"It's our family's way of busting out with excitement," said Oscar's daughter Jayne. "You take love for granted," her sister Marsha added, "You fight all the time, leave home when you're eighteen. There's only a few moments when you really feel that spark. But that's one of those times—when my father sees his three sons dancing."

The performance of the *kazatske* (pronounced in my family *kazatchka*) goes back beyond the memory of the oldest liv-

Max Wallace, Oscar's father, who learned the kazatske *in Russia.*

ing relative, to the Russian towns and villages my grandparents left as children, towns that have taken on some of the cast of Anatefke in *Fiddler on the Roof*. ("They do one wedding scene where they do a *kazatske*-like dance with bottles on their heads," Richie said. "I almost broke into tears.") Although these villages and towns included Jews from different social strata and varied lifestyles, the family's images of what life was like "in the old country" or "back in the *shtetlekh*" (the Russian-Jewish towns) have been drastically altered by popular and literary images. In my imagination, their homeplace has even come to resemble Vitebsk, Marc Chagall's hometown on the Russian-Polish border, a town transformed by memory and imagination into paintings in which all the accouterments of my ancestors' rough lives—the clocks, fishes, and menorahs—are transfused with beauty, turned upside down, floating dreamlike above the village square.

Somewhere between Chagall's mythical Vitebsk and Sholom Aleichem's Anatefke lay the small village of Ochremover in Russia, which Oscar's father, Max Wallace, fled. But he painted no magical, dreamy vision of his homeland. "Tell me one thing that was good about the old country?" he would ask his sentimental fellow immigrants. "You froze in the winter, and you died from the heat in the summer, and everybody ate out of one big pot."

My grandmother and her sister Rose came out of Russia at the turn of the century as small children hidden beneath a pile of straw in an oxcart. And my grandfather's family fled into the snow when a raid or *pogrom* swept through their village, leaving their father to guard their home. They slept in the barren woods for days, and when they returned, half frozen, their house had been ransacked, bed feathers floated in the air, and my great-grandfather hung from the ceiling on a noose. His house cat lay whining on the floor beneath the corpse. After three days the cat died. Such is the legacy of stories from that generation of my ancestors.

Yet for all the wretched memories, all the forgettable things, Max kept the tradition going. "Tell me one thing that was good about the old country," he asked, but he kept the dance alive. On every family occasion, he traced those ancient Russian triangles with his feet. "It's old country, but such a wonderful old country," said my raucous aunt Elaine. "When you hear the music you just want to get up and do it.

It's the same way the Italians feel about," and she breaks into song, "La Soooorento. . . ."

Those small children who huddled around that pot of soup and crossed the border in an oxcart came with far more than their meager possessions piled in their arms. They brought with them a whole eastern European Jewish culture, *yidishkayt*, including tunes, dances, and customs which had sustained generations of rabbis and merchants in Russian-Jewish towns. They brought along with them religious observances, festivals, foodways, a culture that was to be far more threatened by their soon-to-be-discovered progress and wealth than it ever was by poverty and hardship.

In America they settled in Philadelphia and became shop-keepers, mostly. They preserved the Yiddish language, the Jewish holidays, and for as long as they lived (well into my childhood) the Passover seder was an event to behold. As Oscar's daughter Marsha remembered the ritual from childhood, "You don't talk, you don't move, and [there's] twenty pounds of gefilte fish in the kitchen." The women cooked for a week: *kneydlekh* (matzoh dumpling), *kugl* (noodle pudding), and matzoh ball soup.

Their children became businessmen, for the most part. They departed the Jewish city neighborhoods for the suburbs, leaving behind many of their customs—keeping kosher, using *tfillin* (a prayer apparatus), observing Purim. They retained only snatches, a few Yiddish words and phrases (none of which can be adequately translated) such as *mentsch* ("a real human being"), *meshugene* (crazy person). They continued to fast on Yom Kippur, but the traditional home-cooked seder gave way to a catered dinner with the whole *mishpokhe* (family) in a rented hall. It was a discarding of the past that occurred in countless families of similar background all across the country, as being American—integrated and homogenized—displaced the old ethnic identity.

Their children's children became more secular still. Some succeeded their fathers in business. Others became doctors, lawyers, accountants, television producers. They moved still further away, past the Philadelphia suburbs to cities like Washington, New York, and Los Angeles. And when today they come together for family celebrations, even the music to that old Russian dance step has been replaced with a newer

My uncle Oscar Wallace dancing the kazatske with his three sons—Mark, Eddie, and Richie.

Uncle Oscar dancing the kazatske
with my mother in 1949.

Israeli tune played by the Ronnie Lewis Band. But still the *kazatske* continues. Still the flurry of feet.

Yet how strange a custom to represent our Jewish lineage! Here is no ritual dating back to an exodus from Egypt thousands of years ago. Family tradition has it (and scholarly research suggests) that the *kazatske* was a dance of the Cossacks, a group of Russian men of no fixed abode or occupation who became a force of permanent irregular soldiery, and whom our ancestors encountered (generally as enemies) in their tumultuous, century-long stay in Poland and Russia. Their dances were called "Cossack" if of a vigorous nature, combined with somersaults, handstands, and flips. They were called "Cossatchok" when less strenuous. These less acrobatic though still arduous steps appealed to the Jews in their *shtetlekh*, and were incorporated into older dances on festive occasions. "The funny thing is," my uncle Jay joked, "that's probably the dance they did when the Cossacks came after them swinging swords and they tried to escape!"

Oscar bends, kicks his legs out, squats, jumps. It's old-country *kazatske,* yes. Suddenly he reaches for a napkin, ties it around his head, and walks to the rhythm like a half-crippled man. Above the instruments blaring out "Havah Nagilah," he whistles piercingly, pretends to be playing a fife in "The Spirit of '76." The ring of dancers, clapping, laughs with delight. A quintessential American image becomes (through a kind of ad libbing) a part of the dance.

And that walk, that "obviously infirm walk," Richie said, "is a take-off on the Ritz brothers. The Ritz brothers are, let's say, an ethnic version of the 'Three Stooges'—you know, Mo, Larry, and Curly were all Jewish—they were Jewish just like the Marx brothers. But the Ritz brothers in a sense came off as being Yiddish. Dey all spoke with a slight accent. . . . They were in the movies in the late forties. And the best surviving example is [a version of] *The Three Musketeers* with the Ritz brothers, where the opening scene is the three of them baking chicken soup. Harry Ritz used to walk with a very strange walk that [my father found] would go easily into 'The Spirit of '76.' "

The *kazatske* is done by few Jewish families as secular as my own, yet it is still common among Hassidic Jews, particularly in the Lubovitch community in New York. Jill Gellerman, who explored these traditions, discovered that even in this enclave of traditional Jewish life, the dance has adapted

Eddie Wallace performs a difficult kazatske step.

to new soil. The band plays what she calls the "*kazatske* medley," and often includes a few bars of "Yankee Doodle Dandy" along with the traditional eastern European melodies. A quintessential American tune becomes incorporated in Jewish custom, perhaps in the same way that a Russian dance step became part of Jewish celebrations a few generations ago.

So many meanings converge in Oscar's simple steps. When he dances, Oscar writes some of the family history with his feet, recalling like far away music weddings danced in Russian villages, and, more dimly still, echoes of Jewish history back to the pharaohs. The tune "Havah nagilah" ("Let Us Rejoice") is a modern Israeli anthem, but, for us, the dance also celebrates what it means to be an ethnic Jew from Philadelphia—Oscar and his wife Sylvia are, in fact, probably the most ethnic members of their generation, observing more of the old customs than their contemporaries in the family. He is a family patriarch, the senior among the second generation immigrants. And whereas my parents, for instance, retained only a few words and phrases of Yiddish, Oscar and Sylvia broke into it fluently whenever they didn't want the children to understand their conversation.

And of course when he dances, Oscar expresses his own distinctive personality. As William Butler Yeats once wrote, "How can we know the dancer from the dance?" Or as my uncle Jay Burg put it, "That's Oscar, that's his *shtik.*"

His sons too now dance in their own inimitable styles. Marsha suggests that each galavants into the center for different reasons. Richie revels in the humorous improvisations. Marc, she says, is the most sentimental, the most conscious of paying homage to his father in the dance. Eddie is the most athletic, the only one who can kick both of his feet out and touch his toes in mid-air (see photo on page 215). He attributes this to heredity. "My leg structure is a lot like my father's," he said, "[I got the] thigh muscles that you need."

Oscar's children will carry the meaning of the dance with them long after their father is no longer able to kick and bend and stretch. Yet they will always, as Richie said, think about their father when they think about the dance. In turn, when Oscar thinks about the dance, he recalls *his* father before him. "It's a remembrance and a thought," he commented.

When we think about our relatively ancient customs we like to emphasize the way they reach down across the generations, connecting us to our great-great-greats. But as with the family dance, customs are often tied most closely to childhood memories, often reinforced by the personality or will of one strong individual. The *kazatske* is perpetuated not only because Richie and Marc and Eddie have such strong feelings about our Russian ancestors, but because they love and emulate their father, who loves and emulates his own.

My grandmother and the other women of her generation performed a different style of Russian dancing at our family celebrations.

Similarly, parents often celebrate holiday traditions like Christmas and Channukah in ways which recall their own childhood. They often decorate the tree, light the menorah, hang the stockings the way their parents did for them. In this fashion, with little regard for the ageless quality of the customs, a chain of interlocking childhood memories forms across the generations. These memories become our "roots."

On one occasion I asked Marsha what was more important to her about the dance — that it was performed by her father or that it was a Jewish tradition. She summed up her feelings by saying, "He's great and we love him, and incidentally it's a Jewish tradition." But in a way my question was beside the point. For there is a sense in which, as far as his children are concerned, Oscar *is* Jewish tradition. From the first moment they opened their eyes, they saw the two together, conceived of them as one.

Recently, our other passionately celebrated Jewish tradition, the family's Passover seder, began to get out of hand as the good-natured conviviality of the cousins reached such a pitch that it started to drown out the service, and the urge to visit made it difficult to keep the whole family seated. Oscar's son Richie, who was presiding over the service, waved his prayerbook and asked for quiet as a cousin at the far end of the table managed to turn the solemn passover question into a humorous quip: "Why should this night be different from all other nights?" Finally my aunt Elaine, teary-eyed, stepped to the center of the rented hall and raised her glass. "I think all of us should remember why we're here," she said, and then mentioned not the suffering of the Jews in Egypt, but a series of names: "Grandpop Harry, Daddy Al, Bobe Rose . . ." For everyone in the family knows — and the toast only served to reiterate — that the tradition continues, even in the rented hall, in memory of the strong, strict, charismatic figures who presided over the seder when we were all younger, and perhaps especially in memory of my grandfather in whose home the passover supper was celebrated. Then Elaine sat down at the catered banquet table, and with characteristic humor, not knowing whether to laugh or cry, she added, "I'll tell you why we're here — because they sold the biggest house!"

The last song of the evening was an old favorite, and all the aunts, uncles, and cousins joined in for the chorus: "*El b'ney, el b'ney . . .*" Then suddenly Oscar and a host of cous-

*"That was a joy for me to see — my father dancing
at my wedding."*

ins began to imitate my grandfather, who had once presided
over the occasion with such style. They rolled their tongues
through the *"rumpt pa ra ra rum pum pum,"* and, dessert
spoons in hand, they flicked their wrists and swung their
arms with a distinctive flourish. "That's the way your grandfather used to do it," Oscar whispered to me as the song continued: *"El b'ney, el b'ney, r-r-r-r-rumpt pa ra ra rum pum
pum."*

Oscar's father had a weak heart, and died soon after his first
grandchild was born (if he could have seen his three grand-
sons dance, Oscar said, "He would really *kvel*" — as his
daughter translated, "revel and delight"). A few weeks before
Richie was married, Oscar himself went to the hospital for an
electrocardiogram. The doctors noticed a slight change in
his charts, and suggested he return for a stress test. His
daughter Marsha, a physician, knew her father hated check-
ups and doubted that he would bother with the tests. In her
anxious moments she worried that he would die of a heart attack on the dance floor. He too was concerned and did go in.
He passed and, a few days later, danced at the wedding.

"I'd always thought of a big Jewish wedding where my father did the *kazatske*, and that's what I got" said Richie, who
never knew about the test. "Really, that was a joy for me to
see — my father dancing at my wedding."

SHE COMES BY IT HONESTLY
Characterization in Family Folklore
Amanda Dargan

Wearing a loose-fitting dress, Tuga Peterson, the seventy-eight-year-old woman who had nursed a generation of our relatives, performed for us in the small kitchen that had always been her stage. As my sister and I looked on, she drew a portrait with words and gestures of our uncle Ned. "Now Mr. Ned," she said, "Monday, Tuesday, Wednesday, Thursday, Friday, he's Mr. Ned, dressed in his regular work clothes. But on Sunday, um hm. Miss Cullough gets hold of him and dresses him up so you can hardly recognize him. I can see him right now walking out that front door between those two flags, walking just like this. . . ." She imitated Uncle Ned's long stride, exaggerating it by slowing it down, sliding her feet flat across the floor, clearing her throat and moving her arms, bent with clinched fists, in unison with each step. "And his suit," she went on, pretending to smooth down the sides of an imaginary jacket, "his suit is so smooth, if a mosquito lit on it, it would slide off and break its neck."

In her brief imitation Tuga captured our uncle's most familiar qualities: his stride, his dress, the way he clears his throat. She also captured something about the relationship between Uncle Ned and his wife Cullough: the compromise they have reached between his indifference and her concern with fancy clothes. During the week he wears what he likes, but on Sundays and special occasions he wears the clothes she has picked out for him.

Like much of my family's folklore, Tuga's imitation was a form of characterization which bordered on caricature, heightening and exaggerating certain features of its subject. Like the caricaturist, Tuga drew a humorous, extravagant, and yet ultimately recognizable portrait of our uncle by highlighting and playing on some of his distinctive traits. This ability to characterize, to find an incident, a gesture, or a trait which captures the special qualities of families and individuals, is a skill admired in my family and is integral to our folklore. A story, an expression, a description, a nickname, a photograph, or an object of memorabilia is often valued and perpetuated precisely because it captures the features that make a relative distinctive.

Within our family tradition, the best storytellers are those with an eye for details and an ability to imitate the subjects of their stories. Good storytellers are known not only for the stories in their repertoire, but for the relatives whom they characterize particularly well. They are often called on at family gatherings to "do an imitation of Uncle Sam" or to "tell your Annie Louise stories."

Certain family nicknames are also based on characteristic traits. Ervin Dargan calls his son Benton, "Zig," because Benton's large jaws resembled those of the *Dick Tracy* cartoon character, "Ziggy." Since childhood, Ned Dargan has been called "Fish" by his closest friends among the cousins, because he enjoys fishing so much. Margaret Ervin is called "General" by her sisters and first cousins, because, being the oldest, she tends to give them orders. Often these nicknames are used only by those family members who conspired to create them and who use them specifically in situations where they want to tease their relatives by highlighting a certain characteristic.

This use of caricature in family folklore can carry a great deal of force and power. By conveying disapproval in a humorous way, it can be used to pressure a relative into changing a habit or into taking himself less seriously. When Sam Dargan came home for Christmas vacation with a long beard, his grandmother nicknamed him "Sammy Claus." When another relative came to the Fourth of July picnic several pounds heavier than he had been the year before, he was nicknamed "Minnesota" for the pool player "Minnesota Fats." These carefully selected words, gestures, and voice inflections can change temporarily the statuses of both the storyteller and his subject. A child can mock an elder, a relative can exert pressure on another, and Tuga Peterson can poke fun at the relatives of her employer.

My family takes special delight in stories and expressions repeated specifically to illustrate what sets relatives apart from each other as individuals and what distinguishes them as a group. "We've always been a clannish family," a storyteller begins. "You know how clumsy Sarah is," another says and then follows with an imitation of how she gets up from the table and knocks all the glasses over or with a story about how she broke a jar of pickles in St. Paul's Cathedral in London and had to stuff cucumbers in her pockets as she chased them down the aisle.

We are interested in the differences and similarities between our relatives partly because we are a large network of kin and these stories and expressions help to distinguish individuals and branches of the family, giving each a separate identity. The geographic center of the family is a rural community in South Carolina. It is a community with no fixed boundaries. Its borders have changed as the size and shape of the family has changed and as land has been bought and sold. For us, the community ends where the cousins end, and at present that covers an area of around ten square miles, which includes twenty-two households. Much of our folklore focuses on the last-name family groups that make up our community: the Dargans, the Ervins, the Howards, and the Williamsons.

The humor of our folklore, therefore, depends in part on a shared knowledge of the characteristic traits and habits of family members. Most family members can readily name the prominent characteristics of their relatives. They can also name the traits relatives share with each other, particularly those traits associated with a family name. They will tell you that the Ervins are entertaining, witty, and "non-energetic." They enjoy life. The Dargans are big-eyed and optimistic, adventurous, and gregarious. The Williamsons are smart, peculiar, attentive to details, and reticent about family matters. The Howards are big eaters, big talkers, and expert hunters and fishers. Physical traits are traced to relatives several generations removed. We can always spot Williamson eyes and Williamson feet, an Ervin complexion, and a McIntosh mouth. Poor eyesight is inherited from the Evanses and deafness from the Harts.

This association of stock traits with a family name provided a useful mnemonic device for my relative Bill Howard:

I'll tell you something my mother told me to remember my grandmother's family. There were four McIver sisters who lived in Society Hill. The sweetest one married an Ervin, the prettiest one married a Law, the wittiest one married a Gregg — you know the Greggs are known for being witty — and the one with the most sense married a Williamson.

Some relatives are said to be like their last-name family, while the traits of others are traced to various other branches of the family, which means that inconsistencies can be accounted for easily. A relative who is unlike his father's family will be explained as being more like his mother's or his grandmother's side of the family. Or, the contradiction itself may be explained as a family trait. When confronted with the inconsistencies among members of the Dargan family, one family member said, "Well, that's another trait of the Dargans: they vary more."

This tendency to give genealogical explanations for the behavior of relatives often removes personal blame. Criticism of a relative is often dismissed with the common expressions, "It runs in the family" and "She comes by it honestly," followed by stories about other relatives in that branch of the family who exhibited the same trait.

These explanations also can dampen the credit for individual achievements. No one is surprised that Edwin Dargan is such a skilled woodworker, for after all, his great-grandmother was a Hart and the Harts are known for being good with their hands.

From years of watching them closely, family members also know the characteristics of their relatives as individuals. They know, for instance, that Vannie Ervin will always wear a black tie, whether he is at a dance or fishing on Black Creek, that Ervin Dargan will buy almost any new gadget or invention that comes on the market, that Mary Hart McIver will always be late for Christmas Eve supper no matter how much she insists that this year she will be on time. "If you ever want to surprise Mary Hart," goes a running joke in our family, "just tell her what time it is."

Like the caricaturist who exaggerates the most uneven and awkward features of his subject, family members will often emphasize a relative's most peculiar traits and habits in their folklore. Stories are told of how Rosa Dargan always refused to have her photograph taken and when she finally consented to have her wedding photograph made, covered her face with her veil; of how Mr. Ben Williamson had such a good memory for details that he would tell his son exactly which tobacco stalk on which row had a tobacco worm on it that had to be removed; and of how Joe Dargan's memory was so selective that he would forget that he had driven to town and catch a ride home but could remember the names and addresses of all of his college graduating class. Ervin Dargan delighted his cousins with this description of how their uncle Joe Dargan would overcome his tendency to shake from Parkinson's disease when it came to drinking whiskey:

He'd drink a good deal, but he'd hardly ever show it. And he'd shake. You remember how his hands would shake. But when he got ready to take a drink, he'd go up on it like a bird dog and grab it and not spill a drop. [Imitates gesture] He'd shake everything else. [Laughter]

This kind of family folklore tends to make "characters" out of everyone. The stories highlight a relative's idiosyncracies, making them more visible than his or her "normal" characteristics, and, of course, once a certain trait has been highlighted, it sometimes becomes difficult to ignore. Even those traits which are considered admirable can be placed in a humorous light, if an incident is found which shows that trait carried to the extreme. A favorite family story captures how my uncle Ned once carried politeness too far. Bill Howard told this version:

Ned used to visit Vannie a good bit, and Uncle Hugh said that Ned was the best-mannered child he ever saw. He'd always sit quietly at the table and never interrupt anybody talking. Uncle Hugh said one day he was out on one of the fields talking with Mr. Abbott, and Ned came running toward them shouting, "Uncle Hugh, Uncle Hugh!" Uncle Hugh said, "Ned, I'm talking with Mr. Abbott right now." He said Ned danced first on one foot and then on the other, but he waited until they had finished talking. Then Uncle Hugh said, "All right, Ned, what was it you wanted?" "Uncle Hugh, the house is on fire!"

While family folklore tends to make "characters" out of everyone, for most of its subject this status is only temporary, confined to the playful atmosphere of the storytelling session. The permanent status of family character is reserved for only a few, those relatives in whom peculiar habits and traits predominate. I once overheard two relatives talking about an irritating trait of one of their cousins. "But she's such a character," one said. "If you'd just accept her as a character, those things wouldn't bother you so much." The other relative replied, "She hasn't earned the right to be a character yet."

One who did earn that right in the family was Joe Dargan. Joe was not the most admirable member of the family, although family members will insist that "he was always a gentleman." Joe did very little to support himself throughout his life, and he was notorious for his ability to consume large quantities of food and drink. For most of Joe's life, his relatives had to support him. Yet, we remember him with love and tenderness; his songs, stories, and recitations are favorite family traditions, and the tangled fishing twine found in Joe's cabin after he died have become family treasures. These balls of twine are valued because Joe, like many family characters, was both eccentric and endearing, and because they remind us of two of his most memorable traits: the way his fishing lines caught on tree limbs and unraveled all the way to the place where he fished every Saturday, and the way he saved everything, thus ensuring that there would be several balls of twine left to remember him by.

Given Joe's distinctive characteristics of being entertaining, eccentric, and, as one relative put it, "doing set things, and doing them over and over," it is no wonder that Joe became one of the favorite family characters. Even his most noticeable weaknesses became the subject of a great deal of family humor. Bill Howard, for example, told an anecdote based on Joe's chronic laziness and history of unemployment:

My great-uncle Joe Dargan, a "'classic family character.'"

You remember when Joe was living in the Darlington Hotel. Well, after the hotel burned, I asked Joe if he had lost anything in the fire. He said, "Confound it, William, I escaped with only my working clothes." (Shakes his head and laughs) *He never did a lick of work in his life.*

Outside of the family, however, some people were not as tolerant of Joe's idiosyncrasies, an attitude which shocked one of Joe's great-nephews:

The idea of showing disrespect to one of my relatives, well, I just never thought about it or never heard about it. It just really was a shock to catch people off-guard that didn't know that he was my uncle and to hear them say things about him. And it upset me really bad because I felt like saying, "You have no privilege to talk about this man, because he's, he's Uncle Joe, and he's a classic character.

Another established family character was McIver Williamson. Unlike Joe Dargan, Mr. McIver became known as a character outside the family as well. Many persons claim, in fact, that he is the chief legendary character in the area. As

*Two of the Dargan children, pictured here, married two Ervin
children and started the Dargan-Ervin clan.*

A small gathering of our relatives.

his neighbor Earl Gandy put it, "There are more stories about him than in the bible."

Traditions attribute to Mr. McIver many accomplishments in agriculture and nutrition, but most anecdotes about him focus on his idiosyncracies. The portrait which emerges from these stories is that of a brilliant but eccentric man, consciously unconventional, benevolent to those whom he considered deserving, capable of great severity as well as great kindness, and totally dedicated to the causes in which he believed.

Mr. McIver's dress is described as peculiar, especially for a man of his means: his shirts held together at the neck with a large safety pin and cut off at the waist with a drawstring through the hem; his ragged pants with the pockets sewed up to allow only two fingers to fit through; his mismatched shoes with tire treading tacked to the soles; and his entire wardrobe soaked in linseed oil to preserve it. These are the subject of family descriptions and tales about Mr. McIver.

As with Joe Dargan, most relatives insist that Mr. McIver "was always a gentleman" in spite of his unconventional dress and peculiar habits, although Hugh Dargan told about an exception:

We [Hugh and his father] were talking about McIver earlier tonight, about how he was never really considered weird, just eccentric. And that people really liked him. And daddy said, "You know, I never"—he was talking about giving him such a good character reference—"never knew of anybody that would have disliked him," and all this. He was a real gentleman. But the only time I ever heard of him being crude was when he was down at Harriet Swink's. Harriet's mother was having him for dinner. My grandmother was down there too. She said they were having steak, and the steak was tough, but it wasn't bad enough for anybody to say anything about it. They were just going to go ahead and eat it and be polite. McIver didn't say a word about it either. He just reached in his pocket and pulled out his file, took his teeth out and filed them down to a sharp edge, put them back in his mouth, and started eating again.

Mr. McIver also tended to buy things in quantities—large quantities. Ervin Dargan told of how Mr. McIver got tired of losing pliers, so he bought a bushel of them and scattered them around the house. Another story tells of how he went into a store and asked for a bushel of carburetors. Probably because of this trait, a well-known joke has become attached to Mr. McIver:

Mr. McIver wrote Sears and Roebuck, like he wrote them about pliers, and said, "Dear sir, send me a case of toilet paper." And they wrote him back and told him that he would have to order a catalog. He would have to order it out of the catalog. He wrote them back and told them that if he had the catalog, he wouldn't need the toilet paper.

Once a family member is established as a bonafide family character, traditional stories and jokes become attached to him rather easily. As Mr. McIver's great-nephew, Ben Williamson, commented, "People will believe anything you tell them about Uncle McIver."

Whether it is through a single story or a full-blown legend like McIver Williamson, my relatives seem to enjoy seeing themselves made into characters. "Family character" is a special category used by the family for any of its members whose behavior differs from expected values and norms, but no family member is immune from having his habits made to look comical in a family story. While family stories and expressions are often used to exert pressure on relatives to conform, they are also used to convey acceptance of those who do not conform, to place their weaknesses in a different light. Stories about family idiosyncrasies are used along with stories about family traits to express forgiveness for a member's faults, to play down his nonconformities, and to accept him into the fold. In the same way that we can forgive a relative's stubbornness because "she comes by it honestly," we can accept her flamboyance because "she's such a character."

One of my relatives said to me, "Some people think that being part of a big family would restrict your freedom, but I think it gives you more freedom. Some of our relatives wouldn't have any friends if they acted the way they do somewhere else. But here they have a whole family that accepts them no matter what they do." The worst thing that can happen to you in the family (some might argue the best thing) is that you become a family character.

GETTING THE BUTTER FROM THE DUCK: Proverbs and Proverbial Expressions

in an Afro-American Family

✔ Dennis W. Folly

Grey-haired and full of spirit, my great-grandmother is a woman deeply attached to the land. A mother of two children, grandmother of nine, and great-grand-mother of thirteen, she is a wellspring of stories and wise sayings. Granny was born in a log cabin on April 20, 1898, and has lived all of her life in Hanover County, Virginia. Born Clara Wilson Tolliver, she married Walter Abrams at age eighteen and became Mrs. Clara Abrams. In her own tenacious way my great-grandmother has always reminded us that this life and this earth is ours to love and to celebrate, and that even in slavery times members of our family stood up for this. "Yeah," she said, " 'cause they would walk right over you if you didn't have spunk. They couldn't do nothing with grandma because she had too much spunk."

In her lifetime, my great-grandmother has seen the countryside, the community, and the world change in drastic ways. She remembers the days when there was only a horse and buggy for transportation, and people were warmly and intricately related, continuously visiting one another, an entire network of black souls loving, squabbling, singing, praying, gambling, dancing, being born, and passing away as one family. The yards were full of children and the sounds of barnyard animals: ducks, chickens, pigs, goats, peacocks, dogs, and cats. She remembers especially the beauty of the peacock feathers, and misses the sense of sharing and community that has all but disappeared. On land where houses once stood and life's pageantries were acted out, there is now woods and thick patches of honeysuckle and wild berry vines. "You could stand in this yard and yell over there to Betty's and talk then," Granny recalls.

This small community, like many plots of land throughout the south, was parcelled off by slaveowners when Grant took Richmond and the big freedom bell was rung. The hill where our house now sits was known as "Canaan's Hill," indicating a settlement of freed people, of people who had emerged from their bondage in "Little Egypt," the slaveowner's domain. My great-grandmother has often told us the story of when the slaves were freed.

They had a big celebration. Blowin' the horn and celebrating.
See they took Richmond, Grant, the man took Richmond then

232

. . . well Lincoln and Grant . . . the two was together you see, and I don't know who else but they were the head two. And Grant blew the horn for the slavery band was broke. People was free! Say you could hear that horn . . . miles and miles, and people was in the fields they threw their hoe away and start to marchin'. They couldn't do nothing with 'em then, them people, some of 'em just jump up in the field and just scream and hollered . . . they went just running. [She slaps her palms together dramatically.] So glad they was free!

My mother, Mrs. Jean Folly, was born on January 15, 1934, also in Hanover County. Shortly afterwards, her mother, Arlene, left the county for New York City, leaving her to be raised by my great-grandmother. She also has a deep attachment to the land which she has passed on to us. Raised by Granny and spending most of her time around older people, she shares much of the knowledge and sense of tradition reaching back to plantation days. When my great-grandmother forgets a particular detail, no matter how far back, my mother can usually help her to remember.

It is out of this background that my family's oral traditions emerge, and one very important element of that tradition is the genre of proverbs. As others have pointed out, the proverb plays a vital role in African societies.[1] Used in domestic situations, particularly to impart morals to children, as well as in legal and ceremonial contexts, proverbs in African societies are appreciated for their ancient wisdom, their concise character, and for their poetic, artful qualities. As is characteristic of African and African-derived cultural groups, eloquent speech is highly regarded, and the man or woman who can accurately apply proverbs is applauded.

Both my mother and great-grandmother have always been known for using wise sayings, and seem to have some such expression for any possible situation. Many times my great-grandmother used them as a way of letting us know that in spite of our formal education or our familiarity with the modern and mechanized world, there is another level of knowing that we need to pay attention to. "If it's for you, you'll get it," she'd sometimes say if we became obsessed with a particular goal.

Many parents used similar words to instruct their children, to provide a moral code to which one could adhere. "You reap what you sow," Granny might say, or as my mother once wrote me in a letter, "a word to the wise is sufficient." But we also had special proverbs which brought together our family's history. By using expressions that reflect on certain individuals, the spirits of our ancestors are kept alive; by using expressions that are associated with particular periods of our history, the past is made present.

When I interviewed my great-grandmother and mother, my sister, Angie, and my brother, Levi, joined us as we sat in the livingroom, warmed by the crackling wood stove. The informality and spontaneity that characterized our usual gatherings prevailed. The simple mention of many of the proverbs prompted gales of warm-hearted laughter from my mother and great-grandmother. They laughed not only at the proverbs themselves, but at the memories they brought forth.

: Sewed Up in a Salt Sack[2] :

GRANNY: *That's a saying ah, just like Angie at times, she gets her mother to believe just like all children do. Sometimes they are doing things they don't want their mother to really know they're doing 'em, and they will put off a front. Tell you different things, tell you something different. They won't come right out and say. They're trying to fool you.*

Lots of people say, "She just got her mother sewed up in a salt sack 'cause her mother believe everything she says. She ain't doing nothing but foolin' her to death."
JEAN: *Basically, though, it's somebody taking advantage of you, fooling you.*

: Buying a Pig in a Bag[3] :

JEAN: *Oh, now that is like paying for something you don't see.*
GRANNY: *That's right, you don't know what you're getting until you get home and open it.*
JEAN: *I've heard many older people use that in my growing up, Granny among them. People said that just like, it's used for a lot of expressions, like getting married. People say, "Well he*

Mrs. Abrams, "Granny," on her porch in Hanover County, Virginia, 1979.

certainly bought himself a pig in the bag." It means that he didn't really wait to get to know the woman before he married her. Then once he married her it was like the bag was opened up, and he got to see all of it.
GRANNY: *And he was received.**

: CARRIED HIS DUCKS TO THE MARKET AND GOT A POOR PRICE[4] :

"Buying a pig in a bag" reminded us of this proverbial expression which is used in my family to refer primarily to marital situations. My mother said of this, "That's an old one."

GRANNY: *That's like getting married and getting received. You can get received and the woman can get received. It's on both sides.*
JEAN: *I've used both. All right, say for instance you're going to the market. There was a time everybody carried their wares to the market to sell. All right, you're not exactly selling yourself. But when you are going out to get something you want to get the best for it.*

: GETTING THE BUTTER FROM THE DUCK[5] :

Perhaps because my family kept ducks, there are numerous expressions which utilize the duck imagery. This one is my favorite. My great-grandmother learned it from her mother, and the expression is still used by several relatives. When I asked about it, my mother and great-grandmother burst into

---

* There is evidence that "received" may have been used systematically in place of "deceived" in the Afro-American traditional southern speech, yet how many researchers have "corrected" their informants when transcribing conversation. See Mississippi Fred McDowell, *I Do Not Play No Rock 'n' Roll*, Capitol Records. In the introductory comments on side one, McDowell clearly says, "Your friends will receive you," and yet in the liner notes this segment of his comments is transcribed as "deceive" you.

laughter, mainly because of my well-known, longtime interest in the phrase. I have attempted to use this expression on several occasions, sometimes embarrassing myself by substituting "goose" for "duck." "Dennis is certainly anxious to get that one," my great-grandmother laughed this time.

I first remember my great-grandmother saying this when several of us were splitting wood to take in and keep the next few days' fires going. When my mother had just finished splitting a particularly difficult piece and breathed a deep "whew!," my great-grandmother, who was sitting nearby said, "Boy, that done got all the butter from the duck now!"

JEAN: *You have to realize that a lot of these sayings are interchangeable things. They happen to mean something different to any given situations. I first heard it I think when people were cutting wood, and you come upon a tree that was really hard to get down. You know when he was able to get it down, or whatever the job accomplished, he would say, "I tell you that thing really got the butter from the duck!"*

See the fat on the inside of the duck doesn't come away easy. You can't pull the fat from the duck like you can from a chicken, or the other fowl. I think the older people associated their everyday activities with these animals and what not. It's between the skin and the meat, see? And sometimes you even rip the skin trying to get that fat out of there. But it's so rich and fat it's just like butter. You can use it in cakes and all those kind of things, just like you would use butter.

GRANNY: *Yes, Lord, my momma used to use that one. 'Cause she used to go in the woods and cut wood. And sometimes when she'd get through cuttin' she'd be sweatin' and going on. And she'd have to set down, and she'd say, "Ah Lord, y'all go ahead chillun, that thing done got all the butter from me."*

Although I've never plucked or cooked a duck, this proverb has become a part of my repertoire. It retains a special place in my feelings for several reasons. Besides its poetic appeal, it reminds me of a moment of special warmth and closeness to my mother and great-grandmother. It also links me to my family history, and to experiences of my childhood when ducks and other farm animals were about.

: THE KETTLE CALLING THE POT BLACK, AND THE FRYING PAN STANDING UP FOR WITNESS[6] :

GRANNY: *Momma used to use that at us a many times. If we'd get mad with one another and call somebody black, Momma's say, "Now, where you got the room to call somebody black!? You black too. The kettle calling the pot black now, and the frying pan standing up for witness." Lord! [She laughs.] It was a while before I knew what she was talking about.*

As one might expect, this proverb (which is by no means unique to Afro-America) may sometimes connote the issues of color and status when used by Afro-Americans. When I was growing up, my family always used this proverb strictly for its metaphorical message. Perhaps because of the sensitivity surrounding the race and color issues, I have never used this saying. My mother explained its meaning briefly.

JEAN: *Like people disagreeing and has no right to say the things they're saying, you know. They're in the same boat. So why should you say something about somebody else? And I think you say it more or less out of disgust, you get so tired of hearing 'em say those things, or you feel like they're not justified.*

: A HARD HEAD MAKES A SOFT BEHIND[7] :

JEAN: *Oh Lord, I don't know if children started that or not, but the old folks used to tell us that if they was trying to correct you, and you were going to do it anyway. They'd just warn you by saying, "A hard head make a soft tail."*
GRANNY: *Don't use that much. I used to hear momma say it, especially if you act bully. She didn't only say that to us but she would say it to any child if he didn't listen to her. Like Sarah's children across the road, or John would come here. [These are community members who are now adults who were frequently at my great-great-grandmother's, playing in the yard with other children.] But you know, you can't say it to people's children of this day. You wouldn't dare.*[8]

This proverbial phrase refers of course, to the common practice of spanking children as a disciplinary measure, "soft tail" describing the child's rear end after such punishment.

Both my mother and grandmother indicated that it is used only in reference to children, never adults. Even though I have no children, I still use it metaphorically to describe people of my generation when they are acting hard-headed.

: FOOL WITH TRASH IT'LL GET IN YOUR EYES[9] :

This is one of numerous proverbs in my family which conform to an "If — — —, then — — —" structure. Another is "Play with a puppy and he'll lick your mouth," which generally means that if you become too friendly with certain kinds of people, they will cause you great embarrassment. "Fooling with trash" is close in meaning, but serves as a more serious warning.

GRANNY: *I often heard granddaddy say that about his son. You know, he had been married and he had a son and two daughters. He hadn't heard from Arthur [his son] for years and years, and he say Arthur wrote to him, "Papa, I'd like for you to help me, I'm in trouble."*

He said, "Yes, what you need?" He, "Need some money." So he said he sent him the money. But he wrote him in a letter and told him, "If you hadn't been fooling with that trash you wouldn't got, wouldn't got in that trouble." Say, "You wouldn't listen to me." I hear him say he told him, you was fooling with trash, that's the reason you're in trouble.

Both my great-grandmother and mother agreed that this proverb was used most frequently with children. I have however, heard them use it with people who were not children, at least in age. This may have to do with the way in which older generations in Afro-America traditionally have the social status of elders. In the spirit of this status they might regard anyone of a younger generation as a child, and indeed one is always the child of one's parents. My mother explained it to my seven-year-old sister like this.

JEAN: *Yes, that was a way I guess of teaching your children to learn to pick their associates, understand? It's like "You're known by the company you keep," or "Birds of a feather flock together."*

ANGIE: *Momma, does that mean if you fool around in trash you might find something and you'll get in trouble? Somebody might catch you for finding it?*

JEAN: *You know that trash we pick up for to start the fire and stuff with? Well if you mess around with too much you'll get a piece of it in your eyes. But it also mean that if you mess around with trashy people, people that don't have good ideas and scruples, and things like that, that you'll get in trouble.*

: Lauros Catch Meddlers[10] :

We were talking at Christmas time, with presents lying wrapped beneath our tree. My sister was anxious as most young children this time of year to find out what lay inside the wrappings. This expression had probably been used with her more than usual, and she indicated that she knew it well and understood it.

JEAN: *It's a way of making a child shut up, of evading the issue.*

ANGIE: *When a child wants to know something you won't let the child know!*

GRANNY: *Ah Dennis, Dennis, you know Willie Jones. Willie Jones was a lil' boy you know, and he was working 'round the house. So, my mother was stirring up some, she used to call it sweet bread, just for them to have in the kitchen you know. And he come on in the kitchen.*

Willie: "Aunt Betty what you making?"
Momma: "Lauros catch meddlers."

Well he didn't know, he thought it was so. He went on outdoors, and Phillip's grandfather was the butler at the house there.

Willie: "Uncle Phillip."
Phillip: "What you want Peter?" Used to call him Peter.
Willie: "Is you ever ate Lauros catch meddlers?"
Phillip: "What you talkin' 'bout Peter?"
Willie: "I say Aunt Betty making some Lauros catch meddlers!"
Phillip: "Well, how dey look like?"

At this point everyone broke into laughter. My great-grand-mother has a wonderful way of dramatizing the characters and this line was delivered extremely humorously.

Proverbs have been and continue to be an important part of the oral tradition of my family. Contained in them are reflections of their values, ethics, idiosyncracies, and simultaneously a broader and more universal wit and wisdom. They indicate that Africans in America have remained aware of the enormous power of words, and have used the art of language in shaping a strong and vibrant culture. These few samples of proverbs used in my family reflect the spirit of humor and wisdom which has allowed Afro-Americans to persevere, ultimately scraping "the butter from the duck."

HOW MANY ARE ON OUR SIDE?
Growing Up in Greenwich Village

🖎

Anne Warner

During the forties, in the early years of our married life, my husband Frank and I, and eventually our sons Jeff and Gerret, lived in Greenwich Village—that section of New York City below Fourteenth Street, with Washington Square Park its best-known landmark. More than any other section of the city, the Village has kept its feeling of community. Its streets are filled with old brownstones and eighteenth century red brick townhouses, interspersed with more modern apartment buildings, and with small shops, restaurants, and bookstores. The Village at that time was considered to be the heart of New York's literary and artistic life.

We lived on West Twelfth Street in the ground-floor garden apartment of a brownstone. We had our own front gate, a miniscule front yard with a climbable tree, and even our own backyard. Upstairs, next door, and down the block lived a variety of writers and historians and artists with whom we shared many a pleasant evening, singing old songs and swapping stories.

City life was different then. We used to go away and leave the kitchen door, which opened on the backyard, ajar, so that our cat, manipulating the screen door on his own, could get in or out at will. The front door often was unlocked too. We felt safe in giving our boys the freedom of the neighborhood, and they roamed about on their own by the age of five or so. Gerret was a rover then, exploring a new area every day. He and a friend used to go down to Washington Square, or as far north as Hearn's, the big cut-rate department store on Fourteenth Street, the Village's busy commercial upper boundary, where they would ride the escalator up and down for hours. He excelled in finding treasures in Village trash cans —once, for instance, a beautiful Advent calendar that we still use each Christmas.

Probably the first bit of family folklore concerning the boys has to do with the naming of our elder son, born Jonathan Francis. The week he was born, Frank felt impelled to write a sort of ballad indicating his feelings about the event. Being a southerner, and a collector and singer of folk songs, the first thing he thought of was the ballad about John Henry, the mighty black steel-driving railroad worker. The morning John Henry was born, they say, "the Mississippi River run *up* stream for a hundred and fifty miles." "Jonathan" did not scan, nor fit the black southern speech pattern Frank had in mind, so he took the initials "J. F." and turned them into "Jeff." Bill Benét (William Rose Benét, a neighbor of ours) published the result in his "Phoenix Nest" in the *Saturday Review of Literature* on April 10, 1943, and Jonathan has been Jeff from that day to this.

Well, the mornin' little Jeff was born,
Lord, Lord,
The mornin' little Jeff was born,
Well, New York town swang 'round and 'round
An' the subways run plumb out'n the ground
An' the great big buildin's bowed low down,
On the mornin' little Jeff was born.

On the mornin' little Jeff was born,
Lord, Lord,
On the mornin' little Jeff was born,
Gabriel blowed his trumpet to beat the band,
An' the angels danced 'round hand in hand,
An' the Lord said, "Jeff, you's a natchel man!"
On the mornin' little Jeff was born.

On the mornin' little Jeff was born,
Lord, Lord,
On the mornin' little Jeff was born,
He stretched his legs in the mornin' sun,
An' he said, "Jes' look what the Lord's done done!"
An' he said, "God A'Mighty, I'm your lovin' son."
On the mornin' little Jeff was born.

Gerret and the climbable tree outside our home on West Twelfth Street, 1952.

Before the boys were born—and we were married for a number of years before Jeff's arrival—we began to spend our vacations every summer collecting traditional songs from rural people in out-of-the-way places along the eastern seaboard. I have a couple of dozen notebooks filled with the notes I took on these trips. Keeping a journal, writing down the texts of songs, documenting whatever seemed memorable or noteworthy became, I suppose, a habit. It has long been a habit, I realize, in my own family. Among my many family documents, for instance, I have a long account by my great-great-great-grandfather, the Reverend Gideon Hawley, describing his missionary work with the Indians in the 1750s. I have a journal my mother, Elizabeth Hawley, kept as a young girl in the 1880s during a visit to her grandparents. I have a long-documented history of my father's family, the Lochers, who emigrated from Zurich, Switzerland, in the 1850s, traveling all the way to Sutter's Mill in California. I have innumerable photographs going back for several generations. I am often reminded when this recordkeeping urge comes over me of the White Queen in *Alice Through the Looking Glass*. The king had fallen from the chess table and Alice heard him muttering, "The horror of the moment I shall never forget." "You will," said the queen, "unless you make a memorandum of it."

When the boys came along I began jotting down on scraps of paper things they said which seemed to me unusual and amusing, and eventually I assembled these jottings and copied them into a small spiral notebook. It is not the usual baby book, for it contains no mention of height or weight or first accomplishments, just relevant or interesting comments and observations the children made in those early years. I think of it now as one of my folklore notebooks, as well as an item for the family archives.

Reading it with the perspective of elapsed time, it is clear that many of the boys' sayings were an indication of their effort to assimilate the strange events and inexplicable rules which govern the adult world. These comments are not just bright childish sayings. They all have become, in one way or another, part of our family language, repeated at appropriate moments, referred to by means of a word or just a glance which will recall the incident or the phrase to another family member. There is, I suppose, a sense of pride in sharing these bits of humor and ingenuous wisdom that belong only to us. They tie us together.

At the age of two and a half, Jeff was learning the days of the week. Every morning he would say, "And what day is *this*?" Until one day when I answered "Monday," and he said, "Monday *again!* Does this just go on and on?" We have used that phrase time and again in moments of frustration. It was the first of small Jeff's many remarks which seemed to sum up the human condition.

When Jeff was in the third grade he came home one day and said of a girl in his class, "I just love Sheila. I would like to kiss her. My stomach hurts because I can't!" Thirty years later this phrase lingers in the family's vocabulary and even in the vocabulary of one of Jeff's close friends. Upon seeing a

Visiting with the pigeons in Washington Square Park, 1947.
Gerret is on my right, Jeff on my left.

Christmas card photograph, 1946, at our house on West Twelfth Street. From left to right. Frank's mother, Mabel Preston Warner; me with Gerret on my lap; Jeff with ukelele; Frank with Appalachian wooden banjo. Sullivan the cat tolerates the photographic session.

good-looking woman the friend may turn to Jeff and ask, "Did you bring the Tums?"

Gerret lived more in his imagination, without feeling required to adapt so much to the outside world. He could play games by himself for hours, talking to no one in particular about giants, wolves, witches, crooks, and "ghosties." When he was three I heard him say of one of his characters, "He was speaking Frenchly." That is one of what we came to call "Gerretisms," phrases that the family adopted. After hearing on a record the lugubrious hobo ballad, "May I Sleep in Your Barn Tonight, Mister?" and the verse that begins, "I was back there again this past summer / And they told me my baby had died," Gerret asked reasonably, "Who dyed the baby?" This too became a standard family question.

We have teased him over the years about his overheard comment when he was perhaps four, and was chinning himself on a bar in the backyard: "I have dimples . . . and muscles." "Dimples and muscles" is a useful reminder when anyone in the family is showing a bit of ego.

About this same time Gerret asked a mind-boggling question that has haunted us over the years: "I wonder why no bad people have ever tried to rob this house . . . you know, people on the other side. How many are on our side?" How many, indeed.

I find children are naturally interested in God and in religion—not organized religion, but their own relationship to a supreme being. When Gerret was in first grade he came home one day to announce, "There's a girl in my class who doesn't believe in God How would she like it if I didn't believe in her?" As I was putting Jeff to bed one night when he was two he asked, "Who made me?" I said, "I believe God made you." "Oh," said Jeff, "that was nice of Him." Later some admirer said to him, "I think you are made of sugar." "No," he said, "I'm made of God." One day before his nap he asked me to read him some Bible stories. I thought he was nearly asleep, but when I came to the story of Peter's raising Dorcas from the dead, Jeff took his thumb out of his mouth and observed, "That's a fascinating little drama."

I have mentioned our cat before. His name was Sullivan—he had a twin named Gilbert—and he became a Village character. He would sit outside on the stoop in the morning and people on their way to the subway would stop and talk to him. Some even crossed over from the other side of the street for a friendly word, to which he always responded. If he felt cold, or bored, he would put on a pitiful act of being ejected from hearth and home, and many a passerby, finding the upstairs (parlor floor) entrance more obvious, would climb the stairs and ring our upstairs neighbors' doorbell for him. Sullivan had his name tag, with Frank's name under his, and one day a note arrived addressed to Frank expressing great admiration for his taste in animals and proposing a meeting. It might have been the beginning of a beautiful relationship, if Frank hadn't insisted that I answer the lady's note. Anyway, Sullivan was a bona fide member of the family and a good bit older than Jeff. Friends and even relations sometimes called Jeff "Sullivan" when he was first born—as people, and parents, frequently confuse the names of siblings. So I suppose it wasn't too surprising that as I was tucking Jeff into bed one night he suddenly asked, "Did Sullivan and Gerret really grow in your tummy?" Some years later, when Sullivan died, Gerret wept bitterly and said, "That's two people gone from our house." His grandmother—who was living with us—had died the year before.

One day in the fall of 1949, Frank was away, and while I got our dinner together the boys were taking a bath and playing in the tub. Unwisely, I had let them play with some little glass bottles. Somehow one got broken and fell into the tub, and Gerret leaped up, cutting his foot badly on a fragment.

Sharing secrets under the wings of the eagle at New York's Central Park. Gerret (left) and Jeff (right), 1949.

The first thing I knew they were both out of the tub—Gerret standing there dripping blood, and Jeff, stark naked, running around the room saying over and over, "This is too much for me! This is too much for me!"

I finally calmed Jeff down and bandaged Gerret's foot. Feeling he deserved special attention, Gerret, who wasn't four yet, announced that he wanted some junior baby food for dinner, so I said I would go to the store and get some. I left them looking at the pictures in one of their favorite books, *The Wizard of Oz*. Whether it was a picture of the Wicked Witch of the East, or, as Jeff now says, they looked instead at a "blood-thirsty" comic book, something made them panic and they rushed out in our front yard, barefoot, to look for me. It was now nearly 6:00 P.M. and people were coming home from work—which meant the store was crowded and I had a long wait. Many stopped to tell the boys they would catch cold and should go inside, but they just stood there by the gate calling "Mommy! Mommy!" By this time Gerret's foot began to bleed again. This was once more too much for Jeff, and he started out alone down Twelfth Street to find me. When I came around the corner, there was Jeff coming toward me, barefoot and in pajamas, clutching his toy rifle for protection. Behind him stalked our friend and neighbor George Lord, an apron tied around his middle. He had caught sight of Jeff from his apartment window and decided he ought to get into the act. When we got back we found Gerret upstairs with the Lord children, calmly eating a cookie and listening to a story.

"This is too much for me" has served us well. I particularly remember a letter Jeff wrote us when he was out of college and on active duty with the Navy. One night when his ship was in the South Atlantic he went on deck and was overwhelmed by the unending ocean and the brilliant stars overhead. All he could think of, he said, was "This is too much for me. . . ."

Norman Rockwell's famous *Saturday Evening Post* cover showing a group of youngsters, dressed as cowboys, having a shoot-out, expressed perfectly the cowboy mania which swept the country during the forties. Jeff, in due course Gerret, and all their friends were caught up in it. My mother took Jeff to a cowboy movie at Loew's Sheridan Theatre on Seventh Avenue and Eleventh Street when he was three years old, and he never came off the range until he was ten. He

Battle fatigue. An after-the-range-war candid of Jeff, age six, 1949.

used to go around muttering to no one in particular, "bullets and smoke," and he insisted on our strapping a gun to Gerret's hip when his small brother was still in diapers. When Gerret was reproved for making too much noise one day, he said, "My *west* mommy would like it!"

One facet of Jeff's pragmatism was his insistence that before a game of any kind could be played all details must be correct, especially his own costume. One day he was going to a party at a friend's house, dressed as a cowboy, of course. He found that the only gun he had on hand was a toy World War II .45—not a western type at all. Frank and I had no enthusiasm for buying another gun, until Jeff said in despair, "You might as well try to go dressed as a witch without a broomstick!" We went out and bought the gun.

Both Jeff and Gerret heard music of one kind or another from the time they were born, classical as well as folk music. As soon as we could travel again after the war, they went on collecting trips with us, and very early they began to sing with Frank. When Gerret was three or four, hearing the pots and pans rattling in the kitchen, he said, "You know you can hear a tune in everything if you listen hard. Did you hear the tune in the pans? But you have to listen *hard*."

Gerret at the height of the cowboy era, 1950.

If we are to appreciate the value of family sayings—by children or others—one must "listen hard." They are ephemeral, spoken spontaneously and often without conscious thought, and they are quickly forgotten. Yet, remembered and considered, they illuminate individual characteristics that otherwise might never be realized. Too, they can recall a whole period of family life, as a photograph does but with a different dimension. Remembered, they warm the heart and tie the family together with a sense of recognition of ourselves as a discrete entity. That is why I am glad that I kept these records, even in a somewhat haphazard fashion. I always knew they would be valuable and important to the family later on, as indeed they have been.

One night as I was putting Gerret to bed he said something that made me feel I had been awarded a medal. "Is it fun having children?" he suddenly asked. There were times when, in answer to such a question, I might have said "yes" and times when I might have said "no." But I was amazed and touched by his thoughtfulness, and could only answer with real conviction, "Yes, of course it is." "Well," said Gerret, "it's fun being children, too."

BLESSING THE TIES THAT BIND: Storytelling at Family Festivals

✒

Margaret Yocom

Storytelling has long been a way of life in my Pennsylvania German family. Tales of Grandfather Keck getting kicked by a bull as he walked the stubborn animal back to his father's slaughterhouse in Pottstown, Pennsylvania, and Grandmother Yocom's recitation of how, as a 1908 graduate of the local business college, she left her parents' farm with money her brother loaned her to hunt a job in the big city of Philadelphia are standard fare at family gatherings. My parents, too, tell tales: dad, about growing up on a farm in the 1930s; and mother, of childhood summers in the central Pennsylvania mountains.

Like any family's stories, those of my family highlight the unusual habits, unique talents, fateful accidents, and characteristic sayings and actions of our relatives. Some of the stories document not individual feats, but, by telling about the birth of a child or the first meeting of a husband and wife-to-be, recount how the family in a sense became a family. And always between the tales flows information about the family as it ages, oral history that places the people and events in context.

Often, the stories burst forth unannounced, as a part of everyday conversation. But the finest tale-telling sessions come at those festive times when the whole family gathers together, whether at life-cycle events such as weddings or funerals, or holiday celebrations. Storytelling is an integral part of these festivities, but not necessarily a deliberate one. Rarely does a relative say, "Well, let's talk about some of the things that have happened to us." Rather, one topic of conversation leads to another and without realizing the choice, someone pulls an example out of the past and reminds everyone of how Uncle Dave or Aunt Catherine reacted to a similar situation. Then, the family easily turns to other escapades of Dave and Catherine, or to comparable activities of other relatives.

It is no accident that families tell stories during celebrations for, stimulated by seeing everyone together, storytellers recreate in words the physical gathering that stands before them. Although a story may feature the activities of only one of the relatives present, most family members listen anyway because they enjoy hearing about someone they know or are related to by blood or marriage. Some nod their heads as they hear the oft-told tale, and others who may be hearing the narrative for the first time, form an opinion about the actions of the men and women in the tale. Thus, through the shared memory and participation of all present, the stories convey new information to some, reiterate the familiar to others, and help celebrate the family itself.

Since festivals and celebrations are recurring moments of special significance, junctures that seemingly exist outside of normal time, the day-to-day pattern of family activities halts.[1] Relatives break from work or from pleasures with non-related friends and, laden with food and warnings to behave and be cheerful, come together at an agreed upon location to celebrate or witness a special occasion. Because these are special times, family members often pause and look around at themselves, their growing children, and their aging parents. As they pull out photographs of one another, they ponder the future and reconsider the past. Stories appear, then, because through them relatives can reassess the past and feel able to believe that whatever is yet to happen, the family will be there as it always has been.

Stories also appear at family festivals because relatives see any one celebration as an appropriate and important time for stories about any other. After all, no matter what the event, family celebrations do resemble one another. Whether a birthday party or a funeral reception, the same core of relatives gathers to eat together, bestow gifts on one another, and exchange good wishes. These similarities, then, among all life-cycle events and celebrations—past and present—stimulate family storytelling.

Although storytelling relatives may say they are just "telling lies," their tales told during festive occasions do more than just fritter away the time between dessert and dishwashing. Their tales unite them, teach members about their family heritage, and remind all that they, as parts of one another, should help each other. They also set family members apart from everyone else, emphasizing unique qualities relatives should be proud of and promoting a cohesiveness which comes from such differences with the outside world.

Joyful family life-cycle celebrations, like weddings and all the events that lead up to them, are especially filled with family stories. One Sunday evening, for example, while most of my immediate family finished off their supper and talked about my sister's upcoming wedding, our cousin Scott called to invite my parents, Norman and Betty, to a fifteenth wedding anniversary dinner in honor of Norman's brother, David, and his wife, Marie. "Fifteen years, boy," my brother exclaimed after Scott hung up. "Doesn't seem that long." "Well, look at all that's happened," Betty reminded him. "All your marriages, and their kids. Why, we were married in forty-six and Dave and Fern before us, and then Don and Jean in forty-nine or was it forty-eight."

"It was forty-nine," Grandfather Elmer Keck spoke up. "It might have been forty-nine," seconded Norman. "We were building [this house] in forty-nine. Remember, we hid their car up here so nobody would do anything, but Rufus put Limburger cheese on it. . . ."

"And David," Elmer broke in. "David Fry."

"Imagine that!" Norman turned to his son-in-law, George. "Ugh, that smelly cheese melting all over the car engine. What a mess."

"Yes," Elmer said, "when Donnie got married, what Ruf (Rufus) does, he and David Fry, they bought some Limburger cheese and they put it on the manifolds, smeared it on the manifolds of the car and different parts of it that would heat up at different times as the motor got hotter, you know. And, of course, Donald thought everything was fine. His car started. But the stink of this Limburger cheese as the car heated up — and of course, he couldn't get this off. It had melted; the hotter the car got, the worse it got! And they had put it on the exhaust pipe, on the manifold, and everything else. All over the car! He had this for a long time, and he finally had to get out to clean the car off all over.

"But," Elmer continued, "it all goes back to what they did to Rufus, you know, when he got married. Well, Harold had the wedding, you know, in that old church up there outside of Shireman's town where they had services once a year. So Rufus got married and everything was just hunky-dory; everything was fine. So what we did was: we crossed the wires on his car at the back so when he got in the car to start it, the car wouldn't go. And then we had the exhaust pipe plugged up, you know, so it'd run, but it would go "kaput-kaput" if he would get the wires fixed. So people got out [of the church] and the car wouldn't start. Well, right away he started looking, and he found the wire and got the wires fixed up. But he got in the car, and it wouldn't go again. And, of course, he got out again and got to working. They lost a lot of time. They wanted to get going, you know. He finally got it started, but it took another hour and a half, two hours. So, of course, Donnie knew about this."

"You talk about things — the worst I ever knew was a trick they played on Wilmer, my cousin. Did I ever tell you that? Well, Wilmer had his house bought at 22 West Fifth Street. He had the house all furnished and everything, and he went away on his honeymoon with Stelletta. Well, Wilmer had it coming to him because he had played tricks on Elmer Breuninger, his brother-in-law, and Harve, Elmer's brother. So they decided that they would fix Wilmer when he got married. They didn't do anything to him right after he got married. But, when he went on his honeymoon, they got the keys to the house, and they put the upstairs downstairs, and the downstairs upstairs. Everything upstairs and the bedroom, downstairs! The only thing they couldn't change were the bathrooms. And they had signs up: 'Milkman stopped here,' 'Baker stopped here,' 'Butcher stopped in.' They had them all over the house, on the outside. And when Stelletta came home and saw it, she just sat down and cried."

"Did they help Wilmer move it back?"

Storytelling at family festivals: Marie Yocom delights the family at a fiftieth wedding anniversary celebration.

"Oh, no. Oh, heck no. No, they didn't lift a finger!"

"But wasn't he sore at them?"

"What could he do? He had played tricks on these others. I guess Wilmer figured that if you gave it out, you had to take it." [2]

Although storytellers and their tales of family antics may at first seem more fitted to joyous family life-cycle events, it is actually during moves from a homeplace, funerals, and other family crises that family stories seem most needed and, in the end, quite appropriate to both tellers and listeners. Family stories and history buoyed up the Yocom-Keck family when, in the spring of 1976, the home of Grandmother and Grandfather Yocom, so often the gathering place for the family, was sold and its contents put up for auction. Grandfather Isaac, because of illness, had moved to a nursing home and Grandmother Bertha went to live next door with her daughter Gladys and family. The auctioneer's sign went up on the front lawn in early May; and Bertha, preparing to sell most of the goods she used during her life as a farm wife and mother, walked back and forth from her house to Gladys' trying to give away her most prized possessions before the auctioneer's gavel put them in the hands of some stranger.

Storytelling at auction time: Bertha Yocom talks as she prepares household goods for sale.

In anticipation of the sale, everything was laid out on tables. Kitchen utensils spilled off the table and into the boxes on the floor: dishes, vases, plates, and silverware filled every inch of the dining-room table; sofas, benches, and chairs of all sizes littered the livingroom; and boxes of books, bedding, and mementos stood like silent sentries over the stone house on Yocom Road. "Did you see the sign for the auction?" Bertha pointed to the front yard:

"Your daddy put it up the other day. Oh, I never appreciated the house enough when I lived there. I never appreciated the farmhouse either, but when I had to leave, I was so worked up—and weak—that the girls did all the packing for me. I just couldn't do it. You know I'm not going to the sale, are you?"

Remembering that previous move and seeing many of the possessions spread before her, Bertha shared much family history with me, which I recorded in my journal. As we entered the livingroom, she mentioned,

"This couch! It's so good, so sturdy. You see, the nurse slept on this when Grandpop Yocom [great-grandfather Albert] was sick, and then, for grandmom. It's a shame that no one can take it." On the couch lay a brown woolen scarf. "Oh, this muffler! You know, it saved Oscar's [Bertha's brother's] life! One day —bitter cold—he was coming back from the city with friends. It was a car with no top. He would have frozen to death if it hadn't have been for the scarf. Imagine! This scarf!! Can you use it?"

Up the stairs to the second floor she went, leaving one of her two canes behind. In the hallway she opened up a few small boxes lying on the day couch. "Look here, Peggy," she called. One box had several quilting patterns, flax, and lead vices for a quilting frame. "Why, these must be Grandma Yocom's. I wonder where the quilt frame is? Here, take these. Do you want them?"

She walked over to the old hatboxes: "Oh, here's Grandmom Yocom's fox [stole]; she always wore these." From a trunk she took a linen tablecloth and gave it to me: "Here, it's nine feet long; you can cut it. Grandmom Yocom gave this to me. Once I took care of them when they were sick; they wanted to give me

*money, but I wouldn't take it. So she gave me this. I always
used it with my best china."*[3]

Although an emotionally difficult event, the auction gave
birth to a humorous family story, as several relatives wit-
nessed a memorable event and reported it to family members.
I recorded it in my journal as follows:

*Just after Aunt Edie bought a white steel cabinet, she saw auc-
tioneer Victor Rhoads hold up a pair of brown riding boots she
wore as a girl. No one would bid even a quarter. "What about a
quarter?" Vic thundered. "A quarter?" But no one would bid
even that. Edie jumped up: "For a quarter, I'll take them!" As
she ran forward to get them, her two brothers laughed. "For a
quarter!" she exclaimed later. "Why they're good, yet. Look at
the leather. I couldn't see my boots going to somebody who
couldn't wear them anyway!"*

*Similarly, toward the very end of the sale, my father Nor-
man reached for an old rubber baby doll among the litter of
items on one remaining shelf of things to buy. His sister Gladys
caught his hand: "Oh, that thing. Don't sell that!" "No, put it
up," his brother Dave advised. "I saw some people eyeing it a
while back." As the doll went up for sale, Norman whispered to
me, "Why Pop used that doll; he tied it in the cherry tree to
keep away birds." And the auctioneer who had just sold a rock
for a dime, sold the rubber baby doll, too.*

*Family members immediately fashioned these two events
into stories. After the sale when my father and I visited Grandfather Isaac, Norman said that the sale had gone well and,
smiling, he told Isaac about Edie and her boots and about the
doll. "That and the doll were the best," Norman repeated.
"You know, that doll brought a dollar seventy-five!"*[4]

Norman told the stories not only to his father, but to his
father-in-law and his children, even though they were all at
the sale and had seen Edie buy back her own boots. Grandmother and Grandfather Yocom did not want to talk much
about the sale, but they did enjoy the stories. After all, they
confirmed that the sale had gone well: if someone was fool
enough to buy a twenty-year-old dry and cracked rubber doll,
surely the best furniture brought a good price. Also, the objects themselves brought back memories of a cherished past

on the farm when they were young and the children were home.

Although the story of the doll was great fun during and immediately after the sale, it is the story of Edie's boots that family members still tell more frequently. Perhaps it owes its life to a kind of tension: just as the auction mingled the joy of family fellowship and the antics of the auctioneer with the sorrow of the death of a homestead, so the story fuses the apparent silliness of buying back your own boots with the sober awareness that you had to do it before strangers walked off with your own past.

A new family story begins: Edie Yocom buys back her own boots at the family auction.

Like the death of a homestead, the death of a family member also brings relatives together to comfort one another and to rejoice in the family bonds that remain. Unlike other celebrations, funerals impart a sense of urgency to their storytellers, for here the sorrowers especially need to feel family about them. And storytelling, which may last from the moment relatives hear about the death until long after the funeral reception, brings family members close together. Even in the midst of such solemnity, there is laughter, at least at Keck funerals.

One Saturday afternoon in early June as I visited with Grandmother Louisa and Grandfather Elmer Keck, we were talking about Elmer's brother Dan, when the phone rang.

Immediately after he hung up the receiver, Elmer told us that his first cousin Bessie Keck Klein had died. Once again I recorded the conversation in my journal:

"Her father," Elmer explained to me, "was Jonathan Keck, my uncle. So she is your cousin. I've got to go call a few people."

Elmer spread the news to several branches of the family. He called his first cousin Leidy Gaugler; then he talked to another cousin, Mary Hipple. He also called his sister Martha long distance. When Leidy and Elmer made plans to go to the funeral together, I asked if I could go along. Elmer quickly agreed. "It would be nice for you to see the relatives you haven't seen in a long time," Louisa smiled.

Three days later, Leidy and his Chevrolet pulled up in front of Elmer and Louisa's. Elmer, his black suit, white shirt, and red tie freshly cleaned and brushed, and I hopped in the car.

After he and Leidy discussed the best way to travel the twenty miles to Lutz's Funeral Home in Reading, we left. Leidy, just back from visiting his son David in California, talked of his two grandchildren there and how old they were. "I have five brothers and sisters," Elmer replies, "and do you know how I remember their ages? Simple. 3–3–5–3–3. Alan was born in 1890, me in ninety-three, Rufus in ninety-six, Dan in 1901, Mim in 1904, and Martha in nineteen aught-seven."

As we eased into the parking lot, Elmer pointed, "Oh, there's Mary and Elwood [Hipple] and Sadie and Harold [Ziegenfus; Elmer's first cousins]." As we talked about the last time we saw each other at the Keck reunion several years back, Elmer herded us all inside. There among the brocade and velvet drapes and the thick maroon carpet stood Mildred, Bessie's daughter. "Well, Mildred, you're looking good. How's your leg?" Elmer laughed and clasped everyone's hand. Then, after some words of comfort to Mildred and her husband Dick, Elmer and I viewed Bessie, her white hair and pink skin in stark contrast to the shiny satin lining of the bed-like coffin.

As we signed the guest register, Elmer asked me, "Do you know? All the family is represented: me from David (Elmer's father), Bessie from John, Leidy from Cora, Sadie from Emma, and Mary from Hen (Henry)." During the day, he told this fact to several people, including Betty, his daughter, when we got home.

As we sat down in the second section of seats, Harold Ziegenfus walked over, pulled a bedraggled piece of newsprint from his wallet, and stuck it in front of Elmer's face. Elmer read it, a "One Hundred Years Ago" column from the Reading Eagle, *about William Keck and Dutch Liz who, in 1871, were arrested for keeping a "disorderly house." As Elmer laughed, Harold winked, "Black sheep of the family, say Elmer?" The clipping traveled through several more hands until the minister walked to a small lectern.[5]*

After the service, the funeral men closed the coffin and called for the pallbearers. "That's Dick's son," Elmer whispered as the men filed by, "and that's an intended bridegroom."

The car was hot as we climbed in for the trip to Forest Hills Cemetery. "Boy, this reminds me of something that happened to Uncle Bill when we were out on the farm," Elmer said as he turned to Leidy. "It was a hot, hot day; and he was up in the hayloft. All of a sudden he fell out and landed in a big pile of hay, underneath. In a minute or so, he dug himself out, and said, 'Bissel kiel heit!' (Little cool today)."

As we all laughed, Elmer observed that Bill and other Kecks like to joke. "Once," Elmer continued, "Bill tried to play a joke on me with a horse, but the horse kicked him instead. And one day a cousin of mine came over, and Dad told him, 'Bumblebees don't sting today.' So he picked up a bee and got stung. Boy, did Mom yell at Dad. Yes, we Kecks had a lot of capers; but you know, it was all good fun. You remember the good times we had with that Grafanola in the front room?"

Leidy laughed as we drove on, closer and closer to the burial site.

Celebrating life-cycle events and holidays often sets the stage for family storytelling. And anyone who would like to collect family tales and history would do well to watch for and collect during such settings.

Although these many narratives provide much family history, a collector would be wrong to see the tales only as enjoyable efforts at keeping the past alive. Tales are not told simply to jar our memories. A bride and bridegroom do not forget the tricks a cousin pulled at their wedding. A mother hardly needs to be reminded where her children were when she gave birth to her youngest. And relatives do not forget especially embarrassing childhood incidents. Such tales are, rather, the sound of a family very much in the present celebrating, renewing, and reestablishing itself through its stories.

How to Collect Your Own Family Folklore

We hope that the stories, photographs, and accounts of traditions in this book have inspired readers to collect the folklore of their own families. But where do you start? Through the years we have developed some guidelines, which may be adapted to your own needs and circumstances. You might want to get started before the inspiration slips away, and even to jot down some of the stories and traditions this book has brought to mind.

Before you begin. Because family folklore belongs to a living family, it is constantly evolving. Each generation will forget and alter the lore that it has received; on the other hand, that same generation will add new verbal lore and new traditions. This creative aspect of family folklore affects the researcher in several ways. First, no matter how hard you try, you will never record the entire body of your family's folklore since there will never be a time in which it will be totally static. Don't despair. Get down what you can and encourage other family members to do the same. Just think of collecting family folklore as a pastime for which you have an infinite supply of raw material close at hand.

Second, think about your time orientation. The family folklorist cannot be so absorbed in preserving the past that he neglects to record the present. Keep your eyes, ears, and mind open. A tradition does not have to be old to be worth recording. In fact, a good part of any family's tradition is ephemeral and may not last long enough to pass from one generation to another. Collecting family folklore is one case in which too much is better than too little. Tapes can be edited and transcripts can be discarded, but the tradition, story, or expression that you neglect to record today may be lost.

Finally, remember that family folklore exists as part of the day-to-day living of a family, changing and moving with that family. To separate it abruptly from this natural context would rob it of its vitality and its existence as folklore. It is essential to remember that the story itself—including where, when, and how it is told—is as important as the information it conveys. This is the essential distinction between family folklore and the closely related disciplines of genealogy and family history. The following suggestions are designed to help you focus on these folkloric aspects of your family.

As self-appointed family folklorist you now have two tasks ahead of you: to learn your family's folklore and to record it for others to enjoy.

The equipment. Note-taking and tape recording are the usual means of recording family folklore. The tape recorder is the means of choice. Writing during an interview or family event has a number of disadvantages. Most people find note-taking to be both tedious and difficult. It is hard to maintain a conversation or participate actively in the ongoing activities, especially since you can't look at your subject. A complete, accurate account of the story — especially if it is long and detailed — is difficult to obtain. Although the words may be written down, the subtleties of the performance are inevitably lost.

Although both you and your informant might be uneasy and uncomfortable with a tape recorder, you'll probably soon get accustomed to its presence. A small cassette machine with a separate omni-directional microphone will give good results. It is easy to use and so inconspicuous that its presence will soon be forgotten. A sixty-minute cassette (30 minutes per side) is a good choice since it is economical, unlikely to tangle, and long enough to record substantial segments of an interview without interruption.

The microphone should be placed so that all voices, including yours, can be picked up. Run a test before you begin the actual interview and adjust the machine accordingly. The end of a two-hour interview is no time to discover that the volume control was too low! Read carefully any instructions that come with the particular tape recorder you are using.

As far as possible all extraneous noise should be eliminated. Turn off the radio, close the window, move away from the window fan. A few minutes spent finding the proper spot for the tape recorder can save you many hours when it comes time to transcribe the interview and you struggle to distinguish grandma's voice from the roar of a passing truck. The recorder should also be placed where it will not be disturbed during the interview and where you will have easy access to it when it becomes necessary to change tapes.

Although not as essential as a tape recorder, a camera is a useful piece of equipment. It provides a visual record of the

Four generations of one family. From left to right. Brady Dickerson, Katie Dickerson Greene, Mildred L. Henderson Maiden, and in the center, Beverly J. Robinson, as a baby.

interview and the informant. It can also be used to copy any documentary records that the informant might offer, such as letters or scrapbooks.

Family tape recordings and photographs that are worth collecting are also worth preserving. Although professional archival techniques are rather elaborate for home use, some simple, commonsense measures will enable future generations to enjoy your research efforts. Heat, humidity, and light, especially sunlight, are the principle causes of deterioration of tapes, photos, paper, and other artifacts. Storing material in a damp basement or a hot, unventilated attic is not recommended. In fact, people and research materials do best in about the same environment—a temperature between sixty to seventy degrees farenheit and a relative humidity of fifty percent. If you're comfortable, your research material is probably safe. The problem of light is more difficult, especially for photographs which are often displayed under damaging conditions. The best solution is to display only copies, keeping the originals in albums and boxes.

At the present time, you can't assume that color photographs and slide transparencies will be permanent images. Black and white copies should be made of those photographs that you wish to preserve indefinitely. Most commercial photographers can provide this service, but it is possible for an amateur to do an adequate job at home. Thomas L. Davies gives detailed descriptions of simple home copying methods in *Shoots: A Guide to Your Family's Photographic Heritage* (Addison House: Danbury, NH, 1977). For best results, the black and white film should be archivally processed, that is, thoroughly washed at the time of developing to remove any residual chemicals that could eventually damage the film. Again, both professional photo labs and the family photographer who processes his own film can perform this essential step. Acid-free file folders, photo albums, scrapbooks, and storage boxes are available from office and library supply companies and are worth the extra cost because of the added protection they provide.

The people. With whom should you start? Your oldest relative? The one you feel most at ease with? No. The place to begin is with yourself. You are just as much a bearer of your family's traditions as any member of your family. Use yourself as an informant and ask yourself the questions that follow on pages 269–71. You may be surprised at how much you know about some areas and how little about others. It is very likely that you will know more about one side of the family than another, for instance. Once you have collected family folklore from yourself, use your answers as a starting point for questioning other family members. Try to remember family structure. Who are your relatives? Which ones are most likely to have information and be willing to share it? Who gets along with whom? What topics are likely to be sensitive? These are all essential questions that you have to tackle yourself, first.

The first outside person that you interview should be someone with whom you feel very comfortable. Interviewing is not easy and you would do well to get your introduction to it in the presence of a friendly face. A parent or sibling might be a good choice. Young children often have great success with grandparents.

As you continue your interviewing you will pick up clues that will help you find potential narrators: "You should talk to Uncle Joe about that," or "Aunt Jane is a much better story-

M. A. LEARY

CAROLYN MITCHELL

teller than I am." Whenever possible ask directly for sources: "Can you tell me who might know more about that?" As you become more and more involved with the search you will meet relatives that you never even knew you had! Don't neglect non-relatives, either. Your grandfather's best friend may be able to tell you things about him that no family member would know. Don't overlook other members of the household who were not relatives, such as nursemaids or longterm boarders. Try not to be misled by terms of address. Aunt, uncle, sister, brother, and cousin are especially troublesome words since they can indicate respect, affection, and brotherhood as easily as blood or marriage relationships. And although they won't be much help as sources of information on family folklore, don't forget family pets since they can frequently be found as characters in family stories.

The interview. The most productive family folklore interviews are those that take place in a natural context for the reasons explained at the beginning of this guide: family folklore is a living part of a family and cannot be successfully separated from the everyday activities of that family. This can present problems since it will be impossible for you to be present during every naturally occurring folkloric event. You should make use of such opportunities whenever possible, however. Some common natural contexts are family dinners, picnics, reunions, and holidays. These are the times at which families would tell stories whether or not you are there with your tape recorder. Under these circumstances you will probably not even have to conduct an interview — just adjust the recorder, relax, and participate as you would ordinarily.

If no spontaneous natural context seems to be available you will have to rely on what is called an induced natural context. The distinction is straightforward. Instead of waiting for a family dinner to occur in the normal course of events, you initiate one. This approach has the added advantage of giving you a degree of control over the situation. For example, you can invite specific relatives who interact well with each other. Try serving foods that you know will bring back memories from the past.

The group interview context, whether natural or induced, has one major characteristic that makes it extremely fruitful.

The interaction that occurs as a matter of course serves to spark the memories of the participants. One story leads into another, one interpretation elicits cries of "but that's not really the way it happened at all!" The end result of such an interview will differ greatly from private interviews with the same relatives.

Private interviews can also be either natural or induced. If grandma begins to talk to you about her journey to this country while you are washing the supper dishes, fine—unfortunately, you probably won't be prepared with a tape recorder. If you wish to privately interview a relative, try not to do so under formal circumstances. Suggest some activity that will allow you to maintain a conversation easily but will help keep the session natural and low key: going for a walk, sewing, baking. If you know beforehand that a particular activity is usually a time for storytelling, schedule your interview to coincide with that event. Familiar surroundings and routine activities will also help to distract the informant from the fact that he or she is being interviewed and will lessen the unsettling impact of the tape recorder.

Every interview that you do will be unique. The questions on pages 269–71 will supply some uniformity, although you will probably be selective in using them. These brief suggestions should be helpful in most circumstances.

1. Start with a question or a topic that you know will elicit a full reply from your subject, such as a story you have heard him tell in the past. This will give your relative confidence in his ability to contribute something of value to your collection.

2. Avoid generalities. "Tell me about your childhood," for instance, often elicits nothing more than a list of names and dates.

3. Ask evocative questions. Nothing can kill an interview faster than a long series of questions that require only yes or no as answers.

4. Face up to the fact that there will be some information that you will not get. You may be the wrong sex or age. A relative may simply not trust you with sensitive data. If you feel you must have the missing material you may be able to solicit the help of another relative or friend as an interviewer.

5. Be aware that role switching will occur. You have changed from a son or daughter to an interrogator. Both you and your informant may feel uneasy in these new roles. A low-key approach in a natural setting should help relieve some of the discomfort.

6. Show interest. Encourage your informants as much as possible. Interject remarks whenever appropriate. Take an active part in the conversation without dominating it. Learn to be a creative listener as well as a good questioner.

7. Know what questions you want to ask, but don't be afraid to let your informant go off on a tangent. He or she might just touch on subjects of interest that you never thought to ask about.

8. Never turn off the tape recorder unless asked to. Not only does it break the conversation, such action suggests that you think some of your informant's material is not worth recording.

9. Use props whenever possible. Documents, letters, photo albums, scrapbooks, home movies, and other family heirlooms can all be profitably used to stimulate memories.

10. Be sensitive to the needs of family members. Schedule your sessions at a convenient time. Older people tire easily; cut the interview off at the first sign of fatigue. Don't slight

SUSAN MITCHELL

family members who show interest in your project. Interview them, even if you have reason to believe their material will be of minimal value.

11. If possible, prepare some sort of written report for the family as a tangible result of their participation. Remember to save all of your tapes, notes, and any other documentation that you have accumulated. Label everything with names, dates, and places. Ideally, all tapes should be indexed and transcribed as soon as possible after the interview. You will be more conscientious about documentation if you place yourself in the position of your great-grandchild who, many decades in the future, will be using your project as a source for his reconstruction.

12. Before publishing diaries, memoirs, letters, or other written artifacts, you would be wise to find out about copyright regulations. For example, the writer of a letter owns the copyright, not the recipient nor the present owner of the letter. The same principle holds true for tape-recorded oral history and folklore—the speaker, not the tape owner, holds all rights to his material. Most family members will gladly allow you to make use of whatever resources you need for documenting the family's traditions, but it never hurts to be prepared with copyright information. The Copyright Office at the Library of Congress will send a packet of information upon request (Copyright Office, Library of Congress, Washington, D.C. 20560.)

A question of ethics. Most of your relatives will be delighted by your new-found interest in collecting family folklore. Some will undoubtedly wonder if you've gone slightly mad. Unfortunately, a few may be uncooperative and even hostile. Because of the personal nature of the folklore that you will be collecting, you should be very careful to protect the privacy and rights of all family members. Be honest about your intent from the very beginning. Explain your reasons for doing the research. Is it a school assignment? Do you simply want to learn more about your family? Do you plan to publish your findings? The ultimate disposition of the collection may affect their willingness to talk about certain subjects.

You may find it difficult to explain what family folklore is and why you want to record it. Your relatives will most likely equate your research with genealogy and family history. No harm will be done if you explain your research in those terms since the areas are so interrelated. Showing them books like this may help, too.

Don't make promises you can't or don't indend to keep. If you say you will erase part of a tape, do so, even if it means losing some important information. Respect confidences and privacy. Let your informants see anything that will be published before it is too late to alter the manuscript. Although the intimate nature of family folklore places restrictive and sometimes frustrating burdens on the researcher, the bulk of your collection will probably be non-controversial.

Finally, never record secretly. There is no justification for dishonesty and the bad feelings within the family that may result.

One last word. Please do not be discouraged by all the dos and don'ts that we have suggested. Once you have begun collecting your own family's folklore you will realize that the guidelines are based on commonsense and lots of practice. Vary them to suit your own family circumstances. Improve them with our blessing and encouragement. And above all, enjoy yourself, your family, and your folklore.

A possible questionnaire. Every family is unique. Every folklore fieldworker has his or her own special interests and style of interviewing. Because of this diversity, no single set of questions will successfully elicit folklore from all families. The most useful questions will be those that you develop through knowledge of yourself and your family. For your initial efforts the following questions may be helpful. Just remember that they are meant to be suggestive, not absolute. Pick and choose among them as you see fit. By all means change the wording to suit your own situation and personality.

1. What do you know about your family surname? Its origin? Its meaning? Did it undergo change coming from the old country to the United States? Are there stories about the change?

2. Are there any traditional first names, middle names, or nicknames in your family? Is there a naming tradition, such as always giving the firstborn son the name of his paternal grandfather?

3. Can you sort out the traditions in your current family according to the branches of the larger family from which they have come? Does the overall tradition of a specific grandparent seem to be dominant?

4. What stories have come down to you about your parents? Grandparents? More distant ancestors? How have these relatives described their lives to you? What have you learned from them about their childhood, adolescence, schooling, marriage, work, religion, political activity, recreation? Are they anxious or reluctant to discuss the past? Do their memories tend to cluster about certain topics or time periods and avoid others? Are there certain things in your family history that you would like to know, but no one will tell you? Do various relatives tell the same stories in different ways? How do these versions differ?

5. Do you have a notorious or infamous character in your family's past? Do you relish stories about him/her? Do you feel that the infamy of the ancestor may have grown as stories passed down about him/her have been elaborated?

6. How did your parents, grandparents, and other relatives come to meet and marry? Are there family stories of lost love, jilted brides, unusual courtships, arranged marriages, elopements, runaway lovers?

7. Have any historical events affected your family? For example, how did your family survive the Depression? Did conflict over some national event such as the Civil War or Vietnam cause a serious break in family relationships?

8. Are there any stories in your family about how a great fortune was lost or almost (but not quite) made? Do you believe them? Are these incidents laughed about or deeply regretted? If a fortune was made, who was responsible and how was it achieved?

9. What expressions are used in your family? Did they come from specific incidents? Are there stories which explain their origin? Is a particular member of the family especially adept at creating expressions?

10. How are holidays celebrated in your family? What holidays are most important—national, religious, or family? What innovations has your family made in holiday celebrations? Has your family created entirely new holidays?

11. Does your family hold reunions? How often? When? Where? Who is invited? Who comes? Who are the organizers and hosts? What occurs during the reunion? Are there traditional foods, customs, activities? Are stories and photographs exchanged? Are records (oral, written, visual) kept? By whom?

12. Have any recipes been preserved in your family from past generations? What was their origin? How were they passed down—by word of mouth, by observation, by written recipes? Are they still in use today? When? By whom? Does grandmother's apple pie taste as good now that it's made by her granddaughter?

13. What other people (friends, household help, etc.) have been incorporated into your family? When? Why? Were these people given family title such as aunt or cousin? Did they participate fully in family activities?

14. Is there a family cemetery or burial plot? Who is buried with whom? Why? Who makes burial place decisions? If there are gravemarkers, what type of information is recorded on them?

15. Does your family have any heirlooms, objects of sentimental or monetary value that have been handed down? What are they? Are there stories connected with them? Do you know their origin and line of passage through the generations? If they pass to you, will you continue the tradition, sell the objects, or give them to museums?

16. Does your family have photo albums, scrapbooks, slides, home movies? Who created them? Whose pictures are contained in them? Whose responsibility is their upkeep? When are they displayed? To whom? Are they specially arranged and edited? Does their appearance elicit commentary? What kind? By whom? Is the showing of these images a happy occasion?

* We would like to thank Margaret Yocom, who co-authored this section.

Appendix

❧ THE FAMILY FOLKLORE PROGRAM

On the broad lawns surrounding the Washington Monument, a tent city emerges each year, the temporary home for musicians and craftspeople transported to Washington to participate in the Smithsonian Institution's annual Festival of American Folklife. Begun in 1966 as a simple Fourth of July weekend celebration, the festival, now two weeks in duration, highlights the folk culture of America's diverse ethnic, regional, and occupational groups.

The festival is both a huge national pageant and a curiously intimate event. Amid the myriad performance stages and exhibition tents, there is always the opportunity for visitors to speak personally to Navajo dancers, D.C. cab drivers, Appalachian quilters, and regional cooks. It is hoped that each visitor will be able to find at least one event which serves as a link with his own heritage. Staged in the nation's capital, within sight of the White House, and the Jefferson and Lincoln Memorials, the festival serves to legitimize and celebrate individual Americans and their traditions.

The Family Folklore Program, established in 1974, was simultaneously a logical extension of this personalized approach and a reversal of the festival's traditional format. For the first time, visitors who came to enjoy an afternoon of performances suddenly found themselves performing the stories and traditions which had been passed down in their own families. On an immediate level, we wanted to make festival-goers aware that they, like the Cajun fiddlers and the Appalachian balladeers, were bearers of unique folkways. Our long-range goal was to begin study of the family group as a folk culture with its own corpus of tales, expressions, and other creative forms by which to celebrate and perpetuate a shared heritage.

All this was fine in theory, but as we set up our modest tent that first year, we wondered whether a few card tables, cassette tape recorders, and the avid interest of five folklorists would be enough to draw people away from rousing bluegrass music and colorful ethnic dancing. Somehow, the tent, sparsely decorated with patterned tablecloths, a few photos scavenged from second-hand shops, and a hopeful sign reading "Family Folklore—Will You Share Yours With Us?" drew a steady stream of visitors from the first day on.

In some ways, the festival was a truly unorthodox place to collect such private material. Far removed from the dining-room table, the front porch, and the holiday celebrations at which stories and traditions naturally unfold, informants were asked to share the details of their lives in an open tent abutting Native American dancers and capped with the steady drone of jet planes on approach to National Airport. Yet, there were many unforseen advantages in collecting in this atmosphere.

Far from being a distraction, the other events at the festival seemed to inspire our informants. Everything from ethnic foods to regional music elicited reminiscences and stories. We were able to capitalize on perhaps long-dormant memories brought to mind by familiar smells, sights, and sounds. For many visitors, the festival was also part of a summer holiday or an extended family vacation. Not only did they bring their children on this outing, but their older relatives "visiting from Utah." With the extended family in tow, our tent became a comfortable place to exchange family stories.

In the tent, we tried to create, metaphorically, a feeling of family life. Using kitchen tablecloths was one simple device for suggesting a home-like atmosphere. Another more powerful stimulus was our small display of family photos. Seeking only to create a homey ambience, we did not realize at first the ability of photos to bring forth family stories; nor did we know then that home photography constituted a distinct and legitimate genre of family lore. Yet, the reaction to the photos was so profound that within the first few days of interviewing, our understanding of the forms of family folklore unexpectedly broadened.

After the 1974 festival closed, we placed a single ad in the *Washington Post Magazine* asking local residents to lend us their photos, albums, and home movies. The response was overwhelming. Within two weeks, we had received hundreds of letters from people offering their most treasured collections. One hundred families were invited to lend their materials for research and exhibition. From these, we produced elaborate photo displays detailing common themes in home photography. We also produced "Home Movie," a composite film exploring the dreamy visions of family life created by family cinematographers.

Visitors to the 1975 and 1976 festivals found that our tent, much like parts of the Smithsonian museums, had begun to resemble an attic. It overflowed not only with photos, but with quilts, stitched pictures, diaries, poems, and even a "junk drawer" filled with trinkets whose nostalgic associations made them impossible to throw out. Two collections of stories recorded at previous festivals were offered for sale, and in 1976, "Harmonize," a new film based on traditions related to us by five local families, was shown continuously with "Home Movie" in an adjacent tent. Perhaps one of the chief beauties of this project was the way in which informants contributed to our understanding of family folklore. By interpreting their recollections in exhibitions, films, and publications, we, in turn, were able to enhance the educational value of the project and to provide additional stimuli for our informants in the years that followed.

The family folklore interviewing tent attracted an intelligent and self-conscious group of informants, as did the festival itself. About eighty percent were white-collar workers, with an emphasis on teachers, social workers, doctors, and lawyers. Seventy-five percent of those interviewed were living in the Washington, D.C., area, although most of these had grown up in other cities and were not here permanently. Overall, the sample is biased towards the large cities on the east coast and the south. The interviews attracted a disproportionate number of Jews, about thirty percent of the interviews, and Italians, about ten percent. Other significant ethnic groups were Irish, Germans, and Scandinavians. White Anglo-Saxon Protestants were also well-represented. Although the percentage of interviews with black Americans was small, we conducted about forty interviews with members of Afro-American families in the tent.

A common topic of conversation among our staff involved speculation on why so many Russian Jews and Italians chose to be interviewed. Were these groups simply overrepresented in the festival audience? Are these ethnic groups particularly self-conscious, verbal, or family-oriented? We came to no conclusions, but some simple immigration statistics may offer clues.

In the so-called second wave of immigrations, from 1901–1910, a million and a half persons immigrated from Russia and over two million from Italy. This is next only to Hungary and represents the largest groups ever to immigrate to this country in so short a period of time. Those young people who came to America during this time now had grandchildren in their late twenties, many of them still living in the eastern seaboard cities where their grandparents disembarked. Sociologists have long noted the trend of third-generation Americans to take a strong interest in their family origins, which may explain the interest of young Italians and Jews in being interviewed by us. Perhaps it is not coincidental that over three years, seven of our sixteen interviewers were also third-generation Russian Jews.

The fact that our interviewers (most were graduate students in the Department of Folklore and Folklife at the University of Pennsylvania) like our informants were middle class made rapport-building relatively easy. Unlike the folklorist working with more traditional, isolated groups, interviewers and their subjects had much in common. Some of the folklorists even found that an effective technique of eliciting stories and expressions was to share similar ones of their own. Yet, the interviewing situation had some built-in distance that also worked in our favor. We were strangers, but as strangers we were not involved in family feuds or factionalism. Often, informants noted that they were talking to us more freely than they might to their own kinfolk. We were also representing the Smithsonian Institution, and our informants took a certain measure of pride in knowing that the interview tapes would be preserved in the institution's archives.

The interviews were open-ended and lasted an average of twenty minutes each. Many interviews, however, lasted an hour or more. As many as fifty informants returned to be interviewed again, often bringing the family "historian" or raconteur with them. The folklorists had a long list of questions from which to choose (see the Interviewing Guide, pp. 269), but most often, individual interviews tended to focus on one or two areas of folklore, depending on the interests of informants. Besides questions dealing with specific genres of folklore, we asked very general questions such as "What other means does your family use to preserve its past?" The answers to these questions were extremely valuable to us in increasing our understanding of family lore.

Over three summers, we taped interviews with nearly two thousand family members, making this collection perhaps the largest body of such material to have been recorded at this time. Yet we cannot claim that the tapes provide a full and accurate sampling of American family lore. Instead, this collection represents what a self-selected group of informants decided to share with us at an outdoor celebration. It does not necessarily represent Americans as a whole, nor does it touch as deeply as it might on the pathos of family life. The tone of the festival, and of our tent, was decidedly upbeat. And our visitors, however candid in their conversation, related traditions and thoughts which in large part affirmed family life.

For all the stimulation it provided, our tent was quite different from a home where folklore functions in a natural context. Folklore was obtained at the instigation of our collectors, and many of the stories we heard were the ones "Uncle Ned used to tell," not the ones repeated most frequently by the person sitting down with us. The tapes, then, often do not represent the best performances of those stories in the flow of family life. They are perhaps more passive; their occurrences at family gatherings were told to us, not observed by us. There is a trade-off here. To collect as much as we did necessitated being in one place, a very public place, over a period of time. For an unstudied genre, this volume of material makes possible definition and a broad-based system of classification which others may find useful in organizing their own materials. An analysis of performance must be left to folklorists who study selected individual families in-depth.

After each festival, the tapes were transcribed selectively, with an eye towards publication. Inessential conversation, interviewers' questions, and false starts were eliminated. Transcribers listened instead for discrete items of folkloric interest and related thoughts on family life. Conversations between family members were noted when one prodded, amplified, corrected, or contradicted another. Common categories of material emerged throughout the transcribing process, and these categories, once established, helped us to direct our questions to what appeared to be the most fertile areas of inquiry. All of the transcriptions were labeled by year, name of informant, and genre. Predictably, some of the best material was simply unclassifiable; hence our chapter on "Other Stories." For this publication, we and our editors at Pantheon have made minor changes in the original transcriptions only where it was deemed absolutely essential for coherence.

*Visitors to the Festival of American Folklife share their
stories and peruse photo albums in the family folklore tent.*

This book is based primarily on the interviews conducted from 1974 to 1977. It includes parts of two previous publications of stories from the early festivals, and materials from the twelve-week Bicentennial Festival, where we taped at least three times the number of interviews we had during the first two festivals combined. Much of the 1976–1977 material is published here for the first time. Very little collecting has been done since 1977, but over the past five years we have all conducted additional research, written several articles on parts of the collection, and participated in many workshops, panel discussions, and professional meetings across the country, which helped us to put our collection in perspective and collect more diverse materials. One of our staff members has also written a dissertation on American family stories, during which he re-interviewed many of the original contributors in depth. All of these activities have further developed our understanding of the material and are reflected throughout this book.

The family folklore interview tapes and copy negatives of all photos used in our exhibits are available for scholarly research. The interviews are archived by year, informant, and interviewer, and cross-indexed by subject matter. For further information, contact the Office of Folklife Programs, Smithsonian Institution, Washington, D.C. 20560. The family folklore films, "Harmonize" and "Home Movie," are distributed through the Center for Southern Folklore, P. O. Box 40081, Memphis, TN 38104.

T he earliest and still the most abundant printed sources of family folklore are the regional folklore journals. These publications focus on material of local interest and are rich in collectanea pertaining to family folklore. Many of the following articles were written by folklore students and tend to be collections of folklore items with little analysis or contextual information.

FOR FURTHER READING

Boshears, Frances. "Granddaddy Roberts." *Midwest Folklore* 3 (Fall 1953):151–56.

Brann, Dolly. "I Can Remember: An Interview with Mr. and Mrs. L. D. Brann." *New York Folklore Quarterly* 28 (March 1973):244–56.

Brunetti, Michael. "Italian Folklore." *New York Folklore Quarterly* 28 (March 1973):257–62.

Carbo, Terry M. "The Faith Healing Beliefs of a New Orleans Family." *Louisiana Folklore Miscellany* 2 (August 1968):91–100.

Currin, Martha O. and Barbara C. Smetzer. " 'Blackeye, the Intelligent Bird Dog,' and Other Humorous Stories as told by Joe D. Currin." *North Carolina Folklore* 12 (July 1964):1–6.

Dober, Virginia. "We'll Tell 'Em." *North Carolina Folklore* 4 (July 1956):15–22.

Dobie, Bertha McKee, ed. "Tales and Rhymes of a Texas Household." *Publications of the Texas Folklore Society* 6 (1927):23–71.

Gillin, June Jacobi. "Lore from a Swedish Grandfather." *New York Folklore Quarterly* 9 (Winter 1953):268–72.

Giusti, Rosanna M. "The Life Cycle Beliefs of a New Orleans Family of French-Italian Background." *Louisiana Folklore Miscellany* 3 (1975 for 1973):1–28.

Halpert, Herbert. "Family Tales of a Kentuckian." *Hoosier Folklore Bulletin* 1 (August 1942):61–71.

Hardin, William Henry. "Grandpa Brown." *Publications of the Texas Folklore Society* 29 (1959):58–68.

Hawkins, Beverly. "Folklore of a Black Family." *Journal of the Ohio Folklore Society* 2 (April 1973):2–19.

Hilliard, Addie Suggs. "I Remember, I Remember." *Tennessee Folklore Society Bulletin* 32 (December 1966):121–28.

Holyoak, Van. "Stories About My Dad." *AFFword* 1 (October 1971):10.

Hunter, Edwin R. "My Grandfather's Speech." *Tennessee Folklore Society Bulletin* 8 (March 1942):5–22.

Jiles, Paulette. "Card Players and Story Tellers." *This Magazine is About Schools* 5 (1971).

Justice, Beverly, et al. "Old Time Holidays." *Foxfire* 7 (Winter 1973):326–38.

Kelly, Jill. "The Finlinson Family Reunion Tradition." *AFFword* 4 (Spring 1974):37–39.

Labarbera, Michael. "An Ounce of Prevention, and Grandmother Tried Them All." *New York Folklore Quarterly* 20 (June 1964):126–29.

Lockmiller, Earl. "Tales My Grandfather Told Me." *Tennessee Folklore Society Bulletin* 17 (June 1951):42–43.

Lueg, Maurita Russell. "Russell Tales." *Publications of the Texas Folklore Society* 27 (1958): 160–66.

Lumpkin, Ben Gray. "Folksongs from a Nebraska Family." *Southern Folklore Quarterly* 36 (March 1972):14–35.

Lundman, Della. "My Kin Knew Jesse James." *AFFword* 1 (July 1971):18–20.

Nagorka, Suzanne. "The Life of Felicia Nagorka." *New York Folklore Quarterly* 28 (March 1973):286–92.

Parker, Cherry. "Mother-in-Law Lore." *North Carolina Folklore* 5 (December 1957):22.

Pearce, Helen. "Folk Sayings in a Pioneer Family of Western Oregon." *California Folklore Quarterly* 5 (July 1946):229–42.

Pebworth, Ted-Larry. "Aunt Loda's Legacy." *Louisiana Folklore Miscellany* 2 (August 1968):24–33.

Roberts, Mary Eliza. "Folklore in My Father's Life." *Midwest Folklore* 3 (Fall 1953):147–50.

Simmerman, Alice. "Arizona Stories." *AFFword* 4 (Spring 1974):24–36.

Sutton, Mayte E. "Grandmother's Story." *New York Folklore Quarterly* 19 (March 1963):55.

Taube, Kristi. "Family Folklore With a German Flair." *Journal of the Ohio Folklore Society* ns 3 (Spring 1974):17–19.

West, John Foster. "The Old Musket: A Family Story." *North Carolina Folklore* 20 (May 1972):81–83.

White, Miriam Whitney. "Legends of an Adirondack Grandfather." *New York Folklore Quarterly* 22 (June 1966):132–42.

White, Virginia. "Grandmother Remembers Switzerland." *New York Folklore Quarterly* 10 (Winter 1954):274–78.

Willis, Alice. "Tales From a Mountain Homestead." *New York Folklore Quarterly* 3 (Winter 1947):302–11.

Woodward, Susan Holly. "A Grandfather's Tales of the Lowry Brothers." *North Carolina Folklore* 10 (December 1962):17–20.

Although collectanea does predominate in the literature on family folklore, analysis is by no means lacking. Kim Garrett, in "Family Stories and Sayings," *Publications of the Texas Folklore Society* 30 (1961):273–281, incorporates within her fine collection of her own family's folklore the suggestion that family folklore can serve as a binding force within families. Kathryn Morgan, in *Children of Strangers: The Stories of a Black Family* (Philadelphia, 1981), examines the ways in which family folklore can help families cope with difficult situations. Patrick Mullen's "Folk Songs and Family Traditions," *Publications of the Texas Folklore Society* 38 (1972):49–63, is an analysis of the interrelationships between those genres. Stanley Brandes, in "Family Misfortunes Stories in American Folklore," *Journal of the Folklore Institute* 12 (1975):5–17, and Steven J. Zeitlin, in " 'An Alchemy of Mind': The Family Courtship Story," *Western Folklore* 39 (1980):17–33, classify and examine specific types of family folklore. Francis Haines, Sr., looks at stories of westward migration in "Goldilocks on the Oregon Trail," *Idaho Yesterdays* IX (1965) 26–30. Mody Boatright's "The Family Saga as a Form of Folklore," in his *The Family Saga and Other Phases of American Folklore* (Urbana, 1958), pp. 1–19, is still the classic article on the subject and describes the components usually found in a family's traditional history.

Family folklore has now been accepted as a distinct genre by academic folklorists. At least three doctoral dissertations have been prepared on the subject:

Baldwin, Karen L. "Down on Bugger Run: Family Group and the Social Base of Folklore." University of Pennsylvania, 1975.

Yocom, Margaret R. "Fieldwork in Family Folklore and Oral History: A Study in Methodology." University of Massachusetts, 1980.

Zeitlin, Steven J. "Americans Imagine Their Ancestors: Family Stories as a Folklore Genre." University of Pennsylvania, 1979.

Just as the academic discipline of folklore is closely related to other subjects, the field of family tradition has been examined by scholars with a variety of professional affiliations. The following references are just a sampling from these other approaches. Anthropologists have tended to emphasize the social activities related to family traditions; a study of this type is Millicent Ayoub's "The Family Reunion," *Ethnology* 5 (1966):415–433. An early sociological study of the rituals of everyday life is by James H. S. Bossard and Eleanor Boll, *Ritual in Family Living: A Contemporary Study* (Philadelphia, 1950). Genealogists occasionally examine a specific tradition to determine its validity and usefulness as did Stanley Perin in "A Tradition in Search of Its Origin," *New England Historical and Genealogical Register* 121 (1967):29–36. Onomastics, the science of names, often deals with family traditions. An excellent example is Robert Rennick's "The Inadvertent Changing of Non-English Names by Newcomers to America: A Brief Historical Survey and Popular Presentation of Cases," *New York Folklore Quarterly* 26 (1970):263–282.

The literature in the field of oral history is full of references to family folklore. Three very good family-oriented histories are William Lynwood Montell's *The Saga of Coe Ridge* (New York, 1972), Dorothy Gallagher's *Hannah's Daughters: Six Generations of an American Family: 1876–1976* (New York, 1976), and *Jewish Grandmothers* (Boston, 1976), edited by Sydelle Kramer and Jenny Masur. A related genre is the family saga or memoir, based on oral tradition but reworked into a literary format. Alex Haley's *Roots: The Saga of an American Family* (Garden City, 1976) falls into this category. *The Land Remembers*, by Ben Logan (New York, 1976), centers on the life of a Norwegian farm family in Wisconsin and is one of the best examples of the genre. Willard R. Espy's *Oysterville: Roads to Grandpa's Village* (New York, 1977) traces a family's migration from Ireland to the northwest coast of the United States over the course of several generations. *Spoonbread and Strawberry Wine: Recipes and Reminiscences of a Family*, by Norma Jean and Carole Darden (Garden City, 1978), is one of the more unusual presentations of a family's heritage, since it weaves stories and photographs from a southern black family around a cookbook of family recipes. Another unique presentation of family folklore is *The Hammons Family: A Study of a West Virginia Family's Traditions*, a two-record album set with booklet, edited and recorded by Alan Jabbour and Carl Fleischhauer, published in 1973 by the Library of Congress, L65–66.

For those people embarking on a search for their family traditions there are a number of guides available. The books listed below are basic folklore and oral history collecting manuals plus more specialized literature focusing directly on the interrelationships of oral history and family history.

Allen, Barbara and William Lynwood Montell. *From Memory to History: Using Oral History Sources in Local Historical Research.* Nashville, 1981.

Baum, Willa K. *Oral History for the Local Historical Society.* Nashville, 1959.

————. *Transcribing and Editing Oral History.* Nashville, 1977.

Cook, Ann, Marilyn Gittell, and Herb Mack. *What Was It Like When Your Grandparents Were Your Age.* New York, 1976.

Davies, Thomas L. *Shoots: A Guide to Your Family's Photographic Heritage.* Danbury, NH, 1977.

Dixon, Janice T. and Dora D. Flack. *Preserving Your Past: A Painless Guide to Writing Your Autobiography and Family History.* Garden City, 1977.

Draznin, Yaffa. *The Family Historian's Handbook.* New York, 1978.

Epstein, Ellen Robinson and Rona Mendelsohn. *Record and Remember: Tracing Your Roots through Oral History.* New York: 1978.

Goldstein, Kenneth S. *A Guide for Fieldworkers in Folklore.* Hatboro, PA, 1964.

Hartley, William G. *Preparing a Personal History.* Salt Lake City, 1976.

Ives, Edward. *The Tape-Recorded Interview: A Manual for Field Workers in Folklore and Oral History.* Knoxville, 1980.

Lichtman, Allan J. *Your Family History.* New York, 1978.

Robertson, James, ed. *Old Glory: A Pictorial Report on the Grass Roots History Movement and the First Hometown Primer.* New York, 1973.

Shumway, Gary L. and William G. Hartley. *An Oral History Primer.* Salt Lake City, 1973.

Thompson, Paul R. *The Voice of the Past: Oral History.* New York, 1978.

Weitzman, David. *My Backyard History Book.* Boston, 1975.

———. *Underfoot: An Everyday Guide to Exploring the American Past.* New York, 1976.

The following books published by the American Association for State and Local History give basic information on the preservation of research material:

Kane, Lucille M. *A Guide to the Care and Administration of Manuscripts*, 2nd edition. Nashville, 1966.

McWilliams, Jerry. *The Preservation and Restoration of Sound Recordings.* Nashville, 1979.

Weinstein, Robert A. and Larry Booth. *Collection, Use, and Care of Historical Photographs.* Nashville, 1979.

If home photography is your main interest in terms of family folklore, you will find an excellent theoretical introduction in the series of articles in *Saying Cheese: Studies in Folklore and Visual Communication* (Bloomington: Folklore Forum Bibliographic and Special Series No. 13, 1975), edited by Steven Ohrn and Michael E. Bell. Richard Chalfen deals specifically with home movies in his "Cinema Naiveté: A Study of Home Moviemaking as Visual Communication," *Studies in the Anthropology of Visual Communication* 2 (1975):87–103. *American Album,* by Oliver Jensen et al. (New York, 1970); *The Snapshot,* edited by Jonathan Green (Millerton, New York, 1974), *Family Photographs: Content, Meaning, and Effect* (New York, 1981), by Julia Hirsch, and "Family Photo Interpretation," by Judith Mara Gutman, in *Kin and Communities: Families in America*, edited by Allan J. Lichtman and Joan Challinor (Washington, D.C., 1979), are further sources of information on family photography.

NOTES

FAMILY FOLKLORE: THE CREATIVE EXPRESSION OF A COMMON PAST

1. For some good introductions to folklore, see Barre Toelken, *The Dynamics of Folklore* (Boston: Houghton Mifflin Co., 1979); Jan Harold Brunvald, *The Study of American Folklore: An Introduction,* 2nd ed. (New York: W. W. Norton & Co., 1978).

THE FORMS OF FAMILY LORE

1. Collected from Amanda Dargan, age 31, Darlington, South Carolina.
2. Collected in conversation with Ross Abrahams, Washington, D.C.

FAMILY STORIES

1. For a useful discussion of how family stories fit within a framework for oral narrative, see Linda Degh, "Folk Narrative," in *Folklore and Folklife: An Introduction,* ed. Richard Dorson (Chicago: University of Chicago Press, 1972). For some of the new research on the personal experience narrative, see Sandra K. D. Stahl, "The Personal Narrative as Folklore," *Journal of the Folklore Institute* 14 (1977):9–30; see also "Special Double Issue: Stories of Personal Experiences," ed. Richard Dorson and Sandra K. D. Stahl, *Journal of the Folklore Institute* 14 (1977). For other useful research on contemporary storytelling, see Barbara Kirshenblatt-Gimblett, "Traditional Storytelling in the Toronto Jewish Community" (Ph.D. diss., Indiana University, 1972); see also Linda Degh, ed., *Indiana Folklore* 1–14 (1969–present).
2. Regina O'Toole Sokas, age 23, Washington, D.C.
3. For a thorough discussion of the relationship between folklore and history, see Barbara Allen and Lynwood Montell, *From Memory to History: Using Oral Sources in Local Historical Research* (Nashville, Tenn., 1981); see also Lynwood Montell, *The Saga of Coe Ridge* (Knoxville: University of Tennessee Press, 1970); Gladys-Marie Fry, *Night Riders in Black Folk History* (Knoxville: University of Tennessee Press, 1975).
4. Susan Meehan, age 38, Washington, D.C.
5. Karl Lamarr Duff, Kent Store, Virginia.
6. Grace McDonald is a pseudonym. We have withheld the name of her grandson.
7. Name withheld upon request, age 30, Brooklyn, New York.
8. See Janet T. Dixon and Dora Flack, *Preserving Your Past: A Painless Guide to Writing Your Autobiography and Family History* (Garden City, N.Y.: Doubleday & Co., 1977), p. 50.

9. From a student paper by Dora Esten, George Washington University.

10. William Stewart, age 53, Belleville, New Jersey.

11. Donald Collins, age 44, Washington, D.C.

12. James H. S. Bossard and Eleanor S. Boll, *Ritual in Family Living: A Contemporary Study* (Philadelphia: University of Pennsylvania Press, 1950.

13. John Giordano, age 33, New York, New York.

14. From a student paper by Rebecca Martin, George Washington University.

15. Ibid., p. 49.

HEROES

1. Woody Guthrie, "Ranger's Command," used by permission.

2. Kathryn Morgan, "Caddy Buffers: Legends of a Middle Class Black Family in Philadelphia," in 1976 *Festival of American Folklife,* ed. Bess Lomax Hawes (Washington, D.C.: Smithsonian Institution, 1976), p. 26. See also Kathryn L. Morgan, *Children of Strangers: The Stories of a Black Family* (Philadelphia: Temple University Press, 1980).

3. Morgan, "Caddy Buffers," p. 27.

ROGUES

1. John Bishop, age 50, Ithaca, New York.

2. David W. Robinson, Seattle, Washington.

3. Nina Bohlen, age 16, Washington, D.C.

4. William Humphrey, *The Ordways* (New York: Alfred A. Knopf, 1965), p. 37, quoted in Patrick B. Mullen, "Myth and Folklore in *The Ordways,*" *Publications of the Texas Folklore Society* 35 (1971): 135.

5. Sue Berryman Bobrow, age 36, Washington, D.C.

MISCHIEF MAKERS

1. Erik Erikson, *Identity, Youth and Crisis* (New York: W. W. Norton & Co., 1968), p. 158.

2. For an exploration of the structure of family stories see Steven Zeitlin, "Americans Imagine Their Ancestors: Family Stories as a Folklore Genre" (Ph.D. diss., University of Pennsylvania, 1978).

3. See "Special Issue: The Practical Joke," *Southern Folklore Quarterly* 38 (1974): 251–331.

INNOCENTS

1. Humphrey, *The Ordways*, p. 21; quoted in Mullen, "Myth and Folklore in *The Ordways*," p. 137.
2. Collected in conversation from visitors to the 1976 Festival of American Folklife.

MIGRATIONS

1. Miriam Fors, age 56, Portland, Oregon.
2. Humphrey, *The Ordways*, p. 58, quoted in Mullen, "Myth and Folklore," p. 138.
3. See Alex Haley, "Black History, Oral History, and Genealogy," *Oral History Review 1973* (1973): 1–25.
4. E. Franklin Frazier, *The Negro Family in the United States* (Chicago: University of Chicago Press, 1966), p. 13. For other examples see the collections of slave narratives from the Federal Writers Project of the WPA.
5. Mody Boatright, "The Family Saga as a Form of Folklore," in *The Family Saga and Other Phases of American Folklore*, ed, Mody Boatright (Urbana: University of Illinois Press, 1958), p. 129. Quoted from Angelina Smith, "Dandy Jim Smith" (unpublished manuscript).
6. Gregory Gay, Washington, D.C.
7. Francis Haines, Sr., "Goldilocks on the Oregon Trail," *Idaho Yesterdays* 9 (1965–66): 26–30.
8. Carl Fleischhauer and Alan Jabbour, *The Hammons Family: A Study of a West Virginia Family's Traditions* (record and booklet), AFS L65–L66 (Washington: Library of Congress, 1973), pp. 3, 4, 27.

LOST FORTUNES

1. Boatright, *Family Folklore*, p. 15.
2. Stanley H. Brandes, "Family Misfortune Stories in American Folklore," *Journal of the Folklore Institute* 12 (1975): 5.
3. Ibid., 13.

COURTSHIPS

1. Helen Trenchi, age 52, Bethesda, Md.
2. Michael Kernan, *Washington Post*, December 29, 1976, p. B3.
3. Suzanne Gibson, age 30, Alexandria, Virginia.
4. Kevin Scott, "Interview with Maria Katzenbach," in "Book World," *Washington Post*, January 15, 1978.
5. Collected in conversation from Amanda Dargan, age 31, Darlington, South Carolina.

FAMILY FEUDS

1. Name withheld, Washington, D.C.
2. Peter Vietze, age 30, Nashville, Tennessee.
3. Amanda Dargan, "Family Identity and the Social Use of Folklore: A South Carolina Family Tradition" (Unpublished M.A. thesis, Memorial University of Newfoundland, 1978), p. 163.
4. Mark Twain, *The Adventures of Huckleberry Finn* (New York: Holt, Rinehart & Winston, 1948), p. 101.

SUPERNATURAL HAPPENINGS

1. Barbara Anthony, age 42, Suitland, Md.

STORIES FOR CHILDREN

1. Regina O'Toole Sokas, age 23, Washington, D.C.
2. See Kenneth S. Goldstein, "The Telling of Non-Traditional Tales to Children: An Ethnographic Report from a Northwest Philadelphia Neighborhood," *Keystone Folklore Quarterly,* 20 (1975): pp. 5–17.
3. Name withheld by request.
4. Name withheld by request.

FAMILY EXPRESSIONS

1. *Christian Science Monitor,* May 9, 1956, quoted in Allen Walker Read, "Family Words in English," *American Speech* 87 (1962): 9.
2. Richard Sackett, age 45, Bethesda, Maryland.
3. *Christian Science Monitor,* June 8, 1956, quoted in Read, "Family Words," p. 8.
4. Read, "Family Words," p. 9.
5. Steven Tauber, age 42, Chevy Chase, Md.
6. Kim S. Garrett, "Family Stories and Sayings," *Publications of the Texas Folklore Society* 30 (1961): 276.
7. Mary Slemp, age 37, Big Stone Gap, Virginia.
8. See Larry G. Small, "Traditional Expressions in a Newfoundland Community: Genre Change and Functional Variability," *Lore and Language* 2 (1975): 16.
9. R. A. Stewart Macalister, *The Secret Languages of Ireland* (Cambridge: 1937), p. 92, quoted in Read, "Family Words," p. 10.
10. Garrett, "Family Stories," p. 274.
11. Nancy Redenbaugh, Fort Collins, Colorado; Ann M. Fleming, Pittsburgh, Pennsylvania.
12. Dargan, *Family Identity,* p. 127.

13. Claudia Fugar.

14. Frederick Erickson, "Timing and Context in Everyday Discourse: Implications for the Study of Referential and Social Meaning," Sociolinguistic Working Paper Number 67 (Austin, Texas: Southwest Educational Development Laboratory, 1980), quoted in Ron Scollon, "Tempo, Density, and Silence: Rhythms in Ordinary Talk," (Unpublished paper, University of Alaska, Fairbanks, 1981), p. 1.

15. Collected in a conversation with Gingy Caswell.

FAMILY CUSTOMS

1. Bossard and Boll, *Ritual*, p. 10.

2. Ellen Kurzman, age 41, Glen Ridge, New Jersey.

3. Bossard and Boll, *Ritual*, p. 28.

4. Mary Dreshter, Hyattsville, Maryland.

FAMILY PHOTOGRAPHY

1. Thomas Schlereth, *Artifacts and the American Past* (Nashville, Tenn.: American Association for State and Local History, 1980), p. 20.

2. Susan Sontag, *On Photography* (New York: Farrar, Straus & Giroux, 1977), pp. 15, 81.

3. Carol Maas, Greenbelt, Maryland.

4. Jonathan Green, ed., *The Snapshot* (Millerton, N.Y.: Aperture, 1974), p. 24.

5. Margaret R. Yocom, "Fieldwork in Family Folklore and Oral History: A Study in Methodology" (Ph.D. diss., University of Massachusetts, 1980), pp. 113–18.

6. Pauline Greenhill, *So We Can Remember: Showing Family Photographs* (Ottawa: National Museums of Canada, 1981), p. 124.

7. Name withheld upon request, Bryn Mawr, Pennsylvania.

8. Audiotape from the film "Home Movie: An American Folk Art," by Steven Zeitlin and Ernst Star, Smithsonian Institution, 1975.

9. Catherine Noren, *The Camera of My Family* (New York: Alfred A. Knopf, 1976), foreword.

10. Corinne LeBovit, Silver Spring, Maryland.

11. Sontag, *On Photography*, p. 8.

12. Marjorie L. Share and William F. Stapp, *Picture It!* (Washington, D.C.: Smithsonian Institution, 1981), p. 80.

13. Joan Bernick, Washington, D.C.

14. Sontag, *On Photography*, p. 8.

15. Nancy Hallsted, Bethesda, Maryland.

16. Martha Ross, Bethesda, Maryland.

1. Alan Ludwig, age 24, Alexandria, Virginia.
2. Richard E. Snyder.
3. Simone de Beauvoir, *Coming of Age*, trans. Patrick O'Brian (New York: G. P. Putnam's Sons, 1972).
4. Ibid.
5. See Barbara Kirschenblatt-Gimblett, *Ashkenaz: Essays in Jewish Folklore* (Philadelphia: University of Pennsylvania Press, forthcoming). See also Barbara Myerhoff, *Number Our Days* (New York: E. P. Dutton, 1979).
6. Suzanne MacKenzie, age 17, Brewster, Mass.
7. Nancy Smith, age 31, Albany, New York.
8. Robert Rhode, age 30, Silverton, Texas.
9. Letters from October 6 and 14, 1861, contributed by Martha Swartwout, John Brandon's descendant.
10. From Andrew Nicholas Conrady to his great-grandson Andrew Nicholas Coyne, contributed by Ruth Coyne.
11. From the manuscript by E. S. Goodwin, "Memories of Our Grandfather," contributed by Mrs. Frank L. Goodwin.
12. Ron Sutton, Washington, D.C.
13. Conrady letter to Andrew Coyne.

GETTING THE BUTTER FROM THE DUCK: PROVERBS AND
PROVERBIAL PHRASES IN AN AFRO-AMERICAN FAMILY

1. See E. Ojo Arewa and Alan Dundes, "Proverbs and the Ethnography of Speaking," reprinted in Alan Dundes, *Essays in Folkloristics*. 1978, 50–70. First printed in *American Anthropologist* 66 (1964): 70–85; see also Peter Seitel, "Proverbs: A Social Use of Metaphor" *Genre* 2 (1969): 143–61, and John Messenger, "The Role of Proverbs in a Nigerian Judicial System" *Southwestern Journal of Anthropology* 15 (1959): 64–73.
2. This proverb does not appear in the following standard proverb references: Archer Taylor, *The Proverb* (Cambridge: Harvard University Press, 1931); Bartlett, J. Whiting and Helen W. Whiting, *Proverbs, Sentences and Proverbial Phrases* (Cambridge: Harvard University, 1968); Archer Taylor and Bartlett J. Whiting, *A Dictionary of American Proverbs and Proverbial Phrases, 1820–1880* (Cambridge: Harvard University Press, 1958).
3. A common proverb, it is usually seen as "buying a pig in a poke" in European tradition. See Taylor, *The Proverb*, p. 187 and Whiting and Whiting, *Proverbs, Sentences*, p. 458.
4. Not found in Taylor, *The Proverb*, Whiting and Whiting, *Proverbs, Sentences*, or Taylor and Whiting, *Dictionary*.

5. Not found in Taylor, Whiting and Whiting, or Taylor and Whiting.

6. Found in Taylor, pp. 13, 158, 170.

7. Not found in Taylor, Whiting and Whiting, or Taylor and Whiting.

8. To "correct" a child means the entire process of telling him or her that a given behavior is wrong, and then reminding or instructing him or her in the socially approved behavior.

9. Not found in Taylor, Whiting and Whiting, or Taylor and Whiting.

10. Not found in Taylor, Whiting and Whiting, or Taylor and Whiting. This may be related in some way to another expression common in my family, "meddlesome madisome." This is said to a child who meddles in something that he should not.

BLESSING THE TIES THAT BIND: STORYTELLING AT
FAMILY FESTIVALS

1. For a discussion of festival, see Robert J. Smith, "Festivals and Celebrations" in Richard M. Dorson, ed., *Folklore and Folklife* (Chicago: University of Chicago Press, 1972), and John B. Bender, "The Day of *The Tempest," Journal of English Literary History* 47 (1980): 235–58.

2. Journal, 30 May 1979; interview with Elmer Keck, 23 June 1979.

3. Journal IV, pp. 4–8, 30 April 1976.

4. Journal IV, p. 16, 3 May 1976.

5. Journal I, p. 55–57 and 73–79, 7 and 10 June 1975.

My sincere thanks to the members of my family who helped me learn the stories: Bertha David Heiser Yocom and Isaac N. Yocom, Katherine Louisa Keck and Elmer Christman Keck, Betty Keck Yocom and Norman David Heiser Yocom, Gladys Yocom Metka and William Metka, Edith Yocom Boyer and Randall Boyer, Marie and David Yocom, Douglas Yocom, Janet Yocom Keck, and Diane Yocom Suptlee. Enjoy.

ABOUT THE AUTHORS

Steven J. Zeitlin was born in Philadelphia, Pennsylvania, and raised in São Paulo, Brazil. He received his bachelor's degree from the University of Pennsylvania, his M.A. in literature from Bucknell University and his Ph.D. in folklore from the University of Pennsylvania.

Born in Hartford, Connecticut, Amy J. Kotkin received her B.A. in American studies at Case Western Reserve University and her M.A. in American civilization from the University of Pennsylvania.

Holly Cutting Baker was born in Fall River, Massachusetts. She has a bachelor's degree from Emmanuelle College and is completing her Ph.D. in folklore at the University of Pennsylvania.

Zeitlin, Kotkin, and Cutting Baker, with the help of Sandra Gross, founded the Family Folklore Program at the Smithsonian Institution in 1974. Steven Zeitlin coordinated the program, and is currently at work on a folklore project with the Queens Council on the Arts in New York City. He has also made several documentary films. Currently, Amy Kotkin assists in producing a touring lecture and seminar series for the Smithsonian National Associate Regional Events Program. Holly Cutting Baker has been an archivist with the American Folklife Center at the Library of Congress and is now at home caring for her husband John and her two-year-old daughter Kate.